OEDIPUS AT FENWAY PARK

OEDIPUS AT FENWAY PARK

· · ·

What Rights Are and Why There Are Any

LLOYD L. WEINREB

Harvard University Press

Cambridge, Massachusetts

London, England

1994

Library of Congress Cataloging-in-Publication Data

Weinreb, Lloyd L., 1936–
Oedipus at Fenway Park : what rights are and why there are any /
Lloyd L. Weinreb.
p. cm.
Includes bibliographical references and index.
ISBN 0-674-63092-0 (alk. paper)
1. Human rights. 2. Civil rights. 3. Responsibility. I. Title.
JC571.W38   1994
323'.01—dc20
94-3060
CIP

To

David Mitchell

Preface

THIS BOOK originated in a question that I was asked after the publication of *Natural Law and Justice* in 1987. I had argued there that the idea of justice is antinomic: it incorporates two distinct notions, to which I referred as entitlement and desert, that are both dependent on and inconsistent with each other. A number of readers, who were generally sympathetic to the argument on its own terms, asked me, "What then?" For we do have the idea of justice, and it powerfully affects us. If it really is antinomic, how do we get on? The answer, which I barely suggested in *Natural Law and Justice* (and did not then fully understand), is the subject of this book.

When I set out to explore the question, I decided without much deliberation to inquire first into the nature of rights, which seemed to reflect our conclusions about the content of justice and also to contain within themselves the combination of objectivity and normativity that is central to the problem of justice. I did not anticipate how deep or how far that inquiry would carry me. It turned out that rights—or some equivalent concept—are at the very core of the human condition and are the means by which the antinomy of justice is overcome. Coming to understand how this plays out and completes the argument that I made earlier has been a source of great satisfaction.

A preliminary version of the general argument appeared as an essay, "Natural Law and Rights," in Robert P. George, ed., *Natural Law*

Theory (Oxford: Clarendon Press, 1992). A preliminary version of the argument in Chapter 8 appeared as an essay, "What Are *Civil* Rights?" in *Social Philosophy and Policy* 8, no. 2 (1991):1–21.

I am grateful to the friends and colleagues who read my work in progress and am glad to record my gratitude here. Dick Fallon read the whole manuscript in an early draft and reread portions of it a second and sometimes a third time; he was as patient as he was persistent while I struggled to get it right. Raymond Belliotti, Scott Brewer, Dan Meltzer, and Cass Sunstein read the manuscript in one or another of its drafts. Each of them helped me to make the succeeding draft better. Zeph Stewart gave me valuable suggestions for Chapters 4 and 8, Nicholas Weinreb for Chapter 5, Sissela Bok for Chapter 6, and Kathleen Sullivan for Chapter 9.

The staff of the Harvard Law School library gave me substantial bibliographic assistance with characteristic good grace. During the very last stage of preparation of the manuscript, I was a visiting professor at the Fordham University School of Law; the staff of the library there helped me to make final bibliographic corrections. Laurie Corzett typed and retyped innumerable drafts of the manuscript with awesome efficiency and equanimity.

Aida Donald at Harvard University Press gave me valuable advice; as the publisher's representative, she has been the best of friends. Ann Hawthorne, who copyedited the manuscript for the Press, helped me to improve it at the end.

I worked on the manuscript while I was a scholar in residence at the Rockefeller Foundation's Study and Conference Center in Bellagio. I cannot imagine more agreeable surroundings for such work.

Contents

OEDIPUS AT FENWAY PARK

Introduction

T HE APPEARANCE OF ANOTHER—yet another— book about
rights will not be the cause of much rejoicing. Rights are currently a glut on the market in both political philosophy and practical
politics. Notwithstanding Bentham's famous dismissal of rights at large
as "nonsense upon stilts,"[1] philosophers take rights seriously, sometimes, indeed, seem to take scarcely anything but rights seriously. In
public forums, rights proliferate like weeds in an empty lot, so that it
is impossible to see the ground beneath. Calling some claim a matter
of right—the right to smoke, the right not to be in the presence of
someone who is smoking, the right of lobsters not to be boiled[2]—is
not so much a characterization of the claim as a bit of autobiography;
it serves mostly to emphasize the claim's importance to the speaker.
So we have reached the parlous state—vide this book, this paragraph—
that one expresses obligatory regrets for adding to the discussion as a
preface to doing so.

Not that we have made much headway in understanding what rights
are in general or what rights there are in particular. Judith Thomson,
who has made the concept of a right a central element of her moral
philosophy, observed not long ago that "moral theorists are not yet in
a position to begin to answer" the question of what rights we have,
because we are not clear enough about "just what it is to have a
right."[3] Although she has recently gone a long way toward providing

an answer to the latter question, she does so insistently without reliance on a prior understanding of what a right is or why anyone should have any. We can describe what it is to have a right, but we cannot explain it; "to have a right" she says, "just *is* its being the case that people may and may not treat you" in certain ways.[4] Similarly, H. L. A. Hart cautioned that despite the emphasis in political and legal theory on "basic human rights," we have not established a "sufficiently firm foundation for such rights."[5] Observing the multitude of different, often competing claims that parade as rights, not to mention basic human rights, few will disagree.

One might expect that there would be a reaction against rights, if only to escape the cacophony. But few persons, following Bentham, question whether there are any (nonlegal) rights after all. On the contrary, rights are pursued the more intensely, as if to confirm that they are real, not imaginary, and that they are important. Rights, whatever and whichever, seem unavoidably to have a place in moral discourse. The most thoroughgoing consequentialist is likely to slip into the vocabulary of rights, only adding not very convincingly that the rights in question prove on examination to have consequentialist underpinning. Often enough, he goes further and suggests (inadvertently giving the whole show away) that the conclusive argument for his consequentialist position is that it accounts for the substance of certain conceded rights.

So, once again, rights, but, I hope to show, with a difference. The two questions that are addressed in the central portion of this book are "What are rights?" and "Why are there any?" The first question, all too familiar as it is, cannot be answered convincingly without the second, which is, however, scarcely ever asked directly. (It is the question that Thomson has argued cannot intelligibly be asked.) Rather, we are told how rights function or how much is lost if they are denied. That is not the question I have in mind. I mean to ask "Why are there rights?" in much the way a small child asks "Why are there elephants?" or rutabagas or rainbows. If we are hardy enough to answer the child at all, we shall probably tell her how it happens that there are elephants—which is not at all what she asked—or, more likely, we shall say, "They just are," and change the subject. No similar evasion will do with respect to rights. For rights are not things the "happening" of which can be explained in the usual way, as the effect of antecedent causes. Nor can we say confidently that they just are. For they are not observably "out there"—not, at least, in the same way as elephants. Rights concern us so much principally because it is not the case that they "just are"; they have to be honored, and they are routinely denied. Only the best magicians can deny an elephant.

The short way with such puzzlement is also the obvious one. Rights are not the same sort of thing as elephants, and the conditions of their "existence," if you want to talk that way, are similarly different. Rights are part of normative discourse. Once that is understood, it is easy to say why there are rights. There are rights because . . . well, because there is normative discourse, nothing more than that. Once we get into the correct "realm," rights "just are," after all. But that does not alleviate the puzzlement. On the contrary. For if the normative realm is where rights have their being, they are a most peculiar feature of that landscape indeed. Not only do they seem to have a quality of objectivity—validity? reality?—that is generally absent from the normative realm. What is worse, rights seem ordinarily to be closed to every kind of normative consideration; a person's right is usually a sufficient reason for allowing her to do something that we think is wrong for her to do and will have harmful consequences. These peculiarities of rights need to be explained in a manner for which none of the familiar patterns of explanation is adequate.

As part of the response to the questions about the nature of rights generally, in the later chapters I address a third question: "What rights are there?" The question is of obvious importance in itself; but it is important also as a test of the answers to the general questions. One of the more disconcerting aspects of the current debate is the lack of connection, or even resonance, between abstract theories about rights and lists of concrete rights. All too often the two inquiries are kept separate, so that theory is untroubled by indigestible practical details, and advocacy of specific rights is accountable only to its own rhetoric. Thomson is among the few who treat the two inquiries as genuinely interdependent; since, however, she concludes that a right is simply what people who have a right have, her argument brings the inquiries together without making a connection. L. W. Sumner has observed: "A standard of authenticity [for rights] must . . . include both a conceptual and a substantive component, the former telling us what rights are and the latter telling us which rights there are."[6] Generally I agree. But our persistent failure in both these respects cautions that there may not be such a definitive standard. I should regard a theory of rights as satisfactory if it provides the ground for rights, which itself accounts for our inability to specify unqualifiedly what rights there are and at the same time explains the origin of actual rights in a concrete context. That is the line that I shall pursue. Although the advocacy of specific rights ought to offer stronger justification than fiat or mere preference for recognizing some claims as rights and not others, I have taken as a central problem, which has to be accepted on its own terms, the juxtaposition of our certainty that there are rights, on one hand, and our inability to validate specific rights without qualification, on the other. The juxtaposition is not, as it is usually regarded, just an unfortunate feature of the discussion; it is an aspect of the phenomenon being observed.

In Chapter One I indicate persistent perplexities in current thinking about rights, those features of rights that seem too plain to be discarded and yet cannot be integrated coherently with one another or placed satisfactorily within a general theoretical framework. Although the approach here is generally analytic, the outcome is not just the analysis of a concept. For we do seem to start from the position that in some sense (which is, as much as anything, what needs to be elucidated) rights are real and that our task is not simply to define our terms but to describe accurately. Explaining what rights are, we affirm that there are rights.[7]

Using the material in the preceding chapter to set the stage, the argument begins in Chapter Two. The conclusion of the argument, summarily put, is that rights and responsibility are one and the same. In a casual way, that is entirely familiar. It is a commonplace of moral exhortation that there are no rights without responsibility, a common-place of political rhetoric that there is no responsibility without rights. I shall argue, however, that the equivalence of responsibility and rights is much more rigorous than those simple formulas disclose. Rights resolve the fundamental antinomy between freedom and cause that defines the human condition, which resolution finds expression as human responsibility. That, and only that, is why there are rights; and from that we are able to conclude what rights are.

In outline, the argument goes like this: A person is responsible, in the specifically human sense that implicates desert, only for his conduct that is self-determined. But conduct cannot be said to be a person's at all unless it is traceable to his individual attributes. If in principle every event in the natural order, including those involving human beings, is causally determinate, it does not seem possible to regard any conduct as self-determined, for it must all be traceable to causes beyond the person's control or to his attributes, which are themselves traceable to causes beyond his control. If, however, it is the case that the personal attributes to which a person's conduct is traced are *properly* that per-son's, that is to say, proper to him and *duly* his *as the person he is,* then it can be said that the attributes and the actions that flow from them are *self-*determined in the required sense. For, whatever their causal origin, normatively they are determined according to that person's self, the unique individual that he is.

If all of a person's attributes were (regarded as) properly his—his due—then everything that happened to him would be determined according to his self and therefore deserved. But that clearly is not the case. On the other hand, if none of a person's attributes were properly his, then there would be no escape from the determinist outcome; all of our actions being traced ultimately to attributes that were not self-determined but simply happened to us, there would be nothing for which we were personally responsible. In order to sustain individual responsibility, therefore, we require a distinction between those per-sonal attributes that are merely a matter of fact, which constitute a person descriptively as a being like other beings within the causal order of nature, and those personal attributes that are his normatively, which constitute him as a responsible person, self-determining and incurring desert.

We make this distinction between descriptive and normative attributes by means of the idea of a right: a quality or attribute, considered as a power, that a person has duly, that is to say, as of right. Such normative attributes may or may not also be a person's descriptively, as a matter of fact. A person, fully constituted descriptively as an individual differentiated from all other individuals, may have more or less than her due in countless ways. Her powers are all more or less subject to infringement by others or may be ameliorated by others, if not directly then in some compensatory fashion. In the first instance, therefore, rights protect fully generally a person's liberty to determine her conduct for herself: to act responsibly. But rights and responsibility alike are specific to conduct affected by the attributes in question. Normatively constituted, having her rights, a person is responsible and incurs desert, not for everything that happens to her but only for specific conduct within the range of application of her rights. If a person has a right that is denied, she is excused from responsibility within its range but remains responsible in other respects. So to speak extends the application of the concept of a right to the full range of individual action, not only that with respect to which the power of the individual is contested (and the right, therefore, in issue), but also that with respect to which individual power is regarded as determinative so uncontestedly that it would be otiose and peculiar to speak of a person's right. Such an extension, I shall argue, does not distort the familiar, central concept of a right, but clarifies it by making explicit what is already contained, albeit ordinarily too obvious to require mention, within it. Having to do with alterable circumstances affecting one's capacity to act, rights speak ordinarily to the conduct of others toward their possessor. But the immediate significance of rights, afforded or denied, is the person's responsibility for conduct to which the right relates; they have a bearing on normative judgments about that person.

Rights may thus be defined as the *normative constituents* of persons, attributes that constitute them as autonomous and, therefore, responsible beings. They are an aspect of personhood itself, and although rights ought to be respected, rights as such are not what a person *ought to have* but what a person *has,* or *is,* simply and entirely as a person. No more is needed to establish the reality of rights than what we know directly and incontrovertibly from experience: that there are, among beings, persons and things and the difference between them. Although rights have normative significance, they are, like responsibility, a matter of fact.

So to state the conclusion is perhaps to invite rejection of the whole enterprise from the start. For it threatens one of the canons of philosophic respectability: that "is" and "ought"—fact and norm—are logically distinct, and nothing is implied, rigorously or unrigorously, about what ought to be exclusively from what is the case.[8] Although my argument does indeed make some inroad on the separation of "is" and "ought," it does not seek to overthrow the canon generally. It only brings into the open what is implicit both in the common understanding of what rights are all about and in most theories of rights.

Chapters Two and Three are a brief excursus into the problem of human freedom and responsibility. I state the central issues simply, without much qualifying detail. The heart of the problem is not, as so much of the literature suggests, getting clear what we mean by responsibility and all the subtle distinctions by which we elaborate what we mean in particular circumstances. Most often we know well enough what we mean, even when we do not agree precisely about its application. The problem is rather making sense of responsibility altogether, in light of what else we know.

The transition from responsibility to rights is made in Chapters Four, "Oedipus at Fenway Park," and Five, which are the heart of the book. We may not have to calculate the earned run average of a pitcher named Oedipus; but we do need to know who, if anyone, has a right to pitch for the Red Sox. For there are a great many people who would give anything for the chance. We need to know, at any rate, if it is right that out of all those people Roger Clemens be the pitcher. And if so, does he have a right to be rewarded so extravagantly for what so many others would gladly pay to do? Answering those questions will take us from Fenway Park to Thebes and back. Roger Clemens and Oedipus have more in common than either probably would have supposed.

One of the most contentious questions about rights I have already answered indirectly. If rights are an aspect of personhood, then only human beings have rights, because only human beings are persons. I address the question "What has rights?" explicitly in Chapter Six. Unsurprisingly, ordinary usage is not so rigorous. Since persons have duties—persons alone having duties—with respect to nonhuman kinds that resemble duties arising from rights, and since duties are the principal payoff of rights, it is generally accurate enough practically, if not conceptually, to refer to the nonhuman object of a duty as the possessor of a right. So to speak lends such a duty the normative force of a right, which is what the proponents of animal and other nonhuman rights mostly want. Nevertheless, all the arguments that the defenders of rights of animals and other nonhuman kinds make in their behalf can be made more clearly and convincingly in terms of duties. To speak instead of rights adds rhetorical heat at the cost of some light.

Chapters Seven and Eight discuss how specific rights follow from the theory. The rights identified in Chapter Seven as human rights are not familiar in the terms in which I state them. They relate closely, however, to ones that are familiar and, indeed, are among those most frequently asserted. These rights follow directly from personhood, and, the categories of human being and person being coextensive, they attach to all human beings as such. Accordingly, they (and only they) can meaningfully be described as natural—inhering in the nature of a human being—or human rights. Taking that position, I address questions about human beings (the yet unborn or recently born, the senile, the condemned) who lack responsibility as persons or who are deemed to have forfeited it. The conventional practice of including such beings generally within the category of persons is connected to the fact that even a fully responsible person is all the while also a nonautonomous being and intermittently only that. Although the ascription of rights to nonresponsible human beings and not to nonresponsible beings of other kinds may look from a distance like "species discrimination," as some defenders of nonhuman rights have called it, it has a plausible, if not ineluctable, basis.

Responsibility is individual and attaches uniquely to a person fully constituted as the individual she is, distinct from all other persons. A person must, therefore, have rights that attach not because of what all human beings alike are, but in virtue of individual attributes that differentiate one human being from another. Such rights are not universal. Yet, attaching to persons constitutively—constituting them as persons—they also are a matter of fact and not merely a matter of policy or preference on whatever basis. In Chapter Eight I locate these differential rights in the deep, established ways of a community, its actual practices as well as its patterns of normative judgment. Their source is convention, not in our sense of the secondary and trivial but in the more profound sense of the classical Greek term *nomos*. It follows that one cannot enumerate fully what rights there are without reference to a particular community. Any theory of rights that does not account for their objectivity is unsatisfactory. Nevertheless, what are perceived to be rights all too obviously vary concretely over time and from one community to another. There may be criticism of any community's catalogue of rights from within or without—a manifestation, indeed, of their objective aspect; but, criticism or no, the catalogues are not all alike. To pretend otherwise or to suppose that the variation is corrigible and will in some future be eliminated is whistling in the dark. The problematic juncture of fact and value considered abstractly reemerges concretely as the question how a given configuration of rights can at the same time be both the subject and the standard of evaluation.

Although these rights, which appropriately enough are commonly designated as civil rights, are not universal, their basis indicates how they are ascertained in practice. Chapter Nine derives some general lessons about how to conduct serious inquiry about the status and scope of specific rights and illustrates the application of the general theory by considering three of the most contentious current issues in the rights debate: rights of the handicapped, gay rights, and affirmative action, or reverse discrimination as it is also called.

Discourse about rights refers familiarly to different categories of rights: human rights, civil rights, rights of nonhuman kinds, and, most familiar of all, legal rights, as well as some others. Rights in each category seem to have certain characteristics different from the rest. Why suppose, as my argument evidently does, that they are bound together by a single characteristic or set of characteristics uniquely applicable to all rights? For example, in some uses of the term, perhaps the most central ones, rights are certainly connected with the autonomy of responsible individuals. But why must all rights have that connection, since many people do talk intelligibly about animal rights without attributing responsibility to animals? Why indeed, if such a connection would seem to dispossess of rights infants, the senile, and others who are not presently responsible? Again, although some rights are so basic that they seem to be somehow "in the nature of things," others surely are not; and the latter, which include a virtually limitless variety of legal rights, vastly outnumber the former. Why, then, urge that rights "resolve the fundamental antinomy . . . that defines the human condition" or are necessarily fundamental at all? Surely some rights reflect only a choice among policies each of which might plausibly be defended. No doubt there is something about all the categories of rights that accounts for their designation as such. But in view of their apparent differences, may they not be related by a number of overlapping similarities, none of which is common to them all?

Although the variousness of rights makes attractive the suggestion that there is only a general "family resemblance" among them, it is striking that few philosophers or theorists about rights have taken that approach. On the contrary, there is quite broad agreement that the concept of a right has specific content that limits what counts as a right, although there are further distinctions to be made. That may, of course, be a mistake; there may be nothing more involved than an ambiguous general term that requires more particular specification. But in view of all the efforts to clarify the concept of a right as such, it seems powerfully unlikely. And it is not correct. Although I am far from urging that every legal right is to be ranked as fundamental, I shall argue that the core of the concept of a right is its connection with responsibility. Understanding that core and the antinomic human condition from which it arises and applying that understanding to the special case of legal rights enables us in turn to resolve the central problem of legal philosophy: the perennial debate between legal positivism and natural law. Similarly, applying that understanding to other special categories of rights, or what are asserted to be rights, leads to a coherent resolution of the conceptual puzzles that they present.

In the course of my argument, I have not always observed the usual separation between the language of ordinary description and the language of normative discourse. Where that occurs, the argument itself will disclose why a distinction of that kind has no application. As I have already suggested, the manner in which rights overcome the division between what is and what ought to be takes us to the heart of the matter. So also, although a central concern throughout is to elucidate our use of familiar concepts, the concept of a right above all, the argument is not, or not only, conceptual. For in a critical respect, the concepts are not up to us but are determined by or—it comes to the same thing—determine "reality," what there is. Rights enable us to overcome a deep *phenomenological* contradiction. Without rights or some equivalent concept, we could not make sense of, or even articulate, a fundamental structural aspect of our experience, on which all our concrete experience depends. It makes no difference whether one says that the contradiction is in the reality that we experience or that it is in our experience of reality. Either way, we cannot get beyond or through experience to an unexperienced "noumenal" reality. The argument has an obvious affinity with Kant's epistemic ontology. Unlike Kant, however, I shall argue that the contradiction is not a barrier to understanding, but itself, contained by the idea of rights, provides the ground of understanding.

One of the reasons why rights so occupy us now, I think, is that transcendent sources of meaning in comparison with which the human condition is a temporary and imperfect state have lost their hold. It is easy to suppose that concern for rights must reflect an aggressively individualistic and competitive world view, one in which having one's own for no reason other than that it is one's own prevails over the needs and wants of others individually or as a group. Rights, it is sometimes suggested, are anticommunitarian. That view of rights misses their true import. Rights may, of course, be abused. But without rights, there is no freedom and no responsibility. Whatever the view from a perspective not our own, from our perspective the human condition is not a limited and less perfect version of something else. On the contrary, its paradoxes are themselves what give meaning to our existence. That is what rights are all about and why they matter.

CHAPTER ONE

Persistent Puzzles

M OST OF THE LITERATURE about rights is concerned either to analyze the concept of a right or to specify the content of particular rights. Since rights have a prominent place in philosophical literature and political debate alike, efforts to clarify the concept and to pin it down concretely are not surprising. But although one might expect the two efforts to support each other, the former setting bounds for the latter and the latter providing testing examples for the former, they do not sit easily together; and although much good work has been done, neither goal is much closer to being realized. Analysis seems to be constrained by some aspect of a right that is recalcitrant to the usual categories and "just is" the case, as if rights are not wholly within the bounds of reason but are simply "given" as part of the furniture of the universe. The description of specific rights, on the other hand, seems always to rest finally on contestable individual or social judgments. Lurking not far below the surface are a number of persistent puzzles about what rights are in the first place, which indicate bafflement at the most fundamental level.

Rights affect interpersonal relations. The practical significance of the rights that a person has is most often how he may properly act in relation to others and they in relation to him. It is not evident, however, whether rights as such are relational or are in the first instance attributive and their relational significance derived from that.

Does one have any rights in the absence of other persons? Or is a right necessarily a right against some other? Again, insofar as a right is relational, it is normative. Is the normative aspect, then, its only content, inherent in the right itself? Or does a right have non-normative content, from which its normative significance is derived? Even when our primary concern is plainly relational and normative, we speak of rights as belonging to their possessor and as if they are a matter of fact: one has, or does not have, a right, as one has, or does not have, ordinary attributes like a strong physique or good judgment. In itself, that linguistic oddity need not trouble us. We speak similarly about having or not having a duty. In the latter case, however, the statement is readily rendered into explicitly normative language: A person having a duty ought to do whatever it is that the duty prescribes. No such rendering is available with respect to rights, which remain insistently in the indicative mode. What is it that a person having a right ought to do?

Indeed, the statement that someone has a right seems to insist more than anything on *not* prescribing what *he* ought to do. We should not ordinarily say that a person has a right to do *x* unless even more certainly he has a right not to do *x*. Likewise, the right to have *x* does not mean that one ought not do without it if he wishes and perhaps even if he does not. We are most likely to point out that a person has a right in just those circumstances in which some consideration points in another direction. It would be odd to tell someone that she ought to take an action (say, contribute to the Red Cross) and add at the end, "and you have a right to do it as well," unless it were supposed that she might not have the right (the money she would contribute being earmarked for something else). Nor does a person who explains that she did something (bought a fancy car) because she "wanted to" add, "and I had a right to," unless it may be supposed that she ought not to have done it (she has two cars already and contributes little to charity) or, once again, that she did not have the right (she has already missed payments on her debts). So although it is sometimes important to note that a person has a right to do the right thing, the right to do the wrong thing concerns us just as often.[1]

Possession of a right thus carries no implication that the possessor ought to exercise it. He may surrender or waive it or, perhaps, give it away. According to its terms, he may lose it. But ordinarily it may not properly be denied or disregarded in the interest of accomplishing some goal with which its exercise would conflict. In exceptional circumstances, the right may not prevail. But such circumstances must be genuinely exceptional; the reasons for disregarding the right must not amount merely to what is preferable on the whole.[2] Even when a right does not prevail, a trace of it remains and prompts what might be called moral regret, a sense that the denial of the right is an unfortunate aspect of the situation despite everything.[3]

Whatever the normative impact of a right may be, it evidently does not implicate an approving judgment about its exercise or the consequences of its exercise. Hence rights have been characterized as distributive. And so it appears. For if Smith has a right to act in a certain way and Jones does not, we are likely to feel obligated ordinarily to sustain Smith's act, even if we feel equally obligated to prevent Jones from doing exactly the same thing. But what is it that a right distributes, and on what basis? And what are we to make of a normative phenomenon that disregards both the moral quality and the consequences of an act, provided only that the actor be a determinate person, as if it refers not to conduct as such at all but rather to something about that person? In what sense can it be morally preferable that Smith do x than that x not be done, even though x is a bad thing for her to do and will have a harmful effect? Of course, it might be preferable to allow Smith to do x, if she chooses, because on balance a rule that allows her to choose will have more good effects than any other workable rule. But recognition of a right does not seem necessarily to depend on such a calculation; frequently it is easier to ascertain that there is a right in a particular case than to theorize about such cases generally.

The strongest rights go even further in this direction. Not only do they attach without any ordinary justification for their exercise. They may be said to be mandatory or inalienable; that is to say, one cannot give them up or assign them away. Although the decision whether to exercise the right or how to exercise it is unconstrained, one is constrained to decide. An unavoidable right, however, sounds more like a duty, which is paradoxical.[4] Nor does the paradox end there. For however problematic is a right to decide whether to do the right thing, it seems a good deal more puzzling to assert that there is a duty to decide whether to do the right thing, a duty that prevails over the duty to do the right thing itself.

The ambiguity of rights and even the uncertainty whether the modal ambiguity is at bottom conceptual or (somehow) phenomenal do not impede discourse about them. Although in other contexts one would quickly be asked whether he is describing what is the case or prescribing what ought to be, when we speak about rights we seem comfortably to do both or, at any rate, to straddle the high fence that usually separates them. The ambiguity is neither suppressed nor inadvertent. On the contrary, it is immediately apparent and evidently deliberate. And, if that is a matter of concern only to those who are philosophically inclined, it is no less within the understanding of ordinary people. Rights are as familiar and as easy to grasp as an argument on a playground. Indeed, the ease with which we engage in talk about rights despite the ambiguity is itself cause for philosophic concern.

Rights and Duties

In order to account for the clear conviction that rights are normative, despite their indeterminacy concerning the conduct of the possessor of a right, it has been urged that their normative significance has to do not with the possessor but with some other person(s), for whom the right imposes a duty. (Rights, that is to say, are essentially relational.) In the same vein, it may be said that the significant thing about possession of a right is not *having* a right but *not having* one. Since not having a right is understood to mean that one has a duty (presumably, though perhaps not necessarily, in consequence of someone else's having a right), it is again the duty rather than the right that counts. The ascription of a duty is a very common reason for calling attention to a right; and locating its normative content there has the virtue of bypassing the apparently descriptive attribution to its possessor. Still, it is at least worth noting that if a person's rights are nothing more than an elliptical reference to other persons' duties, it is a strange way of speaking. Why should we refer to Smith's rights when we mean Jones's duties, unless the former have independent significance and are in some way the ground of the latter?

Nor is it only our pattern of speech that resists this explanation of rights. For insofar as Jones's duty is traced to Smith's right, it also is curiously indifferent to ordinary moral judgment. Jones is not required nor, often, even expected to approve Smith's exercise of her right. On the contrary, his duty is typically asserted because approval may be lacking. If Jones believes that exercise of the right will be destructive, he may urge Smith not to exercise it, so long as the urging stops short of coercion. If, insisting on her right, Smith proceeds, Jones's duty does not bar him from taking steps to avoid the likely consequences, which Smith intends and expects to bring about, so long as the right itself is honored. In this way arise difficult questions about honoring the "letter" or the "spirit" of a right: that is, how much honoring the right requires. In *The Merchant of Venice* Shylock insists on his right to a pound of Antonio's flesh, even though it seems outrageous. Acknowledging the right, Portia appeals to Shylock to renounce it. When he refuses, she proposes to honor the right to the letter, and in doing so defeats him. The duty seems thus to be defined by the right and, like the right itself, not to have a connection with any other normative consideration.

As a practical matter, the view that rights are always connected to a duty is plausible. A right that could be exercised fully without affecting or being affected by the behavior of other persons seems scarcely to deserve the name; it would be a "free good," available as of course. If anything, it would be an ordinary power or capacity, though, since it would be available to all, scarcely even that. Similarly, it would be peculiar to assert a person's right to some state of affairs that was altogether beyond anyone's capacity to bring about. The exercise of a right may not conflict with anything that others ordinarily consider doing or want to do and need not be accompanied by anyone's conscious performance of a duty. Most of us most of the time observe our duty not to assault our neighbors, take their property, or disturb their peace, without giving it much thought. Still, it does not seem inaccurate to acknowledge that our neighbors' rights in those respects give rise to duties, which might become significant if circumstances changed.

There are also, however, familiar situations in which the practical significance of a right is not its bearing on the conduct of others but its bearing on the conduct of the right-possessor. Walking in the country, Smith may wonder whether she has a right to cross an open field, pick flowers by the side of the road, or keep a locket that she finds in a ditch. Her conclusion in each case will have a bearing on how she believes others also ought to behave: whether to block her way, put up a fence, or claim the locket. But any such question may be moot in the circumstances because no one else is about; and Smith may ponder the question of her right seriously all the same. There is a common moral understanding that one ought to weigh one's actions in just that way, without regard to whether one can "get away with it." The point is not that Smith's right, if she has one, does not implicate duties of others, for plainly it does; rather it is that the question has importance for her that is independent of any such duty. (Smith might put the question to herself as whether she has a duty not to cross the field, and so forth, which in turn might raise the question whether someone has a right that she not do so. But it would be at least as natural to put the question directly in terms of her right. One likely answer to the question about the flowers or locket, for example, would be, "I have as much of a right as anyone else.")

Similarly, although reference to a right would ordinarily be otiose if one lacked power to exercise it, which no one else could provide, the right is not altogether empty. There is a felt difference between being unable to do something and being under an obligation not to do it, which difference may affect one's conduct. Concluding that she has no right to take a locket that is wedged under a rock, Smith may regretfully leave it where it is. Concluding that she has a right, she may return later with a bar to pry the rock loose. One may respond that, after all, she did have the power to exercise the right potentially and that only because she did was the right significant. But that conclusion is retrospective. It seems as accurate to say that her acquiring the power was a reaction to the conclusion that she had the right as the other way around.[5]

Rights independent of duties may also be asserted meaningfully not as a predicate for action by anyone in particular but as the basis for a program still to be worked out. It may be said, for example, that some group of persons or all persons have a right to medical care, decent housing, a meaningful job, and so forth. Such statements affirm the substance of the right as an aspiration or goal and usually are not intended or understood to affirm a concrete, present duty of anyone or everyone to provide what is lacking. There is a large difference between such statements and the assertion of an enforceable legal right or even a right that one believes ought to be enforced. But to dismiss the description of such goals as rights altogether is to miss an important distinction between them and other social goals that are based on considerations of the general well-being. Strongly as one believed that the nation's greatest need was increased productivity, controlling inflation, or military defense and promoted it as a social policy, he would not characterize it as anyone's right. To characterize a goal as a right indicates that its justification is not general but individual, a matter not of policy, what is good on the whole, but of what is due the persons in question, that is to say, a matter of right.[6]

We may note parenthetically that duties do not seem invariably to require rights any more than the other way around. Duties count most when a person might otherwise act differently. Ordinarily there is no reason to insist on performance of a duty that confers no benefit on anyone; and it is easy to regard whoever benefits as having a right correlative to the duty. There are, however, duties that depend not on reason but on will, the justification (or explanation) for which is simply authority to command. Ceremonial duties of religious practice are of this kind. For those who acknowledge them, they are duties not because God has a right to their performance—what could that mean?—but because God or someone with proper authority has commanded that they be performed. Other ceremonial duties, like standing while the national anthem is played, also attach because of who one is oneself and not because of one's relation to someone else, whose right the performance of the duty is said to be.

Duties like charity and generosity are owed to no person in particular and can be met in a variety of ways. The very point of such duties is that they go beyond consideration of others' rights and do not depend even on considerations of general welfare. The latter may affect the direction of one's generosity but not the duty itself, which arises out of one's own nature. One may object that ceremonial duties and duties of unspecific benevolence are aspects of moral conduct generally and, as such, different from duties attached to a right. But that simply reinforces the point that duties do not entail rights.[7]

One category of duties requires special mention. Many moral obligations have to do with the well-being of particular nonhuman beings or nonliving things. Most people believe that they ought not to treat animals cruelly, waste natural flora, or spoil great natural or human-made treasures, like the Grand Canyon or the Parthenon. Some obligations of this kind can be explained as broad-gauged utilitarianism that takes into account the good of future generations as well as the now living. Often, however, such an explanation seems far-fetched and in any case superfluous. The more obvious explanation is that the duty is based on concern for its object. That is the case at least with respect to animals, about which it is natural to say that there is a duty not about them but *toward* them. Animals are said to have an "interest" as individuals and not merely as components of the general good. Some of those who recognize interests of animals allow that plants and nonliving entities may also have interests; all that is required, they suggest, is that there be a recognized condition of well-being or flourishing as an individual entity. Putting together the duty and the interest, it may then be argued that the object of the one and possessor of the other has a right to performance of the duty.

In this instance, the question of a right is more often practical and political than conceptual. To deny the right, it is feared, is to deny or at least to diminish the duty. Those who want to sustain the duty, therefore, urge that even if the "right" in question lacks some of the features of paradigmatic rights, whatever those may be, it has enough of them to warrant using that term. I discuss this issue at length in Chapter Six. For the present, it is sufficient to note that such rights, if that is what they are, lack most of the features about rights that trouble us. What is troubling about them is not the facticity and moral neutrality of rights generally, for their dependence on the initial proposition that there is a duty makes them distinctly normative in the first instance. Rather it is the normative assumption on which they are based: that a nonhuman (or nonliving) entity can have an individual claim distinct from and superior to the general good. If the duty toward an animal were based on an authoritative revelation—for example, that the animal is sacred—that would account fully for the duty without reference to any such claim. The explanation would be simply that it was right to treat the animal as the revelation prescribed.

The connection that is made between rights and duties reinforces the central puzzle about rights. Although it is true that a right typically implies a duty of others, at least to the extent of not interfering with its exercise, in many circumstances the right and not the duty is the focus of our attention. Even when we attend to the duty, insofar as it is a corollary of the right, it restates the substance of the right in explicitly normative terms, without explaining it. Although we may, and frequently do, assert that Jones has a duty because Smith has a right, it would be odd in the extreme to assert that Smith has a right *because* Jones has a duty, as if the duty were our main concern and the right an incidental consequence. The most that we could assert in that direction is that *inasmuch as* Jones has a duty, Smith has a right, which states the connection without explaining either the right or the duty. The right, that is to say, remains primary. Calling attention to the concomitant duty emphasizes the ambiguity of rights: Are they attributive or relational, descriptive or prescriptive, concept or phenomenon?

Rights and Rules (Herein of Legal Rights)

The weight of the argument that rights always implicate the duty of another does not rest solely on the connection between rights and duties. It is crucial that both the right and the duty are referred to a rule that provides their justification, whether they are considered separately or together. So, according to Stanley Benn and Richard Peters, "the right of X is the duty of Y. To say that X has a right to *f*5 is to imply that there is a rule which, when applied to the case of X and some other person Y, imposes on Y a duty to pay X *f*5 if X so chooses. . . . The correlation . . . between rights and duties is a logical, not a moral or legal relation. . . . Right and duty are different names for the same normative relation, according to the point of view from which it is regarded."[8] Without insisting on the reciprocity of rights and duties, L. W. Sumner has argued to the same effect. The only defensible ground of rights, he urges, is rules founded on utilitarian premises: "a right is genuine just in case the social policy of recognizing it in the appropriate rule system is the best means of promoting some favoured goal."[9]

Arguments of this kind are exemplified by legal rights, which, extending over the whole range of human affairs, are readily regarded as a model of rights generally. The outcome of a legal controversy is typically expressed by reference to the right of someone or other. If conflicting rights are asserted, the resolution of the controversy dictates which prevails in the circumstances and qualifies the subservient right accordingly. In general, we presume that the parties to a controversy represent and act for themselves and that each can, if he chooses, forgo his claim. Reference to a right makes that general presumption specific; it indicates both that a claim will be enforced at the demand of the party who has the right and that whatever is the substance of the claim is contingent on such a demand, or at any rate subject to cancellation if it is waived. The reference adds nothing to the outcome and is explained by the proceedings, actual or assumed, leading to that outcome—the rules of law as applied.

Broadly speaking, therefore, a legal right stands for the outcome that will be enforced—the state of affairs that will be brought about—at the behest of the party having the right. The potential for enforcement is both necessary and sufficient. The absence of a remedy, it is commonly said, is in law absence of the right.[10] So regarded, legal rights display the distributive aspect of rights and, more particularly, since their enforcement is directed at someone else, the connection between rights and duties. Someone who has a legal right thereby acquires power to bring about a state of affairs that she could not bring about otherwise. The right may consist only of an absence of legal restriction on the exercise of power that one otherwise has: that is, the lack of an enforceable right of others or independent official authority to prevent the person from exercising her power. Or it may include also a restriction on others' exercise of their powers that would interfere with one's own exercise of power. Still more amply, it may include provision of a power that one otherwise lacks. The best known effort to lay bare these distinctions among legal rights is Wesley Hohfeld's. Within his system, an absence of restrictions was designated a "privilege" and a restriction on others' powers an "immunity"; only an empowerment by force of law was a right properly so called.[11] Although the differences among permission, protection, and provision are significant, in the context of civil society in which the government has a monopoly of force, even the first, most restricted form of right constitutes an empowerment; and only insofar as a person is so empowered is it correct to describe him as having a right. The First Amendment right to practice one's religion, for example, is primarily an empowerment against the government; it bars the government ordinarily from restricting religious practice, by all the means otherwise at its disposal, in aid of some policy that it thinks more important.

Like powers generally, legal rights are anticipatory, available to be exercised; but whether they are exercised or not depends on their possessor. Even if not exercised, powers describe actual capacities. One may have the power to run a four-minute mile, to solve an equation, or to persuade a crowd. Whether one does or does not is a matter of fact, ascertained, in principle at any rate, in the ordinary way. A doubter could test the matter by clocking the runner, setting the mathematician a problem, or giving the politician a forum. Similarly, someone who has a legal right has the resources of the law available on demand and can call on them just as he calls on resources of his own. That also is, in principle, an ascertainable matter of fact. Much has been made of the indeterminacy of law, in hard cases if not in every case. Although the extent of such indeterminacy has sometimes been greatly exaggerated (often in support of an argument, itself political, that the law follows politics in detail as well as in gross), there are certainly cases in which a court might "go either way." Once a case is decided, however, provided that the court is duly constituted and has acted within its jurisdiction, the law is, as a matter of fact, whatever the court has said it is, at least with regard to the particular controversy before the court. Whether it will be applied in the same way in the next case is another matter. A good deal of the weightiness that has been attached in this respect to the phenomenon of judicial discretion depends on obfuscation of the difference between "the law" before and after the fact, that is, before and after it has been determined what the law is.

If enforcement is the key, however, legal rights appear not merely helpful but highly misleading as a model for rights that do not depend explicitly on law or some similar set of rules accepted as valid and effective within their range of application. (Believing that enforcement is the key, Bentham drew the appropriate conclusion, that absent such "posited" rules, there are no rights.) For in such a case, enforcement does not seem to be in the picture at all. If anything, it is the lack of enforcement—the absence of a legal right—that typically prompts discussion of rights of another kind: moral, human, or civil rights.[12] If we question whether someone who has a legal right has also one of these nonlegal rights, doubt about the latter often indicates some doubt whether the legal right may not contravene the unenforced nonlegal right of someone else. Confronted by this incongruity, one who relies on an analogy to legal rights to explicate rights generally may observe that the only difference is that in law "must" or "shall" replaces "ought" and let it go at that.[13] But if in law the threatened "or else" is everything, what remains as the content of a right after that has been eliminated?

Thinking of legal rights as empowerments emphasizes this difference between them and rights generally. In the case of a legal right, the availability of enforcement both substantiates the right and establishes the power. So far as nonlegal rights are concerned, however, one may well have the right but not have the power. Or, of course, one may have the power without the right. Possession of a legal right, like a power, is ascertainable as a matter of fact. But what does one have when he has a nonlegal right? How is it put to the test? Such questions are not only, like questions about legal rights, controversial. There is not even agreement about what kind of answers would be satisfactory.

Considering a legal right, one may conclude not only that the person having the right ought not to exercise it, as is true also of a nonlegal right, but that she ought not to have the right in the first place. Just because legal rights can be regarded as powers that are conferred and might be withdrawn, there is no reason why they may not be evaluated approvingly or disapprovingly. The normative judgment is neither redundant nor contradictory. If we have in mind a nonlegal right, however, although the right has normative significance, a normative judgment about the right itself is altogether out of place. Thus, the assertion that, in view of Smith's right, Jones ought (not) to act in a certain way is entirely familiar. But could one comprehensibly assert, without reference to a law or some similar posited rule or convention, that Smith has a right but ought not to have it? What independent bases could there be for the two conjoined propositions? To whom might the latter proposition be addressed? If Smith's right arose out of prior conduct of some other person, one might deplore her having the right. For example, Jones might have made Smith a foolish promise, which one thinks he ought never to have made. Nonetheless, since he has done so, Smith has the right; and to say that she ought not to have it is only to say indirectly that Jones ought not to have made the promise. If for some reason the promise is not binding, the conclusion is not that Smith has the right but ought not to have it, but that Smith does not have the right. (Whether the promise is legally binding and Smith has a legal right is a different question.)

The element of enforcement that assimilates legal rights to powers is at the heart of another difference between legal rights and rights generally, which bears directly on the argument that rights are dependent on rules. Whether a rule of law itself depends on an anterior conception of the right (embodied perhaps in a fundamental document like a constitution) or on a conclusion of public policy about what is best on the whole, so long as the rule is acknowledged as valid it sustains the derived concrete legal right, which is simply an application of the rule to a particular factual context. Even when there is no plainly applicable and dispositive rule, the basis of a decision will be cast explicitly or implicitly as a rule that governs the case at hand as well as other relevantly similar cases that may arise thereafter. The rule will (purport to) be drawn from the materials—statutes, prior decisions, administrative expertise, guided discretion—that other rules make relevant. Although the result in a particular case may by the doctrine of precedent become the source of a rule, that result is itself the product of a rule found to have been applicable to that case. That is true even though the rule may remain a matter of controversy after the result has been announced. In short, however narrowly prior or subsequent jurisprudence confines the rule determined to be applicable, the right constituting the outcome of the case is justified by reference to it. If the outcome is later declared to have been mistaken, the reversal too will be explained as a correction of the rule previously announced.[14]

The direction of legal reasoning thus appears to support the general dependence of rights on rules. Outside the law, however, our reasoning is likely to proceed in the opposite direction. Asked to explain the assertion that Smith has a right to Jones's assistance, one could not satisfactorily respond that Jones ought to help Smith or that persons in Jones's situation ought to help persons in Smith's situation, either of which propositions might be true although Smith had no right to Jones's help. Rather, Smith's right would typically be offered as a sufficient explanation of why Jones ought to help her. Indeed, the very point of asserting that Smith has a right is to obviate consideration whether or not (absent the right) Jones ought to help; and ordinarily, the right overrides the conclusion that (absent the right) Jones ought not. Were no right of Smith in issue, the question whether Jones ought to help her would be answered differently, by consideration of whether doing so would have good consequences or for some other reason be the right thing for Jones to do.

Those who urge that valid rights are derived from rules are not unaware that our usual way of deploying rights in moral discourse is to the contrary. They believe, however, that reasoning from right to rule *cannot* be correct and that it must perforce give way to the modal logic of their argument. Rights, they say, have normative implications. But a normative proposition can validly be derived only from another, more general normative proposition. A valid claim of right, therefore, *must* be based on another normative proposition, that is to say, a rule. (The rule itself being normative and requiring validation, Benn and Peters restrict it to propositions conferring a potential benefit on someone, hence the reciprocal duty; and Sumner restricts it to propositions justified on utilitarian grounds. In either case, the essential detail is that the rule is normative and not its specific normative content.) What distinguishes a right from normative propositions generally is that the former presupposes a rule presumed to be valid and, therefore, regards the question of validity as settled. Thus, according to this argument, a "right" that cannot be referred to a rule either lacks the special claim of validity that characterizes rights (or has no normative implication whatever), in which case it is not a genuine right, or it is invalid.

Each step of this argument, taken by itself, is sound. It is the case that rights have normative implications. It is the case that normative propositions are validated by normative propositions. If rights make a special claim to be valid independently, it must, so it seems, be because the validating proposition is a rule that is taken for granted to be valid and hence breaks the usual chain of normative validation. Legal rights appear to support the argument and to exemplify just how a valid right is derived. If other asserted rights cannot be derived similarly, the argument dictates that they are not true (or valid) rights, whatever our habits of thought or speech may suggest to the contrary.

On closer inspection, however, the example of legal rights demonstrates that the argument does not escape the challenge of its own logic. When the substance of a legal right is questioned, it is ordinarily taken for granted that there is a body of law the validity of which is not in doubt, from which the rule applicable to the case can be derived. An answer to the question does not call for normative evaluation of the content of the rule, but simply a determination of what the rule is.[15] Told that Brown has a legal right to fire Gray, it is inadequate to respond that Brown's business will decline, that he does not recognize Gray's merit as an employee, that Gray's family will suffer, or even that the law on which Brown relies is a bad one. To contest Brown's right, one has to give a ground for argument that the correct rule of law applicable to Gray's employment situation is not the rule on which Brown relies—because Brown's lawyer has misinterpreted the precedents, or because other rules provide for a departure from precedent in this instance, and so forth. Although Gray's lawyer may urge the superiority of the rule supporting Gray on any number of grounds, the issue at bottom is not which is the better rule but what the rule is. If a court orders that Gray be rehired, Brown's supporters may describe the outcome as a change of rule in midstream, a flat-out denial of Brown's actual right. They are entitled to their opinion. The response to the contrary, however, is not, "According to the applicable rule, Brown has a legal right, but it would be better if he did not, so let's ignore it," but "Brown does not have a right, although there are arguments that he does."

So far as the law is concerned, reasons for overthrowing a rule are not reasons for disregarding a right that the rule confers. While the rule persists, the right has priority over normative arguments to the contrary. (It is for just this reason that it is often said that hard cases—in which there are strong normative arguments against the applicable rule—make bad law.) In place of the normative justification for a right that reference to a rule is supposed to provide, there is only the fact that there is a rule. That is precisely the point of the reference. Were the rule itself subject to validation, one would not have a right but only a normative proposition, the validity of which depends on the validity of a further normative proposition, itself contingently valid in the same way.

The whole argument that rights are dependent on rules hinges, therefore, on the implicit premise that the validity of the rule in question is established on some non-normative basis. In the case of legal rights, that premise is contained in the assumption that the question arises in the context of an effective legal order. The general problem of validity is perhaps the most contentious issue of modern jurisprudence, because it obliges us to confront the possibility of factual validation of normative propositions.[16] Brought to ground, the general argument that rights depend on rules is the same. It does not resolve the puzzles about rights but restates them more emphatically.

Rights on Their Own

The preceding discussion does not lead unequivocally to a single outcome. If rules do not provide a way out of the puzzles that beleaguer rights as we now think of them, then perhaps we should conclude that we must think about them differently thus: Propositions about rights are not different from normative propositions generally, and the reference to a right serves only to indicate the certainty with which the proposition is asserted or as a declaration that one is not willing (for the moment) to discuss its validity. Powerful as the argument pointing in that direction is, rights have proved too strong to be dismissed as a mistake or as only a linguistic flourish. Most of the recent discussion about rights takes the opposite tack. Rights are said to be fundamental—so fundamental, indeed, that they stand alone. Their place in moral discourse can be described; but how they occupy that place, what they are and how they escape the constraint of reason, is simply a puzzle without a solution. There being no solution, the puzzle is set aside.

Two important theories of rights, which illustrate this pattern of description without explanation, have classified rights in one instance as entitlements and in the other as claims. Although each writer explicitly rejects the classification of the other, their conclusions are remarkably similar. H. J. McCloskey has argued that rights are entitlements.[17] Relying on that initial classification, he considers many of the issues discussed here: the relation of rights *qua* entitlements to duties, rights as powers, and so forth. His principal reason for describing rights as entitlements, however, is that there are convincing reasons for rejecting all the other plausible classifications (powers, liberties, claims). The virtue of "entitlement" in his view is precisely that it lacks strong descriptive content; except for avoiding the other terms, the reference to an entitlement adds nothing to the discussion and does not itself contribute to our understanding of rights.[18] Joel Feinberg has characterized rights as claims, more particularly as valid claims.[19] He too does not make much of the classification as a descriptive matter; he observes that rights and claims are frequently identified with each other, so that defining one by reference to the other is a "dizzying piece of circularity."[20] Even so, he argues, we shall understand the nature of rights better if we consider the activity of claiming.[21]

Making a claim or claiming that one has a right, Feinberg says, is an activity governed by understood requirements. A valid claim is one that can be justified "within a system of rules." In the case of nonlegal rights, the asserted justification is found analogously in "moral principles, or the principles of an enlightened conscience."[22] The content of the principles is not specified further. Without more than that to go on, however, the analogy on which Feinberg depends to bring rights within the category of valid claims does not work. It passes by the whole question whether rights are not the ground of moral principles and not, therefore, validated by them. If the justification of a right is a moral principle, it is unclear what need or use there is for reference to a right; for the real issues in each case must be the validity of the moral principle and the strength of its application in that context.[23] Elsewhere, Feinberg seems to acknowledge the primacy of rights. He observes that they are "especially sturdy objects to 'stand upon,' a most useful sort of moral furniture," which have "supreme moral importance."[24] McCloskey also recognizes the primacy of rights and makes that a reason for not characterizing them as claims. Rights, he says, are "logically more basic than, logically prior to, claims in general and hence to legitimate claims in particular"; they are "logically primary."[25]

Valid claims, Feinberg says also, are made by a certain sort of creature: "respect for persons . . . may simply be respect for their rights, so that there cannot be the one without the other; and what is called 'human dignity' may simply be the recognizable capacity to assert claims. To respect a person then, or to think of him as possessed of human dignity, simply *is* to think of him as a potential maker of claims."[26] Although this suggests that human beings may be the only creatures that have rights, elsewhere Feinberg has argued that at least higher animals also have rights, because they have sufficient interests— "appetites, conative urges, and rudimentary purposes, the integrated satisfaction of which constitutes their welfare or good"—for claims to be made in their behalf.[27] Without interests, he says, a creature "can have no 'good' of its own," and therefore cannot have rights.[28] Since, however, as Feinberg concedes, such a creature or even an inanimate object can be cared for and preserved in a state of well-being or good repair, it is hardly more of a stretch metaphorically to say that they have interests and an individual good than to say that animals can make claims. Feinberg's conclusions about what can possess rights reflect a common, but far from universal, intuition; beyond that, except for registering his approval or disapproval of certain more or less metaphoric linguistic usage, he leaves obscure just what it is about rights that only certain kinds of beings possess them. McCloskey argues similarly that some rights, at least, must be "intrinsic to their possessors,"[29] by which he evidently means that they depend on the fact that the possessor is the kind of creature it is. He believes that, strictly speaking, only human beings qualify.[30] Like Feinberg, he stops short of the critical issue: Why do human beings (and, if it is true, only they) have rights?

In the end, McCloskey and Feinberg leave the elaboration of rights not far from their starting point. Despite their own efforts, they seem very nearly to acknowledge that rights are *sui generis* and cannot be cabined within a more general classification. Feinberg himself observes: "if a 'formal definition' of the usual philosophical sort is what we are after, the game is over before it has begun, and we can say that the concept of a right is a 'simple, undefinable, unanalysable primitive.'"[31] That is to say, they can only be recognized and not explained.

Other efforts to fit rights within another, more tractable rubric come to the same conclusion.

Coming at the matter differently but coming out in about the same place, some specifically functional accounts of rights explain their significance by assigning them a special role in moral discourse, without addressing the manner in which the role is accomplished. The account of this kind that has had the most currency, at least as a rubric, is Ronald Dworkin's reworking of Hobbes's famous phrase: Rights, not clubs, he says, are "trumps."[32] More particularly, Dworkin argues that rights ordinarily prevail over considerations of general well-being: "It follows from the definition of a right that it cannot be outweighed by all social goals. We might, for simplicity, stipulate not to call any political aim a right unless, for example, it cannot be defeated by appeal to any of the ordinary routine goals of political administration, but only by a goal of special urgency."[33] This trumping quality of rights, Dworkin has said, associates rights with nonconsequential ethical theories. In a rather different way, John Finnis has made the same association, linking "natural rights" to a stringently nonconsequentialist theory of natural law.[34]

Although Dworkin's argument defends the primacy of rights, his dissociation of rights from ordinary considerations of the public good and utilitarian ethical theory in general does not go far enough. Rights do not just favor one kind of ethical theory over another; rather, they appear to be divorced from ethical considerations of every kind, except, of course, those to which they themselves give rise. So far as conduct of the right-possessor himself is concerned, his right is simply independent of the right and the good; a right to do or to have x is also, necessarily, a right not to do or to have it, whatever may be dictated by consequential or nonconsequential arguments either way. So far as the conduct of others is concerned, rights trump *both* the right and the good.[35] The priority of rights over nonconsequential arguments is easily overlooked, because a person's right typically is itself a nonconsequential ground of another person's duty; it is precisely that normative significance of a right that needs to be explained. The deep puzzle about how rights function, which Dworkin's trumping metaphor only half discloses, is that rights have normative consequences but are themselves generally impervious to normative considerations of any kind.

The puzzle is compounded in theory, if alleviated in practice, by the limited defeasibility of rights. With few exceptions (among whom Kant is notable), rights theorists have agreed that in extreme circumstances, a right may give way. The same point is made, perhaps reducing the primacy of rights a little more, by describing them as having only *prima facie* weight.[36] This defeasibility has to do not with the possessor of the right, which is fulfilled however she exercises it and who may, therefore, be subject to any kind of moral argument about how she ought to exercise it. Rather, it has to do with others, who may justifiably ignore the right for the sake of a very large and exigent good. Although rights trump nonconsequentialist arguments also, they are not similarly defeasible by them. Consequences being left aside, a right must either defeat such an argument or be defeated by it in all circumstances. Defeasibility seems thus to depend on a balancing of incommensurables: a nonconsequential "distributive" claim on one side and consequential considerations on the other. And, indeed, the priority of rights in ordinary circumstances does not depend on the perceived weakness of any consequential considerations, which may weigh heavily on the conduct of the possessor; rather, however weighty they may be, they are deemed irrelevant to possession of the right.

In this connection, the assertion sometimes made, that rights are indeed absolute, should be given more respectful attention than it usually is. Judith Thomson's argument that rights, albeit defeasible, leave "moral traces" in the wake of their defeat is a partial recognition that rights cannot be thrown in the balance with other ethical considerations; they can only be thrown over.[37] So also, Finnis' insistence that a consideration of consequences can never require direct invasion of a "basic good" may be understood partly as a generalized defense of the absoluteness of rights.[38] That such absoluteness perforce gives way in practice, buttressed sometimes by unconvincing arguments about "double effect" and the like, is not an indication that it was wrong from the start so much as concrete recognition that the primacy of rights and their limited defeasibility spring from a contest between incommensurables that reasoned argument cannot resolve.

In order to escape this puzzle, it may be asserted that rights do not disregard all nondistributional values but rather give an especially prominent place to a particular value or set of values as components of the good: those associated with individual liberty or autonomy. Dworkin, for example, has observed: "Right-based theories are . . . concerned with the independence rather than the conformity of individual action. They presuppose and protect the value of individual thought and choice."[39] That view of rights is taken up by familiar political rhetoric. Among the rights that are most prized in American society are rights against the government, which reject collective action in favor of the individual. The emphasis on rights in American political theory, it is said, confirms their connection with values that inhere in the individual; in the domain of rights, the individual is the relevant entity.

Historically, the connection between rights and individual liberty is supported by the Lockean tradition. From Locke's Whig point of view, the powers to which individual "natural" rights are opposed are those of the government. As the theory of the "divine right of kings" (against which Locke argued) reminds us, however, autocracy may be and, indeed, usually is right-based as much as democracy. According to that theory, the king's rule was a matter of his right, which was independent of the good of his subjects or any other criterion that measured the effects of his rulership.

The argument that right-based theories as such favor the individual is weak not only historically but theoretically as well. If the issue is taxation or the draft, then the right not to be taxed or conscripted does indeed favor the individual. There is, however, another point of view representing the propertyless, unprivileged masses whom Locke never noticed, from which the liberty of the individual is opposed not by the government but by the power of other persons and protection of the rights in question depends on governmental action to restrain such power. Since in either case the powers that are confirmed are designated as rights, both points of view can be described as right-based; but if the question is which theory favors the individual rather than which individuals are favored, it seems plausible to select the one that relies least on governmental action to alter the prevailing distribution of powers. In fact the most strongly "individualist" political philosophies are generally ones that recognize the narrowest range of governmentally protected rights. The libertarian theories of philosophers like Herbert Spencer in the nineteenth century and Friedrich Hayek and Robert Nozick in this century emphasize powers, not rights. The rights that are recognized consist mainly of restrictions on the exercise of those few powers, mostly involving the use of physical force, that are singled out and characterized as aggression. Beyond that range, persons get what they can and keep what they get. That also is defended as a matter of right, of course; but the right confirms, without altering, the actual distribution of powers.

The rights that liberal theorists like Dworkin have in mind are ones that do not designate particular individuals or even depend significantly on differential individual powers. In that respect, they are egalitarian rights. All the same, as rights, they provide the occasion for exercise of individual powers, which do differentiate one person from another. Necessarily, they favor some persons more than others, on the basis of both their actual powers and their desires. The increase in autonomy that is said to be their object and result is purchased by an equivalent restriction of the autonomy of someone else. Unless there is a prior conception of rights or of the individual that specifies which rights count, the statement that rights-based theories favor the individual either is tautologous or is susceptible to directly contrary specifications. One may conclude that a right is not more than a reminder of the importance of the individual person in any moral equation. But that surely depreciates a right too much. For rights purport not merely to deepen ethical inquiry on other bases, but to override it. Rights are trumps.

Closely related are theories that link rights especially to the political good. Rights are said to be the foundation for the organization of individuals into a political community in which the government, as the organ of the community, has a monopoly of force. So, for example, John Rawls has found the origin of basic rights in a theory of justice as fairness that provides the ground rules of social organization; the theory uses a hypothetical contract to elaborate with considerable complexity what is at bottom defended as our common intuition, after due reflection, of what is fair.[40] Thomas Nagel argues that the justification for basic rights is found in "the nonaggregative, unanimity-seeking conception of legitimacy." Rights, he says, "must be justified by their role in making it unreasonable for anyone to reject a system which protects them, and reasonable for some to reject a system which does not."[41] T. M. Scanlon, I believe, would similarly defend certain basic rights as powers retained by (or conferred on) individuals because, were they denied, a person could reasonably reject an agreement to surrender any of his powers to the collective judgment of the group as a whole. Defending a contractarian moral theory generally, he says, "An act is wrong if its performance under the circumstances would be disallowed by any system of rules for the general regulation of behavior which no one could reasonably reject as a basis for informed, unforced general agreement."[42]

The principal difficulty of such arguments as a theory of rights is that they are premised on the fact they purport to explain. It may be that, however it is put precisely, reasonable persons would not willingly be governed unless they retained certain rights. But why does that matter? Why strain so to formulate the terms of a hypothetical contract that sustains the hypothetical willing agreement of the persons who are governed as parties to it? All sorts of other beings (as well as nonliving entities) are subject to the collective power of the group. Why are they not also among the "governed" whose willingness to be governed is critical?

To be sure, there is something far-fetched about soliciting the approval of all the animal kinds, not to mention vegetable kinds and rocks and waterfalls and . . . But what is it about persons (who invariably are the only parties to the hypothetical agreement) that makes it not only reasonable to solicit their approval but wholly unreasonable, and self-evidently so, not to have it? If, on one hand, it is difficult to see how the various nonhuman kinds could signal their approval, it is not difficult to devise a plausible substitute. The agreement in issue, even of persons, is entirely hypothetical anyway.[43] On the other hand, if the place of persons at the bargaining table were not so obvious, one might speculate about circumstances in which the approval of (some) persons also would be, at best, supererogatory. No one, so far as I am aware, has urged that the expulsion of Adam and Eve from the Garden of Eden was illegitimate because they never agreed to the termination clause in their lease. Nor are we without historical reminders that it is possible to regard the approval of some persons as essential and the approval or disapproval of others as entirely beside the point. The substantial insights of these theorists raise a further question the more acutely: What is it about rights, that persons—all persons? and only persons?—not only can but must possess them?

The tendency to formulate that question as the terms of a hypothetical contract betrays the fundamental limitation of theories of this kind. Since the contract is only hypothetical, the consent that is required cannot be an actual expression of the unconstrained will of any individual; rather it is the reasonableness of the conclusions themselves, the so-called terms of the contract, that are at stake. As to that, none of the theories finally has more to say than that the proposed conclusions are intuitively appealing. The language of contract and consent serves mainly to hurry us past this stage of the argument. What it suggests most of all is bafflement at the inability to find convincing grounds for conclusions that seem so certain in themselves.

Thomson's account of rights comes closest to confronting the bafflement head-on. Rights, she says, can be identified by their function; but their function can only be described as what rights do. To have a right is not more than being in a certain kind of relationship with other people: "To have a right is to have a kind of moral status, so working out what a right is comes to the same as working out what people ought or ought not do, may or may not do, given a person has a right."[44] A right is a summary of such relationships, which form a coherent set in virtue of the idea of a right itself. We need no explanation of rights because we have other ways to identify them experientially, such as the "moral traces" they leave when they are overridden. Not only do they identify rights; they make rights important. Our proper task is not to look beyond rights, which is futile, but to study them as components of our moral experience, with a view toward increasing our understanding and making it more precise. It is perhaps not clear whether Thomson believes that rights literally are the relationships she identifies or that rights explain the relationships but are themselves inexplicable; her generally reductionist approach makes the former more likely. Either way, she regards them as fundamental elements of moral reasoning. She argues forcefully that the search for explanation is self-defeating because the assertion of a right is a normative claim, the justification for which can only be another normative claim, which will itself call for justification. Sooner or later, one can only describe. Accepting the modal logic that makes rights inaccessible to reason, she also accepts them as a phenomenon of our experience and lets it go at that.

When Thomson says that having a right is being in a certain normative relationship with other people, it is not clear what she means. On one hand, she may mean only that in a given society such a relationship prevails and that in that society, therefore, there is such a right. If that is her meaning, then her account of rights does not seem to be about the concept that we have in mind. We refer to rights as reasons for behavior, not merely as descriptions of it. Thomson might accommodate this by suggesting that when we give rights as reasons, we are in reality only observing that behavior in conflict with a right departs from a well-established norm, thus preserving the underlying descriptive character of rights. But that does not capture nearly enough of our intended meaning. For it is entirely familiar to assert the existence of rights that are not generally acknowledged, at large or in a particular community, as a reason for conduct. So also, we may argue that a claim of right that is generally acknowledged is nevertheless mistaken. If this interpretation of Thompson's thesis is correct, therefore, her analysis is not convincing that the normative aspect of rights is not what it appears to be. Alternatively, she may mean that having a right really is being in such a relationship, not as a matter of society's actual practices but as a matter of fact. That is evidently what she intends when she refers to rights as "moral facts."[45] But that term conjures all the puzzles that confound us. In what sense is a normative relationship a matter of fact? Why is this particular kind of normative relationship a matter of fact but not, presumably, other interpersonal obligations? And why does it prevail over other moral considerations? What, in short, *are* moral facts?[46] If such questions are, as she suggests, unanswerable, Thomson's position amounts to a recommendation that we find other topics to occupy our minds—sensible advice, perhaps, but frustrating all the same.

The various efforts to unravel the puzzles about rights bring us out always in the same place. However they are phrased, the puzzles turn on the same theme: that rights apparently disregard the separation between fact and value. They attach to persons like ordinary descriptive characteristics; yet they have direct normative significance. Despite their normative significance, they do not depend on normative premises and are generally unassailable by normative arguments, which are not merely unavailing but irrelevant. They lay claim to a kind of objectivity that we associate with matters of fact; yet they are contentious and subject to challenge in a way that matters of fact are not. For all these reasons, it is not clear even what sort of thing a right is. Insofar as rights are normative, we can describe our bafflement conceptually, in terms of the modal logic that separates descriptive and prescriptive propositions. Insofar as they are a matter of fact, they are in some sense an aspect of our experience, and our bafflement is ontological, a matter of—however odd it sounds—the "existence" of rights. Even to form the questions stretches and distorts our usual patterns of thought. Despite these troubling incoherences, rights are unavoidable. Not only are they ubiquitous in normative discourse. Without them, our moral reasoning would be radically incomplete.

CHAPTER TWO

Human Responsibility

WITHIN THE VARIOUS CONTROVERSIES about the nature of rights, a line is understood to be drawn between human beings and all other kinds of beings and things. Some theorists assert categorically that only human beings possess rights. But even those who ascribe rights more broadly recognize that human beings are a special case. The question about rights of nonhuman kinds typically is their eligibility as a class for any rights at all. We are asked to consider whether animals have rights. Or certain species of animals. Or trees. Or special categories of nonliving things, like natural wonders or manmade monuments. What specific rights any of these kinds may have either is largely taken for granted or is disregarded; it is, at any rate, treated as a separate matter secondary to the general issue. Defenders of animal rights, for example, may be concerned to establish generally that animals have rights; usually, however, it is understood that the right principally in issue is a right not to be treated with cruelty, which, it is urged, all animals in common possess. The closest that one comes to differentiation among animals is the common assumption, frequently left unsaid, that somewhere down the great chain of being, animal life persists without rights.

In contrast, no one doubts that if there are rights at all, human beings are eligible to possess them. Whether there are any human rights, rights that all human beings possess as members of a class, is much disputed; and the most urgent source of controversy in practice is the basis for individual rights that differentiate one human being from another. This radical change of focus perhaps suggests that we are concerned with different concepts when we consider rights of human beings and of other kinds. But it does not seem so; for on both sides of the latter controversy, the rights of human beings are taken as the central case. The defense of animal rights consists mainly of an effort to show that rights can be predicated of animals to the same or similar effect as their predication of human beings; and the rejection of animal rights usually depends on the argument that animals lack some quality in virtue of which human beings have rights. Some progress may be made, therefore, if we start with the central case and move outward from there: Rather than ask, What is it about rights that this or that kind of entity possesses them? ask, What is it about human beings that they possess rights? If we can answer the latter question, we shall be in a better position to inquire whether nonhuman kinds possess rights as well.

It is often urged (though often also controverted) that only an autonomous being, one that is responsible for its actions, can have rights. Put simply, the argument is that only if a being is capable of acting to bring about ends of its own does the notion of a right have significance. Without such capacity, the "exercise of a right" could signify only random or indeterminate behavior, if the behavior were regarded as unconstrained by any externally imposed function, or the receipt of a benefit, albeit not one determined to be beneficial or sought by the recipient. The converse proposition, that only a being that has rights can be responsible, is seldom remarked except in specific political contexts. Whatever basis there might be to affirm rights of a being that is not responsible, it is difficult to imagine circumstances in which one might wonder whether a being conceded to be without rights were not responsible nonetheless.[1] The being lacking any rights, there would be no reason or justification for not doing with it, or seeing to it that it did, whatever is determined to be best, all things (including, perhaps, its own well-being) considered, and eliminating its causal agency altogether.

A being without rights is subject to determination according to ends chosen by others (though not necessarily all others). That is what having no rights signifies practically. Whoever has effective authority or control over the being determines its behavior, whether by exercising control or by failing to exercise it, and is, therefore, the responsible agent. Agency and responsibility may be hotly disputed, as when two persons claim (or disclaim) ownership of the same property; but such a dispute does not include the possibility that the property itself is responsible. Or, no one may have effective authority or control, in which case responsibility is ruled out entirely. So, the dog's owner is responsible for what it does, whether the dog remains obediently by its master's side or, its master paying no attention, it runs along the street sniffing at people. It might be appropriate to describe the behavior of a being without rights as unrestrained or wild, or even, rather loosely, as free, but not as responsible. From the moral point of view, if there is no other responsible party, the behavior of such a being is like natural forces—fair weather, hurricanes, drought, disease—that affect our lives dramatically for good or ill but incur no praise or blame, because they are not responsible.

Would a being too powerful to be restrained not be responsible? If so, does the argument here not lead to the conclusion that might makes right(s)? And if that is not correct, must we not conclude that only power and not rights is essential to responsibility? That is, would such a being not be responsible for how it exercised its power, whether or not it had a right to exercise the power as it did—or, indeed, especially if it did not have the right? (Surely, a person who exercises power in excess of his rights is responsible and will be judged harshly precisely because he has exceeded his rights.) Suppose a tiger invaded a village and was killing people. Despite intensive efforts to capture it, it remained on the loose—a being too powerful to be restrained. Although no one would hesitate to capture and, perhaps, to kill it as soon as possible, it would not be urged that the tiger was responsible in the distinct sense of meriting blame for its depredations. We might say that the tiger had to be killed because it was a *bad* tiger, but only in the same sense in which we might describe an accident in which many people were hurt as a bad accident; no one, I trust, would say that if it was a *bad* accident, there is no point in asking *who* was responsible, since the responsibility has already been determined. When a French homeowner puts a sign "Chien méchant" at his front gate, he is not telling us that his dog is wicked but that it is dangerous; if the dog snaps at an unwanted intruder, it will most likely be patted on the head, not scolded. The suggestion that a being subject to no restraint (except, of course, the limitations of its own nature) is therefore morally responsible is plausible only if one has in mind a (human) being conceded from the start to exercise that kind of responsibility, such as an absolute monarch. Similarly, the familiar, if largely imaginary, personage of the noble slave may be thought to be an example of a responsible being without any rights; but recognition of the slave's moral virtue is implicitly an admission that he does have rights, even if he has no legal rights. Were he wholly without rights, his responsibility for what he did would be eliminated, and with it his nobility as well.[2] We could praise him, perhaps, but only as we praise the well-trained animal or the effective tool. Mere power does not entail responsibility, nor does lack of power entail lack of rights.

The often repeated formula "'ought' implies 'can'" should, therefore, be amplified. One cannot significantly urge that a person ought to do something that she is (known to be) unable to do; for her inability deprives the normative statement of its apparent prescriptive force. Similarly, to assert that a person ought to do something commits one to the view that the person, having the capacity, has also the right to do it. (We sometimes say that a person *ought* to do something, meaning only that she is likely to do it, as we say, looking at the sky, "It ought to rain tomorrow" or, inspecting a knot, "There, that ought to hold." When the detective, having laid a trap for a burglar, says, "He ought to come through the window any minute," he is making a prediction, not prescribing how the burglar ought to act and certainly not suggesting that he has a right to enter in that unusual way.) The right needs to be stated with care. It may not extend beyond the precise situation at hand. Still, it is not merely a case of the person's having the right *since* she ought so to act. It is rather the reverse; it would not be true that she ought so to act unless she had the right, however restrictively it is defined. There are, of course, many kinds of situations in which one might urge another person to do something against the law, something, that is, that she has no legal right to do. Such situations furnish the standard occasion for civil disobedience. The apparent conflict arises because the moral agency implicating the moral right arises within a normative order different from and superior to that which denies the legal right. One urges that notwithstanding the law, the person ought to do and has a superior nonlegal right to do that which legally she has no right to do.[3]

But further, to assert that a person ought to do something implies that he has the capacity not to do it—there is no point in prescribing the unavoidable—and also that what he does is up to him; although he may suffer the consequences, he has a right subject to that qualification not to do what he ought. For otherwise, prescribing to him as to a moral agent or, more generally, prescribing for him would be out of place. Rather, he having no right to do otherwise, it would be appropriate simply to see to it that he does what he ought, or, at any rate, that what ought to be done is done, if not by him then by someone else. Thinking about legal rights, we commonly describe the imposition of a sanction for conduct as a denial of the right to do it. We may say, for example, that inasmuch as the law proscribes smoking marijuana and imposes a punishment for doing so, there is no legal right to smoke marijuana.[4] Strictly speaking, however, unless one imports an independent notion of what consequences are allowable, because they are "natural" or "standard" or something like that, provided that the sanction does not amount to coercion the right is not eliminated altogether but rather qualified or specified as a right to engage in the conduct under certain conditions. (Suppose one were to assert a right to eat his piece of cake. Would that mean that he has a right to eat his cake and have it too?)

Because rights typically specify relations among persons who may have opposed interests, they are easily regarded, from the perspective of someone other than the possessor, as a barrier to a proposed course of conduct. From the perspective of the possessor herself, however, a right confirms that her course of conduct is open and that with respect to the matter in question, she is self-determining and responsible. That is at least part of what having a right means.

The strong connection between rights and responsibility suggests that we may learn more about rights if we consider responsibility directly. For that connection would be powerfully explanatory of the special status of human beings as possessors of rights. Whatever other similarities and dissimilarities there are between human beings and nonhuman beings or nonhuman kinds generally, there is broad agreement that human beings and only human beings are responsible in the full sense that implicates moral judgment. That agreement, I emphasize, serves only as a preliminary justification for turning the examination of rights in the direction of an inquiry into responsibility. What it means to affirm that (only) human beings are responsible is part of the subject of that inquiry. And, once again, nothing that has been said so far is intended to prejudge the question whether animals and other nonhuman kinds have rights. Whether inquiring into responsibility will indeed help us to answer that question remains to be seen.

Human responsibility is a structural fact of our experience. By "structural fact" I mean a proposition that cannot be contradicted without altering the nature of our experience, not merely in some concrete particular(s) but in a fundamental way, making it a different experience entirely. To deny that human beings are responsible is not like denying that they have opposable digits or denying that there are any human beings on an island that we know is inhabited. Those denials would be startling enough, but we would adjust, if only by speculating that the person making the denial were play-acting. The denial of human responsibility does not merely omit some information or contradict something that we had strongly taken for granted. It transforms the very nature of what we, as human beings, experience. So, although one might translate the description of an event that refers to a person as a responsible agent into a description that omits such reference, the translation would not be fully equivalent, because responsibility has no equivalent in those terms. It is, in that sense, fundamental.

Responsibility depends on agency. It is axiomatic that if a person acts as an agent (in the special sense that responsibility requires) he is responsible, and that if he does not so act, he is not responsible. To act as an agent is to be the effective origin of what happens, the person to whom, and no further than whom, the action (or its consequence) is traced. No full account of this agency can be given, for reasons that will become clear. It is, nevertheless, a wholly familiar part of ordinary experience. We know what it is to act as an agent oneself, and we recognize when others act as agents.[5] Although we make a great many more subtle distinctions in particular contexts, ordinary language expresses the general distinction between responsible action and behavior for which one is not responsible by the active and passive verbal voices, the former ("I jumped") viewing the subject of the verb as agent and the latter ("I was pushed") viewing the subject as the object of forces external to, or at any rate other than, himself. The active and passive voices are good but not perfect indicators. "He sneezed," and "he stumbled" both describe something that happened to a person rather than a responsible act. When the passive voice is used, it leaves open the possibility that what happened to the person was caused by something else, for which he is responsible. Another, somewhat more articulate way to express the distinction is to refer to the person *qua* agent as self-determining and to his action as self-determined. When he is the object of other forces, he is not self-determining; his behavior is determined not by himself but by the other forces. The reference to self-determination may implicate an elaborate theory of human action and free will, which some theorists reject altogether. But the term is commonly used more loosely, not as an explanation but only as a descriptive metaphor. In that sense, and for the present only in that sense, responsible conduct and self-determined conduct are equivalent.

In ordinary circumstances, whether conduct is self-determined or not, and hence whether a person is responsible or not, is an empirical question. Most conduct is categorized generally one way or the other:

Answering a riddle or telling a joke (usually) is self-determined, yawning or sneezing (usually) is not. Some conduct is not so easily categorized: Laughing or crying, for example, may be instances of responsible conduct or not according to the circumstances, which need not be very unusual in either case. Almost any conduct may have a misleading appearance in sufficiently special circumstances. One may act *like* a person who is not responsible, deliberately appearing to be drunk, to trip, or to make a slip of the tongue. Or one may give every appearance of deliberate action but in fact be under hypnosis or subject to a compulsion. Although the question whether conduct is self-determined or, more familiarly, whether a person is responsible for particular conduct often is controversial and may have great practical consequences, most of the time the situation speaks for itself, and the question is answered simply by observation. There are a very large number and variety of indicators that we use to answer the question in specific circumstances. Ordinarily we know what evidence is relevant and where to look for it.

At a more general level also, the question is empirical. A kind of conduct that had been thought to be self-determined may prove to have physical causes or to be "compulsive," that is, to satisfy the criteria of behavior that is other-determined. So, for example, recent studies have indicated that a propensity to get drunk or to become enraged, which unexceptionally invites reproach, may have significant genetic or physiological components. A shift in the other direction is unlikely as a practical matter, not because the absence of responsibility is conclusively established but because empirical evidence other than one's own experience of responsibility tends always toward establishing effective causes. Still, it is theoretically possible that some kind of conduct that had been thought not to be self-determined would prove to have elements of responsibility. Evidence that refuted previously accepted explanations of conduct and revealed inexplicable variation might perhaps be interpreted that way.[6] A conclusion one way or the other may be hotly contested. Usually, however, we are able to formulate tests that count, or would count, as evidence. Most obviously, we are likely to ask whether a person persists in the conduct despite very good reasons to act otherwise or, on the other hand, provided with good enough reasons, proves to have an effective choice after all. Confronted by the defendant's claim that his act was the product of an "irresistible impulse," the judge in a celebrated Canadian case observed to the defendant: "If you cannot resist an impulse in any other way, we will hang a rope in front of your eyes, and perhaps that will help."[7]

There is, however, another level of inquiry, at which the issue is not empirical and the fact of human responsibility itself is called in question. It may be urged not that specific conduct was not self-determined or that a kind of conduct generally is not self-determined but that no conduct at all is, or could be, self-determined, except perhaps as a wholly descriptive category without normative significance. All human behavior, that is to say, no less than other occurrences, is fully determined by prior causes, which immediately or mediately are beyond the individual's control. Not only full-scale behaviorists and some philosophers may espouse such a position. At some time in their lives, most persons are likely to be struck by an argument of this kind, in one form or another. But even when we entertain the abstract argument, we order our concrete experience differently, recognizing and taking account of individual responsibility as a matter of fact. The most committed behaviorist does not disregard the distinction between responsible action and nonresponsible behavior in the conduct of his life. If he did, we would lock him up.

The convinced determinist does not look around and fail to see what others see or see what they overlook. He is not unaware of the ordinary evidence of agency or lack of agency in his own conduct and the conduct of others. Nor is he noticeably more able to predict how persons will behave. Rather, all such evidence to the contrary, he challenges the very idea of self-determination as incoherent. Focusing on the normative significance attached to it, he rejects the possibility of a "free will" as the essential predicate of individual responsibility. Will, he argues, cannot be a spontaneous, self-generating phenomenon, apart from and independent of the individual's own circumstances. Unless a person's will is tied uniquely to her, to the person that she is, in what sense is it *her* will? But she is that person in virtue of what she was in the past. The person she was in the past in turn was that person in virtue of what she was before that. And so forth. Yet, in that case, in what sense is her exercise of will now free? The familiar phenomena that we describe as manifestations of the will—to exercise will power, to be weak- or strong-willed, and so forth—are not said not to occur. Rather, it is argued, they too can only be reflections of a person's past, if they are that person's at all. Hence the conclusion: We are determined to do what we do and only think we are free and responsible. The concrete experience of responsibility for our own actions and evidence of the responsibility of others may lead us to suppose and to act as if it were otherwise; but they cannot stand up against the logic of the abstract argument. We are in the situation of a puppet performing onstage and congratulating itself on its performance, all unaware of the strings that control its movements, or a robot intricately programmed to perform certain operations and, in its way, to reflect on its performance. If it is not quite accurate to call *self*-consciousness a delusion, it is, at any rate, misleading; for there is no undetermined self to be found.

The determinist's argument is illustrated by the practice of excuses, the significance of which is to deny responsibility. Although we usually rely on observation to decide whether a person is responsible for particular conduct, self-determination is not a distinct, observable quality of the conduct itself, like swiftness, grace, or agility. We may say that a person's performance was marked by determination but not that it was marked by self-determination. Rather, if conduct is of a kind that in the circumstances is generally characterized as a person's own action, the conclusion that she is responsible follows, in the absence of evidence of some other explanation that provides an excuse. Or if conduct is of a kind for which persons in the circumstances typically are not accountable, it will be so regarded unless there are special grounds to believe the contrary, like motivation to dissemble. The most fully elaborated practice of excuses is in the criminal law, which allows a small number of specific excusing defenses. Although the defendant's general responsibility for his conduct is an element of every crime, the prosecution is not required to prove that as part of its case. Rather, the defense has the initial burden of proffering an excuse, which the prosecution must then refute. The burden of proof may rest with the prosecution or the defense; but wherever the burden lies, the prosecution is not obliged to go beyond refuting the specific defense and to prove responsibility at large.[8]

For the most part, we regard as excuses conditions that have a recognized, identifiable etiology and place a person outside the endless variety of the normal. Not regarded as an excuse are any of the ordinary qualities that one has from birth—intelligence, good looks, physical strength, and the like, or their lack—or any of the ordinary circumstances that surround one from birth—loving parents, wealth, education, and the like, or their lack—which significantly affect our life careers. Of course, some make more of their natural capacities than others; and some, as we say, rise above their circumstances while others fall below theirs. But whether we make more or less, rise above or fall below, also depends on personal characteristics that originate in one's actual life history—perhaps even, as scientists are beginning to discover, in the chemical composition of the body, but at any rate in such factors as whether one's parents were themselves hardworking and instilled the virtue of industriousness, and so forth. In fact, the determinist argues, are not all our attributes, not just those few that we allow as excuses, links in a chain of cause and effect, circumstance and consequence, that is unbroken in principle, even if not (yet) fully apparent to us? In any case, he says, if it is otherwise and a person's actions are not, however indirectly, the determinate product of individual attributes that are themselves fully determined either by her individual nature or antecedent circumstances, are they anything but happenstance, not *her* actions normatively at all but only events in which she happens to be embroiled, for which she is no more responsible than anyone else.

In order to make sense of responsibility in these terms, we need to break out of determinism sufficiently to characterize an action as free, while at the same time retaining enough of what is determinate about it and the person whose action it is to characterize it as hers and not, from a normative point of view, a random happening. But that does not put the problem strongly enough. For unless the action is fully undetermined, then it is not free in the necessary sense. And unless what is determinate about the person is also determining, unless, that is, it is sufficient to determine the action fully, then the action is not hers in the necessary sense. What requires explanation is not an exercise of will that is partly free and partly determinate, but one that is wholly free and wholly determinate. Nor is even that enough. Suppose it were possible to separate some conduct from the causal order and to regard it as an act of free will, for which the actor is responsible. Itself self-determined, the act nevertheless takes place—takes its place—within the natural order, as the cause of other effects. Otherwise, there would be nothing to be responsible for. If it is thus effective, within the range of its effects it seems to rule out subsequent acts of free will that are not so determined. Whether we regard it as effect or cause, the will cannot be at once outside the natural order and within it.

The difficulty of the problem is indicated by the extraordinary, not to say desperate, solutions that have been proposed.[9] One might reject the requirement of full self-determination as a condition of responsibility and conclude that a person may be responsible for actions that, as the determinate being he is, he is bound to perform. Classical Greek literature presents such a view. So, in Sophocles' Theban tragedies, Oedipus accepts his responsibility for the course of events even though, as the oracle revealed, he was the person bound to kill his father and wed his mother and had done all that he could to avoid the oracle's prediction. Later, Creon accepts responsibility for the death of his son, Haemon, although that too was what had to happen.[10] Similar statements appear elsewhere in the literature, often accompanied by wonder at the human predicament. However we understand the argument, it does not seem possible to regard that notion of responsibility as resembling our own; we appreciate it as a deeply felt but unexplained affirmation that the human experience of striving and acting is meaningful in human terms. Some modern accounts of responsibility that urge one way or another that it is sufficient for responsibility if the will is involved at all, without explaining how the will can be both individual and undetermined in its effects, are at bottom no more than pallid, deracinated reflections of the original Greek argument.

The solution of Christian theology is different only in its introduction of a specific Being to whose reason and will all difficulties are referred. The strictly intellectual limits of that solution are indicated by the controversy, present from the beginning, whether divine will or divine reason predominates. Christianity removed the issue from reason to faith, with an assurance that a providential, omnipotent God reconciled the determinate order of nature and individual responsibility. But faith aside, the problem is the same, with God or without.[11]

The solution of Kant is instructive. He accepted as postulates both the determinate nature of a being in the natural order and the free nature of a moral being. There can be, he said, no reconciliation between the two. But, he insisted, we apprehend persons, like all that we experience, only as phenomenological beings in the natural order. It is, therefore, a mistake to suppose that we can apprehend the free, undetermined moral being phenomenologically. Such a being is rather an idea of reason, arising from our awareness of the possibility of morality and necessarily beyond actual experience. The argument is elegant and gains strength from the rest of Kantian ontology and epistemology.[12] It has important implications for ethical theory, which Kant elaborated. Even so, it does not address human responsibility as we understand it concretely. Kant is convincing that as a responsible agent, a person must be regarded as unaffected, that is to say, undetermined, by his (phenomenological) situation. When all is said and done, however, that is a statement of the problem, not a solution. Talk of a distinct, undetermined "noumenal" self is in the end not more than a personification, ineffable at that, of the original contradiction.

The currently fashionable philosophic solution does not seek a reconciliation between freedom and cause; instead, it urges that none is needed. The phenomenon of responsibility, we are told, as we speak of it in connection with human conduct, does not pin us on the horns of the determinist's dilemma at all. The apparent contradiction is not within a single, concrete entity, the person unique and entire. It reflects only a difference in the point of view from which the person is regarded. He may be regarded from a "scientific," causal perspective, in which case his behavior is subject to an explanation that in principle does not refer to his will or to him as agent. Or he may be regarded from a distinctly human, moral perspective, in which case we think of his conduct as an exercise of will; we study the motives and reasons for his acting as he did and hold him responsible accordingly. There is no unified perspective that integrates both, no "objective" person regarded, as it were, from no perspective. Nor can we even suggest what such a perspective, such a person, would be like.[13]

That solution—or dissolution—of the problem is attractive so long as the issue remains abstract or, in a concrete case, if it is agreed from the start which of the two perspectives is to be applied. It treats the apparent dilemma as if both perspectives were equally available and one had only to choose which he prefers, according to his interest of the moment. Most of the time, however, we do not regard both perspectives as alternatively available; it is not a question of selecting a point of view but of describing accurately the event in question. Whether the person is responsible or not, actor or acted upon, is a matter of fact and an aspect of the event itself, not a stance that the observer takes, as if he were shifting his weight from one foot to the other. If the conclusion is in doubt, we are sometimes able to avoid opting definitively either way. But that does not mean that both conclusions are equally available and it is up to us to choose which we prefer.

So, to use a recurrent, deeply troubling example, one may regard deliberate acts of child abuse as peculiarly immoral conduct that merits blame and punishment. In many cases, however, there is persuasive evidence that such acts are a product of the abuser's own past, when he was himself the victim of abuse, for which, as for his own conduct, he is to be pitied rather than condemned. There is, at least, firm statistical evidence of a strong correlation between having been a victim and being an abuser. Thinking about the matter abstractly, we may alternate between one perspective and the other. When it is time to respond concretely, however, we must choose between them. Having concluded that the person is responsible and imposed punishment, it would be grotesque thereafter to lament him as an unfortunate victim and express our compassion. Nor, if we conclude that he is a victim and not blameworthy, can we then, shifting the perspective, blame and punish him, without victimizing him further. One may urge that we punish not because the person deserves to be punished but to deter, him and others like him. But (aside from the fact that that misdescribes our actual attitude) the person who is undeservedly punished is no less victimized because it is not done out of gratuitous malice and has a worthwhile purpose. Sometimes it is possible to narrow the focus of the inquiry, so that one or the other perspective is adopted with respect to some aspect of conduct without committing us to that perspective altogether: Even if the child abuser was himself a victim, he could have (tried to) overcome the consequences of his own trauma, or he need not have acted with such cruelty, or he could have sought help. The problem of choosing a perspective may be broken down into smaller parts in this way; but the problem remains with respect to each part. In that concrete context, which is the correct perspective, actor or victim, with respect to his failure to try harder, or his cruelty, or his failure to get help? In practice, we often split the difference, our uncertainty whether the person is truly responsible at all mitigating the punishment. But unless we are prepared to assert generally that persons who are relatively more able deserve to be punished more severely when they fail (and, presumably, to be rewarded less generously when they succeed), splitting the difference between freedom and cause only makes the difference all the more evident.

Attending to the reconciliation of freedom and cause in a concrete case makes plain the inadequacy of the "point of view" approach considered abstractly as well. In effect, it argues that since there is no unified "objective" perspective by way of a solution, there can be no need for a reconciliation by way of a problem. The plain fact, however, is that we do reconcile the two conflicting perspectives, if only by systematically disregarding one or the other. Not only do we reconcile them; we must reconcile them if we are to order our experience at all, because they are not alternatively superimposed on experience otherwise complete but are an aspect of experience itself. How they are reconciled in a concrete case is something that we regard as governed by reason, not by will; it is a matter of fact, correct or incorrect, and not something for us to choose. We may agree that the abstract contradiction between freedom and cause cannot be overcome. How then is it overcome concretely, as an objective matter of fact?

We are thus brought repeatedly to this impasse: Moral agency requires that an action be self-determined, that its origin be one's self—autonomy rather than heteronomy. But however the point is formulated, it seems impossible to segregate the self in question from an array of circumstances that are not self-determined and are determinative, without unmooring the self from any determination whatsoever. The responsible self is either the composite effect of many causes or a chance composition of various attributes. In neither case can we give an acceptable account of responsibility.

The issue about human responsibility is not whether persons are responsible or not. The fact is that they are. The fact is not falsifiable by experience, because our experience is ordered by it. Nor is the issue precisely how to make intelligible to reason what is given in experience. The argument of Kant, which yielded nothing more definite than freedom as an "idea of reason," may fairly be regarded as having pursued the inquiry in that direction as far as it can go. The antinomy of freedom, the opposition between the natural order and the moral order, is complete and unavoidable. As an idea of reason, freedom is not within our grasp. If abstract reason thus fails decisively, there remains an issue that is all the more pressing: how within our experience the antinomy is resolved. For, perforce, it is resolved.

CHAPTER THREE

Individual Responsibility

HOWEVER URGENT MAY BE the antinomy of freedom as an abstract matter, we regularly attribute responsibility and could not otherwise order our experience as we do. In ordinary affairs, one does not wonder about responsibility at large; our concern is not whether anyone is ever responsible but whether someone is responsible for specific conduct or, simply, a specific occurrence. Still trying to bring rights into focus through the lens of responsibility, we may be able to approach the general issue from another angle by attending to how such specific judgments are made.

The question of responsibility does not arise unless a person's conduct—action or inaction—is connected to an occurrence causally, as a link in a chain of occurrences, of which the occurrence in question is an effect. For the most part, that means that the occurrence must have been different had the person's conduct been different.[1] Were someone to observe that Blake, who lives in another city, was responsible for an automobile accident down the street on the previous day, a likely response would be, "I didn't know that she was here at all." If the first speaker were to respond that Blake had not been there, the other person would wait for an explanation of how Blake could be responsible if she was nowhere in the vicinity. (As it turns out, Blake's teenage son, driving her car, was involved in the accident. Had she not loaned him the car to make such a long trip . . . and so on.) Accordingly, only an infinitesimal portion of everything that happens (whatever that means), the bounds of which are fixed proximately or at some remove by the spatial and temporal trajectory of a person's physical being, is even possibly her responsibility.[2] A great many ordinary questions about responsibility are resolved without difficulty on that basis, because it is concluded that the person had nothing to do with the occurrence, responsibly or otherwise. An alibi takes this simple form.

Even this simplest of cases may raise further issues that are not resolved empirically, as a matter of physical causation alone. Within a broad range, one is generally responsible for his "spatial and temporal trajectory"—where he is and when. It may be, therefore, that although a person had nothing to do with an occurrence, he is responsible for just that reason: He ought to have had something to do with it and, if he had, it would not have happened just as it did. Although nothing that he did, as such, is a link in the causal chain, his conduct generally is regarded as connected to the occurrence causally by reference to what he failed to do. Only if we are able to conclude that a person had nothing to do with an occurrence and that nothing he might have done could have altered it (or that he did not know and could not have been expected to know about the occurrence or his capacity to affect it) is his lack of responsibility certain. Nonetheless, over a vast range, persons are exonerated of responsibility for occurrences that they are able to predict and that their actions might affect. For the most part, if knowledge and ability are widely shared, responsibility depends also on having some "responsible relationship" to the occurrence or the persons involved. The occurrence itself does not disclose whether or not there is such a relationship, which is a matter of the community's relevant conventions; but its conventional nature is likely to be overlooked unless it is explicitly challenged. So, for example, a parent's failure to attend a child will be a basis of the parent's responsibility if the child has an accident, even though others who might also have prevented the accident are not regarded as responsible. The parent's responsible relationship is not likely to be an issue, although the parent may be excused from responsibility (and another person held responsible) for another reason.[3]

Although it is the case that but for a person's conduct an occurrence would have been different, the question of his responsibility may be deflected and resolved negatively within a factual account of how it happened. Which among the myriad features of an occurrence is its cause and which are only attendant circumstances is itself a question. When human conduct is involved, causation and responsibility may be intertwined, not only when a failure to act is involved but generally. (Theoretically, the failure to act of every person whose action might have affected the outcome is an attendant circumstance, not regarded as a cause because of the absence of a responsible relationship.) Typically, the stronger the indications of responsibility and the weightier the moral judgment, favorable or unfavorable, *if* one's conduct is the cause, the greater the likelihood that it will be regarded as the cause and not merely a circumstance. Thus, conduct that is morally neutral is less likely to be regarded as consequential than conduct that has moral significance. Especially when personal responsibility is implicated, selection of the cause from all the circumstances of an occurrence but for which it would not have happened as it did calls not simply for observation but for judgment, based on conventional understandings; we learn how to do it in practice and by watching how others do it. Were two persons to agree that an occurrence would not have happened as it did but for each of two circumstances and disagree about which was its cause—Blake loaned her son the car, but his father urged him to make the trip—closer observation and more detailed description of the occurrence itself would be no help; the agreed fact that each circumstance was necessary to the outcome exhausts what can be learned in that way. Rather, unless they agreed to disagree, they could only consider how others view the occurrence, possibly compare their own views about other similar occurrences, and let it go at that. And indeed, unless a question of responsibility was involved, it would be difficult to make sense of their disagreement at all; from a wholly descriptive point of view, the distinction between cause and (necessary) attendant circumstance has no significance. If responsibility is in question, the disagreement must perforce be resolved, because one is not responsible for an occurrence unless it is caused by his conduct. But what, if anything, besides the question of responsibility we address when we consider whether conduct is the cause or an attendant circumstance is unclear.

If a person's conduct is connected to an occurrence (and another circumstance is not identified as the cause), the question of his responsibility may arise. But even if his conduct was crucial to the outcome, he may have no responsibility; for he may have been connected not as an agent but only as a natural object. If Green throws Rourke out the window and Rourke lands on Blum, we may want to say that the cause of Blum's broken arm is Rourke's falling on her; but (unless Rourke should not have been there in the first place and provoked Green and . . .) no one will blame Rourke. Most likely, even if we say that Rourke's falling on Blum caused her injury, we shall not say that Rourke caused it; the cause is the responsible act of Green. (Or perhaps it was Blum's "own fault"; Green and Rourke are practicing something or other, and Blum ignored the signs advising people not to walk below the window.) Indeed, Rourke's fall will not be described as his act at all, in the sense that is relevant to responsibility; it is not something that he did but rather something that happened to him.

In most of the ordinary incidents of our lives, questions like this present no special difficulty, not because the general basis of a considered judgment about responsibility is so clear but because, even though the observable facts are not dispositive by themselves, the situation taken as a whole speaks, as it were, for itself. If one were asked to explain a conclusion in a particular case—say, the conclusion that Rourke is not responsible for Blum's broken arm—he would probably just describe what happened. Were someone to say that he still did not understand and ask for further explanation, unless the first speaker were to call attention to some fact that he thought had been overlooked or given too little attention, he would probably be puzzled and not know how to proceed, except to repeat the key facts with greater emphasis. ("But Green *threw him out the window!*") For ordinarily, there is nothing more to say. The occurrence as described just is (not) what counts as being responsible. The same is true if responsibility depends on a responsible relationship; all that one would ordinarily say to explain responsibility is that there was a relationship of such a kind—she was his mother; she had promised to keep watch—without going on to say why that relationship in the circumstances made the person responsible. Sometimes responsibility remains problematic, not because specific facts are lacking but because the facts, however complete, do not speak clearly enough. Had Rourke not been pushed but gone out the window under his own steam, it might be difficult to tell even with a movie of the whole event (and a record of his interior monologue as he took off) whether he had jumped or fallen. Even so, a resolution of that issue, however uncertain, is likely to be built into a description of what happened. For although we can accommodate an unresolved doubt by mitigating the consequences, favorable or unfavorable, of a conclusion that Rourke is (not) responsible, we cannot describe the occurrence completely without resolving at least tentatively the issue of responsibility: to jump and to fall are entirely different behavior, although the result may be the same either way.

Most of the time, therefore, a question of responsibility is answered within a descriptive account of the occurrence, as a matter of fact. If a person is found not to have been causally connected to an occurrence or if the connection is not something that he did but something that happened to him, he is not responsible, without further inquiry; and a description of what happened will so indicate. If the connection is something that he did or ought to have done, and nothing more is said, he is responsible and may deserve praise or blame, reward or punishment, accordingly.[4]

Sometimes, however, it may be urged that, although the person's conduct is described as his action—"Rourke jumped from the window . . ."—and he would ordinarily be regarded as responsible, that is not so in this case, because of something not about the occurrence but about him: the particular aspect or attribute of the person that explains why he acted as he did is not within the scope of his responsibility—". . . because he was hallucinating and thought he was parachuting out of an airplane." Although the explanation for his action is something about himself, the action was not *self*-determined. In short, he has an excuse.

The strongest, most readily accepted excuses are closely analogous to an external determining cause and make the occurrence seem less like the person's action than something that happened to him. Indeed, some of what we ordinarily think of as excuses are nothing more than an altered description of the event. ("I didn't jump. I fell.") The excuse may be short-term and focused on the particular occurrence, like hypnosis or duress, or it may be a more or less permanent and far-reaching condition, like insanity. Provided that we accept the explanation and the descriptive label attached to it, excuse from responsibility follows, unless the person was responsible for being in that condition and his conduct was a foreseeable consequence. We may not accept them, for just that reason. The hapless lover who steals a diamond bracelet because he was "hypnotized by her blue eyes" will most likely have time in prison to come out of his trance. Most of the time, when criminal responsibility or some other specific assignment of praise or blame is not involved, both the description and the conclusion about responsibility that depends on it can be left somewhat uncertain and ambiguous.

We move beyond the range of such excuses, which typically carry their exculpatory significance on their face, if the person offers as an explanation for her conduct some attribute that is not regarded as external to, or other than, herself but on the contrary is so much herself that, so she avers, she could not have been expected to act differently. She just *is* lazy, or careless, or high-strung. (Rourke just is clumsy.) The same kind of explanation might be offered to account for a praiseworthy act; but persons rarely try to explain their good deeds on such a basis. Were someone to do so, her intended modesty might understandably be mistaken for bragging or what we disapprovingly call "false modesty." When an excuse is of this kind, the issue of responsibility cannot readily be contained, even metaphorically, within a description of the event. For even though we accept the person's description of herself, it does not alter the description of the occurrence as something that she did.

On its own terms, such an excuse is not without force; it seems to be a straightforward application of the general premise that one is not responsible if she "couldn't help it," no less applicable in this case than in the case of her being nowhere around when the occurrence took place. Whatever the cause of what happened, whether "she" as natural object was implicated or not, she was not implicated as a responsible agent. But if the argument is accepted in any case, it seems as though it must be accepted in all. For indubitably a person is who she is. (If not, who is responsible?) And if just being this or that counts as an excuse, because it explains why one does whatever she does, then surely just being something else again must also count as an excuse, because that too must explain why one does whatever she does. The argument, in short, is a specification of the determinist stop: "I am not responsible for who I am. My very constitution as the person I am happened to me and not by me. Therefore, insofar as the occurrence is traceable to me as I am, I am not responsible for it. Needless to say, insofar as it is not traceable to me as I am, I am not responsible for it either."

Some explanations of this kind we are sure to disallow. The person who fails to rescue someone in distress does not let himself off by declaring that even as a child he was a coward. Nor does a diner who leaves no tip impress the waitress more favorably if he says on his way out, "The service was fine, but I've always been a tightwad." Some other such excuses may be more acceptable. "I'm just forgetful," for example, may be allowed a little. We may "make allowances" for someone who has a "hot temper," at least if he is contrite afterward. Or it may be that such explanations do not excuse conduct any more than the others but that the attributes to which they point are not regarded so clearly as moral failings. So, we may not blame the person who always forgets but still hold him responsible in another way; he may have to bear the cost of his forgetting or make amends. The person who always blows up may be forgiven; but he is expected at least to offer an apology. The criminal law generally allows nothing for such dispositional states, even though it takes into account in some circumstances other kinds of idiosyncrasy.[5]

On the whole, we accept excuses that have to do with physical or mental capacities, like strength and intelligence, and not (usually) those that have to do with character, like courage and generosity. There is, perhaps, some support for such a distinction in ordinary experience. People seem less able to change their capacities than to change or at least to regulate their ordinary dispositional traits. But that is not so clear. The difference may be only that the former are more palpable. We know, at any rate, that character, no less than one's capacities, is strongly determined. Character, in the appropriate circumstances, *is* capacity, as the hare learned from the tortoise. How was the hare to know that he would lose the inevitable race if he concentrated on acquiring the musculature for bursts of great speed instead of the habit of steady persistence? One can't do everything. Furthermore, whatever a person's character might have been had he worked to change it, at the moment when he acts his character is what it is. If we regard him as responsible for his character, why do we not regard him as responsible if he is physically too weak to effect a rescue? If he had exercised more in the past, he would have been stronger. No doubt he did not anticipate that he would find himself needing the strength to save a life. But almost certainly, he did not anticipate that his courage would be crucial either. So why do we praise him if he tries as hard as he can but is too weak to do more, and blame him if, strong as an ox, he does not try hard? (To be sure, "ought" implies "can." But suppose he tells us that he always tries to persevere, but somehow seems not to. Or that he tries to try to persevere.) Even with respect to one's character, an excuse may be more acceptable if there are special circumstances. The person who failed to attempt a rescue might have been traumatically injured on a similar occasion in the past, or he might have a "phobia" about that particular kind of danger. The stingy person might have suffered extreme economic deprivation as a child. Why do some circumstances count in this way and not all the others, whatever they may be (even if the particular circumstances are unknown)?

A great deal has been written about the practice of excuses, stimulated by John Austin's classic essay, "A Plea for Excuses."[6] As he and others have pointed out, the excuses that we allow or do not allow in one circumstance or another are often context-specific and make a variety of subtle distinctions that bear on their excusing or extenuating effect. Taken together, they provide what might almost be described as a map of responsibility. But although as a practical matter we usually know which excuses count and which do not, explanation and justification scarcely go beyond the practice itself. Cowardly or stingy conduct just is the sort of thing for which one is responsible. If not that, then what? But the latter question, with only slight change, may be asked by the determinist as well, to quite different effect: If that, then what not? In this way, our responses to specific questions of responsibility lead us back to the general issue. The whole edifice of responsibility appears to be threatened, not so much by the determinist's abstract argument but, more concretely, by distinctions that we make all the time, as a matter of course. It is threatened similarly by the steady encroachment of scientific knowledge on aspects of human conduct that were previously thought to have been up to the individual; even dispositional states, the likelihood of acting one way or the other, are traced to causes other than individual will.

The ambiguity and uncertainty of our responses to concrete questions and the absence of anything that could be regarded as a general theory of excuses give point to the suggestion of P. F. Strawson and others that our conceptions of freedom and responsibility do not refer to a uniquely privileged objective state of affairs but only reflect a distinct human perspective, which may alternate with a natural perspective, according to our interest. So, adopting the former, we assess a person's desert; and, adopting the latter, we explain what caused him to behave as he did. If we are uncertain and our answers are ambiguous, that only reflects a failure to make clear what we have in mind and what perspective it is therefore appropriate to adopt. But that hardly seems adequate to dispose of the theoretical issue. For although specification of the scientific perspective will lead us to exclude consideration of responsibility, specification of the human perspective does not exclude recognition of causal factors that may account for the person's action. On the contrary, if responsibility is challenged at all, we are obliged to consider such factors and, if responsibility is sustained, to contain them within the human perspective. What we want to know is precisely whether, in view of such factors, the person is after all responsible. Most of the time, a full description of an occurrence dictates an answer to the question of responsibility, so that one perspective or the other seems to have a privileged status as the fact of the matter. But even when the question is contentious and calls for an exercise of judgment, it presents itself as a question for which there is a correct answer. The question is "Is he responsible?" and the appropriate response is "He is responsible" or "He is not responsible," not another question: "Why do you want to know?"

CHAPTER FOUR

Oedipus at Fenway Park

THE FAMILIAR TYPOLOGY of responsible and nonresponsible conduct leaves even the most ordinary and obvious ascription of responsibility open to challenge; just when a person's act is most characteristic of her, she may claim that being the person she is, she could not have acted otherwise. To say that a person is responsible is to say that a reference to her individual "will" is necessary to account fully for the occurrence in question, that an account that makes no such reference is incomplete. Yet, within the description of an occurrence, whatever we mean by a person's will may be as fully displaced by her actual personal attributes as it is by external causes with which she had nothing to do at all. Once the attributes (themselves ultimately consequences of causes over which she had no control) that account for her action are fully set forth and understood, there is no room left nor any need to refer to her will. So, altogether unexceptionally, the more we know about someone, the more easily we can predict what she will do in a given situation. Since we do accept the argument that a person "couldn't help it" if it refers to an alibi or to physical or mental capacity, there is no reason not to accept it if it refers to a definite, confirmed dispositional trait. Thus we are led to the brink of the determinist challenge to responsibility as such. At that point, we may conclude that something surely has gone wrong. But just what it is, and how we may escape the challenge, are not so clear.

In order for us to deepen that inquiry, it needs first to be expanded outward. If we acknowledge at all that a person may be excused from responsibility, not because external circumstances prevented him from acting otherwise but because he, constituted as he is, was bound to act as he did, there does not seem to be any reason to restrict the issue to specific actions or failures to act. For whichever of a person's attributes account for this or that action, collectively his attributes account for all that he does. If he may claim that he is not responsible for specific conduct, he may claim similarly that he is not responsible for any of the unfavorable aspects of his life history that are traceable to those same attributes. So, for example, if a person is excused for failing to effect a rescue because he is not strong enough, one supposes that he is also not responsible for other consequences of his lack of strength: being beaten up in the school yard, coming in last in athletic contests, not being hired as a stevedore, and so forth. And just as his lack of responsibility exempts him from deserved consequences—blame or punishment—in the former case, so also it should exempt him from all the other unfavorable consequences, at least so far as individual desert is concerned. If desert depends on responsibility, he deserves the latter no more than the former. Pressing the determinist's case, therefore, one may ask why the same claim that a person is not responsible for and therefore ought to be excused from—or at any rate does not deserve—the consequences of conduct that was not within his control does not apply to any of the aspects of his life history that he wishes were otherwise. Of course, someone may point out to him that if his argument is correct, he is not responsible for—and does not deserve—those aspects of his history that he likes more. But he is in a Miniver Cheevy–ish mood and does not care.

The same question about individual desert, or simply justice, is raised if instead of asking how a person can be responsible for being the person he is, we compare one person with another. Although as members of the same species we have a great many features in common, as individuals we are not completely alike. The differences among us are large in some cases, small in others. They may be expressed as distinct attributes or as a difference in degree. We may say, for example, that one person is strong and another weak or that the former is stronger than the latter. However it is expressed, except by comparing one difference with another there is no way of saying whether a difference is significant or not and what its significance is. The greater the similarity in other respects, the more significant a particular difference is likely to be. Large or small, our individual differences not only describe us; they also explain us. They account for what we do. What we do, in the end, is what we are. Of course. What else could it be and still count as what we, as individuals, do? Yet how can persons be regarded as justly situated and having their due, if their very constitutions, which differentiate them one from another and on which everything that they do depends, are not of their own making?

Suppose a young man presents himself at the spring training camp of the Boston Red Sox and declares that he wants very much to make the team. He quickly establishes that he has all the necessary traits of character: he is a team player, comes to practice early, stays fit over the winter. His only drawbacks, it turns out, are that he is a bad batter (although he practices a good deal), cannot catch the ball (but he is trying to overcome his fear of it), and has a weak throwing arm (he is doing weight training). When the manager refuses to sign him, the young man observes, "It doesn't seem fair. I want so much to be a Red Sox and I have tried so hard. It shouldn't be held against me that I am not very good at the game."

Most likely, however regretfully, the manager will not sign the young man even so. There is another fellow right behind the first who declares that he ought to make the team even though he does not try hard: "I have never tried hard at anything. It doesn't seem fair to hold that against me. I'd much rather try hard, but I just seem not to." We may take no notice of him for the moment. Although we do not blame the young man for striking out consistently—it is not a moral failing— neither the Red Sox nor anyone else is under obligation to disregard his lack of ability or make it up to him. (Some disgruntled Red Sox fans may believe that the Red Sox management thinks it is under such an obligation.)

No doubt life as a Red Sox is not all it is cracked up to be. But the same issue arises elsewhere—everywhere, in fact. The young man who wants to play in the major leagues has a sister who wants to be a research chemist but is rather weak at math and a cousin who wants to sing at the Met but cannot carry a tune. We may be born free, as John Locke assured us;[1] but (as Locke was not slow to recognize) we are also born and raised smart, good-looking, strong, industrious, charming, wealthy . . . or only some . . . or sometimes none of the above. Given a checklist, which of us would not check them all?

When the conversation takes this turn, we seem to have left responsibility far behind. Who is to say whether the young man is responsible for his limited eye-arm coordination? What difference does it make? Playing for the Red Sox depends on having the necessary ability, which a person either has or does not have. Roger Clemens is a great pitcher and makes the team. The young man is not much of a player at any position and has to look elsewhere.

"But," the young man insists, "I can't help it."

"Maybe not," the manager replies. "All the same, Clemens is a great pitcher and you are not even third-rate. Therefore, he makes the team and not you. The rest don't matter."

Put that way, the young man's claim does not sound so unlike a question of responsibility after all; but if that is indeed what it is, the manager's response is more portentous than it appears. In fact, although he would no doubt be surprised to be told so, his reply to the young man is the very stuff of Greek tragedy. Sophocles affirms that Oedipus' tortured history is what had to be, his due because he is Oedipus, even though he was powerless to prove the oracle wrong. Might one not describe the young man's argument as a claim that he is not responsible, because he couldn't help it, for all the missed pitches, bobbled ground balls, and wild throws (actual, if he managed to try out, or hypothetical) and, therefore, does not deserve to suffer the consequences—specifically, not making the team—any more than Oedipus deserved his awful fate? And is not the manager cast in the role of Teiresias, affirming that the young man's lack of responsibility for his ineptitude "don't matter"? Whatever they think about Oedipus, most people would probably agree with the manager that Clemens belongs on the team and the young man does not. If so, however we express it, do we not conclude in effect that they are alike responsible for their ability as baseball players or, at any rate, that their ability or lack of it is their own responsibility, happily in one case and unhappily in the other?

From our own point of view, the brief objection to the Sophoclean solution is that it solves nothing; it merely internalizes the very contradiction that is the source of the original problem. Desert is a function of responsibility, which attaches only to acts that are self-determined. The notion that someone can deserve at large, as it were, without reference to anything that he has done or failed to do, is not so much mistaken but rather, even as a hypothesis, incoherent. But if that is true at Thebes, why is the same not true closer to home, in Fenway Park?

Well, one may object, for one thing seeing baseball as Greek tragedy makes too much of it for even its most ardent fans. Fenway Park is a long way from Thebes and crucially different in at least this respect: Sophocles' tragedy concerned the whole course of Oedipus' life, for which there is no test of what is due except individual responsibility and desert. Baseball may be the national pastime. Still, it is only a pastime, a game, for which there are established rules and conventions, not only the kind that specify how the game is played but also the kind that indicate generally how players are selected. No one asserts that Roger Clemens, simply as a person, is more deserving than the young man. They assert only that if we are talking about major league baseball, Clemens belongs on the team because he is the better player and that is how players are selected. According to the rules and conventions of baseball, and that alone, Clemens is *entitled* to make the team. If you have something other than baseball in mind, who knows what is Clemens' due, or the young man's?

If baseball is thus set apart from "life" and we look no further than the conventions of baseball itself, Clemens' entitlement is plain. For it is certainly true (whatever the occasional appearance to the contrary) that the teams consider ability first and last and are expected to do so. And it may seem entirely obvious that baseball should be set apart.

Isn't it precisely the significance of calling it a game that it be set apart from, well, "life" and have its own rules? We cannot dispose of the matter so easily, however, once the young man has come on the scene. He evidently does not regard baseball as just a game, for which any rule is as good as any other; at any rate, he does not regard the question whether he plays as just a move in a game. On the contrary, he tells the manager, it is a matter of life and death.

"Not my problem. I got troubles enough," the manager will interject. Yes, it is the young man's problem. But it is not resolved simply by pointing out that baseball is a game and concluding on that basis that entitlement according to the rules and conventions of the game is all that counts, desert having nothing to do with it. For if the reason the young man does not make the team is that he is black, we too should respond, "It isn't fair."

"That's different," the manager's legal counselor declares. "The color of a person's skin has nothing to do with the game of baseball." No doubt. But how do we know that? Not from the rules and conventions of the game itself. For it was once the well-established convention that black persons do not play in the major leagues. And while that convention was still in place it was intelligible (and, as we now think, correct) to say that the convention was wrong and that a black player who was good enough deserved to make the team. Although we may, and commonly do, refer no further than an established rule to justify an entitlement, we cannot rely on the rule to justify itself. Nor is the practice to which the rule relates self-justifying, although its perceived purpose—baseball as a competitive sport—may explain the rule as a means to an end.

Although if they are well established they will not always be called in question, at some point the rules and the practices on which, hived off from the rest, we rely to justify entitlements have to be reintegrated into the whole and satisfy the demands of justice more broadly considered. In order fully to approve Clemens' entitlement, we must be satisfied not only that the rules have been applied according to their terms—during tryouts, Clemens was not given weak batters against whom to pitch, nor was the young man put up against especially strong pitchers—but also that the rules themselves are fair: Major league teams *properly* choose players according to their ability (and not, say, according to their desire to play). Suppose the owner of a major league team, reacting to the Brooklyn Dodgers' signing of Jackie Robinson, had said, "Major league baseball is not a competitive sport. It is a business. And we shall all suffer at the box office if we start signing black players." If he had been correct about the consequences at the box office, would that fact have established that the Dodgers had made a mistake?

It may seem odd to look beyond the conventional way of choosing players because the status of baseball as a game, a limited practice governed by conventional rules, is unusually clear. But "life" is in large measure a composite of just such practices, not something different and separate from them. Nor is it self-evident what is and is not a game, governed by special rules. Why, after all, should Sophocles' play not be regarded as a comedy, Oedipus running afoul of the rules of the game as prescribed by something or other—the oracle or *moira* (fate)? His parricide and incest and their aftermath would be only a bit of cosmic slapstick, someone slipping again and again on a giant banana peel. Or, returning to our young man, change the venue only a little, from Fenway Park to Harvard Yard across the river. Is who is admitted to the university also just a matter of entitlement, governed entirely by whatever conventional admissions policies are in place? If so, then any practice at all may elude the demands of justice, provided only that it conform to its own well-established rules. But if not, why do we regard the carefree career of an undergraduate as "life" and the hard schedule of a professional baseball player as only a game?

Why does a baseball player's ability count so much and other attributes, like the young man's effort and desire, count so little? For aught that appears, he is no less deserving in a general way. Why is he not entitled to some handicap to compensate for his (undeserved) lack of natural talent? The handicap might be in the form of different scoring for him and Clemens; or he might be equipped with a device that, with a little effort on his part, fires fast pitches across the plate.

"But you can't play major league baseball that way," the manager will expostulate. "Who would come to watch?"

To be sure, were teams put together on the basis of effort and desire instead of ability (as some junior little league teams are) major league baseball would be even more tedious than it is. But we do not defend Clemens' position in the lineup as a matter of social utility—the spectators' greater pleasure—alone. We regard it as a matter of right. In view of his ability, he is entitled to make the team; and if his entitlement so determined is not required as a matter of individual desert, it is, at least, not inconsistent with desert, his or anyone else's. Insofar as that is a matter of utility, the maximization of satisfactions, there is no consideration of right or justice that inhibits a choice on that basis. The young man is simply, as we say, out of luck.

On the other hand, Clemens' entitlement is not unlimited. Were the manager to decide that the Red Sox had too many pitchers and needed a good shortstop, Clemens (unless his contract provided otherwise) might be released or perhaps traded to another team, even though he were the better all-around ballplayer and wanted to remain in the northeast. More generally, the rules of the game provide that in some circumstances, one team has a preference over the others in signing a player, however the player himself would choose. Once again, it might be argued that that is the nature of major league baseball, justified in the end by the social utility of having teams more or less evenly matched. But if so, on what basis do we conclude that that is all that counts? Why should that override the players' own preferences or length of service on a team? Similarly, if Clemens is entitled to a place on the team, how far does the entitlement extend? Are the "consequences" of his entitlement—all or most or any of what the owners are willing to pay him—part of the entitlement, his to use however he wants? Or may his salary be taxed, perhaps to provide the young man a scholarship to law school?

Such questions ought to be answered, if only to defend the national pastime.

CHAPTER FIVE

Responsibility and Rights

BRIEFLY TO REVIEW what was said in Chapter Three: When we consider whether a person is responsible for some occurrence, we need to settle first of all whether any conduct of his had an effect on the outcome; there must be a causal connection between his act and the outcome or, if inaction is the basis of his possible responsibility, it must be the case that he might so have acted that the outcome would have been different. Unless that minimum condition is met, his responsibility is excluded, because there is no conduct of his to which responsibility can attach. We may also praise or blame someone for conduct that has no consequence, good or bad, that we regard as significant; we should then say that he is responsible for his conduct, even though one might say, in another sense, that he has nothing to be responsible for. If the condition is met, he may nevertheless not be responsible, because the conduct involved no agency on his part: His participation in the occurrence was as a natural object, moved by other forces. If what is at stake is inaction, there must be grounds, such as relationship to another person involved in the occurrence, for regarding it as a failure to act and hence as "conduct" at all. And even if the conduct was, so to speak, self-propelled, the person's own motion, he may not be responsible, because there is an explanation for it that excludes his agency. The line that is drawn shifts from one that is wholly external, between the person and other animate or inanimate entities, to one that views the person as subject or as object, and finally to one that is wholly internal, between attributes that implicate his agency and those that do not.

Most often, when a person is found not to be responsible, it is on one of the former grounds, and the latter, internal distinction need not be reached. If it is reached, on which side of the agency/non-agency line the conduct belongs usually is not contentious and is taken for granted. Nevertheless, a conclusion that a person is responsible always depends on the validity of the distinction in general and its application in the specific circumstances. The only reason for making the distinction, furthermore, is to settle whether or not the consequences of a person's conduct or the conduct itself is attributable to him as his responsibility. The basis for the internal distinction is problematic. But if we are unable to explain or defend it as an independent matter, we are nevertheless able to recognize its application. Concretely, if not abstractly, its reality as descriptive of our actual experience is not in doubt.

As the encounter at Fenway Park illustrates, however, if we press deeper it is evident that this account of how we attribute responsibility leaves unexplained a large issue, which is hidden by the unelaborated references to "a person" and "his conduct." For even if we exclude external causes and some internal causes from the scope of a person's responsibility, we need still to ascertain who—what—is the *person* who is responsible. We noticed in Chapter Two that an attribution of responsibility has two requirements: The act must be undetermined by other causes, and it must be the act uniquely of the person who is held responsible. Tracking the explanation for an occurrence to a person's agency seems to deal only with the first requirement or, at any rate, to take for granted the constitution, or composition, of the person whose conduct is being considered.

The response of common sense is immediate. The person—the self—who is responsible is the person whose conduct it is: who struck the match, who overslept, whatever it is that we are talking about. Who else could it be, after all? But that begs the question. For we are not concerned with the person simply as a physical being, but rather with the person as a moral, that is, responsible, being. And the question that needs to be answered, which the internal distinction highlights, is: How can anyone be responsible for anything that he does if he is not responsible for who—what—he is? From that point of view, so far as concerns responsibility and the desert that goes with it, striking the match is no more attributable to the person who strikes it than being hit over the head. Likewise, the young man at Fenway Park. To be sure, it was he who struck out all the time and missed all the ground balls (or would have, if he had been given the chance). But since his bad eye-arm coordination and all of that happened *to* him, so he claims, and not *by* him, it is not his fault. He does not deserve the consequences, because he is not deservedly who he is at all—even though, merely as a matter of cause and effect, it is certainly true that he is the one who struck out and all that. His claim is that in a just world, a world according to individual desert, he would not be so unfortunately constituted.

The premises of the most ordinary question about a person's responsibility for some occurrence and the young man's much broader question are the same. The difference between them is only that the former question is concerned with specific conduct of a specific person. If, then, the claim is accepted that it was not that person's conduct after all or that he had an excuse, the conclusion that he is not responsible leaves no further question that needs to be answered. We might want to know who was responsible if he was not or if anyone was responsible; but the conclusion about him does not depend on an answer to that further question. Desert being individual and only that person's conduct being in issue, that is an end of the matter. The desert in question, that is to say, is retributive. The young man's claim reaches further. For if it is true that he does not deserve to be who—what—he is, one cannot well avoid the question, Who does? One might benignly suppose that no one deserves to play baseball quite so badly as he. But the matter cannot be left there. For nothing will satisfy his claim except sending him into the clubhouse to put on a uniform. (He will undoubtedly argue no less fiercely that he doesn't deserve it if he *almost* makes the team.) Yet, if the young man's claim is accepted, what of all the others who could and would make just the same claim? What of Roger Clemens? In this case, the question of desert is not confined to a specific person. It is distributive. In a world limited by natural causation, in which there is not enough of everything for everyone, who deserves what? How do we identify the individual, deserving self, differentiated from all other individual, deserving selves? Because each person's desert must be related to the desert of others, the vocabulary of responsibility and excuse, which focuses attention on a particular person, is not adequate.

If the young man went beyond lamenting his (undeserved) misfortune and actually asserted a claim to be on the team, what might he say? Merely to deny his responsibility is not enough; for that leaves him no better off than all the other would-be players. Nor, certainly, can he assert that it would on the whole be socially useful; it is most unlikely that his performance will either improve the standing of the Red Sox or enhance their fans' enjoyment of the game. He might appeal to the manager's generosity and urge that although it would not be useful to put him on the team, it would nonetheless be a thoughtful and kind thing to do. But the manager does not seem the sort of person who would respond to such an argument. Almost certainly, what the young man would say to make his claim is, "I have a right to play."

There is no doubt about what the manager would respond (if he responded at all): "You got no more right to play than . . . than Madonna!"

"Then who does?"

"Roger Clemens, that's who. Now beat it. I got work to do."

The manager's response may be peremptory, but it is likely to strike the rest of us as all that the young man can expect in the circumstances. Moreover, it is precise. Although the underlying issue is the same, when the question of desert shifts from the retributive aspect to the distributive aspect—from "What does the young man deserve?" to "Who deserves what?"—our way of putting the question shifts also.

Our long detour by way of responsibility has thus brought us back again to rights. Responsibility and rights are alike responses to the

puzzle of individual desert in a causally determinate world. Responsibility answers the retributive question: Does this person deserve (well
or ill) for this occurrence or this conduct? Rights answer the distributive question: What does this person, in relation to other persons,
deserve? Although the questions focus our attention differently, they
are inextricably linked. There is no point in asking whether Rolf is
responsible for having started a fire unless he is identified not just as
an object but as a deserving being, capable of responsibility and desert.
Similarly, there is no point in asking whether Rolf is what he deserves
to be or, more familiarly, has what he deserves—that is to say, what
rights he has and whether he has what he has a right to—except as it
may bear on his individual responsibility in some respect. We may ask
what rights Rolf has because we want to know how Alice ought to
conduct herself toward him; but unless we entertain the possibility of
some responsible action of Rolf himself, there will be no occasion to
formulate the question in terms of his rights rather than in terms of
Alice's duties. When we ask about the latter, we ask also about Alice's
rights and, plainly, about her responsibility in that respect. Neither the
self as a subject of desert nor conduct as a predicate for desert is
intelligible without the other; one could speak only of causes and how
far back in the causal sequence it was useful to go. In sum, responsibility and rights are respectively the retributive and distributive responses to a single question: How, in a causally determined natural
order, can persons be justly situated? More simply, what does a person
deserve?

The tight connection between a person's specific responsibility and
specific rights is manifest in how we think concretely about both.[1] If
a person is responsible for specific conduct or a specific state of affairs,
then it is also the case that she has rights with respect to it, her exercise
of which is dispositive to the extent of her responsibility. If a person
has rights with respect to specific conduct or a specific state of affairs,
then, those rights being respected, she is responsible for it to the extent
of her rights. Likewise, to deny that a person is responsible in a

particular respect is to deny that she has rights in that respect; and to deny that she has rights is to deny that she is (rightfully) responsible. It follows also, as a distinct matter, that to deny a person's rights is, to that extent, to make her not responsible, although rightfully she is.

These reciprocal relationships are not often remarked explicitly, because they are ordinarily taken for granted; our attention is drawn in one direction or the other, and the issue is stated in those terms. Or the relationship may be obscured because some other feature of the situation is critical. Attending to a person's failure to meet his responsibility, we are likely to notice his duty and not his right to act as we think he ought to have done; but (although the duty may conflict with a superior or inferior duty of a different kind) unless he had the right, he could not have the duty. So, if we fault Rolf for not walking Ginger (and for the mess that Ginger made in the kitchen) we shall mention that that "was Rolf's job" or that he had promised to do so and do not need to add that he had a right to take the dog down the street. Upholding a person's right in some respect, we are likely to have in mind a potential interference with his exercise of the right, most likely someone else's conduct for which that person is responsible, and not to be thinking about his own responsibility for how he exercises it. If we remind Alice that today it is Rolf's turn to take Ginger for a walk, it is because we want her to let go of the leash; we shall worry about it later if Rolf takes Ginger for a walk through the neighbor's prized flowers. When we consider whether a person has an excuse for some conduct and is, therefore, not responsible, we are concerned with his actual capacities; but had his rights been appropriately different, insofar as they were fulfilled he would have lacked an excuse. Or, if we hold a person responsible for exercising powers in excess of his rights, we probably shall disregard the fact that if we had limited his rights still more, he would have lacked the power to act as he did and, incidentally, would not have been responsible. In both situations, although the person's rights may be regarded as settled and, therefore, are unnoticed, they are reflected in his responsibility. Were Rolf handicapped and unable to walk, he would hardly be responsible for failing to give Ginger her exercise; but if he had a right to have some special assistance, perhaps a wheelchair, and the right were honored, then he might sensibly be required to share that responsibility with Alice. And if she could not be persuaded to let go of the leash voluntarily, it might be taken from her and she might be sent to her room; (temporarily) having no right to go about freely, she is not responsible for Ginger's being exercised, whether Rolf exercises her or not.

The connection between responsibility and rights is indicated in another way, by the symmetrical arguments that are made to sustain or reject one or the other, when each is considered by itself. Just as a person must be attached causally to an occurrence to be responsible for it, she must also be so attached for it to engage her rights. One is not responsible for an occurrence that her conduct does not in any way affect—if, for example, she is nowhere in the vicinity. Nor is one responsible for an occurrence in which she is involved only as a natural object, acted upon rather than actor. Likewise, if one is not at all affected by an occurrence, her rights are not in issue. Patterson, who lives in New York, may deplore the conduct of the police in Los Angeles. But unless she has some interest there, she cannot complain that her rights are denied. And even if one is affected, favorably or unfavorably, by what happens, if she has nothing to say in the matter— whatever her interests, the outcome is not up to her—no question of her rights is raised.[2] Although the young man is deeply troubled when the manager asks him to leave the ballpark, he is denied no right; it is just "his tough luck." A woman who is raped does have something to say in the matter; it is rape precisely because her consent is crucial and she does not consent. The outcome is up to her, as a matter of right, and her assailant is guilty of rape because, overcoming her resistance, he has denied her right. (When the lord of the manor exercised his *droit de seigneur*, it was not rape, because the soon-to-be bride had nothing to say in the matter; if we assert that rape is indeed what it was, that is because we reject out of hand the notion that the lord could have such a right.)

Similarly, the internal distinction on which responsibility depends has a parallel in the context of rights. If we conclude that a person is not responsible because he has an excuse, we do not deny that his conduct was as alleged or had the alleged effects; we deny only his agency, which is excluded by the explanation constituting the excuse. Likewise, a person may have power to affect an outcome, which is subject to a specific duty in the circumstances. The duty bears the same relation to the person's rights as the excuse bears to his responsibility generally. (If the right in question is not one that we regularly have occasion to identify specifically, we may refer generally to the person's liberty. The liberty at stake is, however, comprised of the right or rights to which the duty relates, whatever may be the extent of his liberty in other respects.) If no more is at stake than performance of the duty, which is not itself problematic, the duty displaces any right that he might otherwise have, and the responsibility lies with those who imposed it. So a police officer tells an irate motorist that he "is just doing his duty," even though, as the motorist knows, the officer *could* tear up the ticket. The officer's statement is a disclaimer of both the right to do as the motorist wants and the responsibility for not doing it. On the other hand, having no excuse, a person's action is attributed to his agency and he is responsible. And likewise, if he has power to affect the outcome and is constrained by no duty, the matter is remitted to his agency; and whatever he decides to do and does, that is the outcome. He has not only the power but also, explicitly or as embraced within his general liberty, the right, and with it (provided that the causal connection is established) the responsibility.

In a number of unexceptional contexts, this connection between rights and responsibility may appear to break down. So, for example, we may believe that all children have a right to education, without regard to race or poverty. Someone who was kept out of school on such a ground and nevertheless became highly educated is esteemed more, not less, than those who did not face such obstacles, precisely because, having been denied her right, she made it her responsibility and did it "on her own." A person living under a totalitarian regime may have no right to express political dissent. We may nevertheless believe that he has some responsibility to oppose the government's dictates, and honor him if he does (or blame him if he does not). On the other hand, we might assert that an ordinary citizen has a right to oppose or even frustrate the more outrageous policies of an illegitimate regime, without intending to hold him individually responsible for the effects of the policies' implementation. In more ordinary circumstances, a robber has no right to take his victim's wallet; but he is responsible for taking it and we lock him up for just that reason. A passerby is not responsible for the victim's loss; but, although we are not likely to speak in just that way, he surely has a right to prevent the crime if he can.

In all of these instances and other, similar ones, different strands of responsibility and rights are woven together. If the strands are unraveled, the tight connection between them emerges all the more clearly. We need first to notice the difference between having a right, on one hand, and the right's being honored, on the other. If we say that someone was denied her right to education, we do not assert that she does not have such a right, but that she does; for if she does not, then no right was denied. Nor does the denial of that right indicate that she does not have a right to educate herself, whatever that may be worth in the circumstances. If she did not have the latter right, we could hardly admire her for doing so; there is nothing to admire about doing what one does not have a right to do. (Suppose, for example, a child were not allowed to attend a particular school because she lived in another district, a policy that we believed was correct. Would we admire her parents if by insisting and wearing down the school authorities they obtained permission for the child to attend that school? Suppose, on the other hand, she were not allowed to attend the school on account of her race, contrary to what we believed was her right.) If an acknowledged right is denied, we do not hold the person responsible for the consequences of its denial, even though she has the right; but that is because there is no conduct of hers to which responsibility can attach. The most basic condition of responsibility, that her conduct have affected the outcome, is not met. Although she has a right and, as a matter of right, is responsible, denial of the right in fact is also a denial of her responsibility in that instance.

Second, we need to notice that rights may pertain to different levels, or ranges, of responsibility. The person who lives under a totalitarian regime most likely has no legal right to oppose it; he has also no legal responsibility to oppose it (and, indeed, will probably be legally liable if he does). If, notwithstanding the absence of a legal right, we affirm that he has a responsibility to oppose the regime and blame him for failing to do so, we commit ourselves to the proposition that, notwithstanding the law, he has a (nonlegal) right to oppose it; for it cannot be the case that he ought to do what he has no right to do. Just such an issue, about which there is no consensus, was presented dramatically by cases of German citizens who complied with horrendous Nazi decrees. It was presented more recently by the trial and conviction for manslaughter of an East German border guard who shot and killed someone fleeing from East Germany; under East German law at that time, the guard was required to fire on the fleeing person.[3] As those cases well illustrate, the absence of a legal right to oppose the regime or, more precisely, the legal duty not to oppose it may conflict with a more general nonlegal right; and if it does, the latter prevails.[4] Having the right, a person also is responsible, although the circumstance that he must disregard the law may affect his desert, increasing his praise if he meets his responsibility and mitigating his blame if he does not. Furthermore, if we hold a person responsible for failing to act against the law, we must suppose that he retains some freedom of action and that his (nonlegal) right so to act is not altogether denied; were he confined or always under guard, whatever we thought about the law his responsibility would be out of the question. In the latter situation, whether he is not responsible because he has no right or because, he having the right, the right is denied, depends on the legitimacy of the measures that restrain him. One might conclude that the measures are legitimate under the positive law, in which case he has no (legal) right to oppose the law, but are morally illegitimate, in which case he has a (nonlegal) right, which is, however, denied.

Third, we need to notice the difference between having no right and having a right subject to qualifications. Ordinarily, it is sufficient to say that there is no (legal) right to engage in conduct that the law prohibits. Similarly, we may refer to a right in general terms, without mentioning qualifications that either are understood or are irrelevant in the circumstances. But all rights are qualified in some respect, and, strictly speaking, a prohibition is a qualification on the vast range of residual rights to which we refer generally as a right to liberty or, simply, liberty.[5] In an ordinary sense, of course, the robber has no right to take his victim's wallet. He does, however, have all the rights that allow him to be on the street, unconstrained, when his victim walks by. It is in virtue of those rights that he is able to accost his victim and even finally to rob him; and it is in virtue of those rights also that he is responsible. His situation is far different from, say, that of a chimpanzee in the zoo, who not only has no right to take the grocer's bananas but is not allowed to go into the grocer's store or anywhere near it. It may seem extravagant to make much of the difference in the usual circumstances; but that is because the array of rights that are comprised by the robber's ordinary liberty is so much taken for granted. Were we to entertain the possibility of his being monitored or shackled or kept off the street altogether, the difference would not be without significance. Being prohibited from engaging in specific conduct is not the same as being prevented from doing it or being quarantined. (In that connection, consider proposals that were made at one time to confine persons carrying the AIDS virus, or some group of such persons, to certain quarters of a city.) It is a measure of the strength of individual rights, or liberty, in general that we rarely think of the matter in those terms.

The passerby is not responsible for the loss of the robber's victim. But being on the street when the crime occurs and having the right to prevent it, he may indeed be responsible if he fails to try. Whether he is responsible or not depends on the usual conditions of responsibility: whether he was (or should have been) aware that a robbery was under way, whether he had the means to prevent it, and so forth. (The robber's responsibility might also be excused on the usual grounds: if he were under hypnosis, or subject to coercion, or possibly if he or his children were desperately hungry.) His right is similarly qualified. If he had an unqualified right to prevent the robbery and failed to do so—if, for example, it was his duty to keep the robber under guard and supervise his actions—we should assuredly blame him for the loss. The right and the responsibility are conditional on the same basis.

It was noted above that a person's rights may be qualified by a specific duty, which relieves him of responsibility for the outcome of its performance, because that responsibility is borne by the source of the duty. All the same, he may be responsible for a failure to perform the duty, but only because as a responsible person he has rights. If he did not, rather than impose the duty it would be appropriate simply to constrain him to act as required; and the responsibility for his not doing so would rest with whoever, having authority and power, failed to constrain him. If no one had such power, he might act as was required or not; but having neither rights nor duty, he would have no (moral) responsibility either way. So, the police officer who does his duty and tickets the motorist is not responsible if the speed limit is set too low and traffic moves too slowly. Were he instead to "fix" the ticket, he would be responsible and be blamed for his failure to act as the duty required. The duty having been noted, there is ordinarily no occasion to mention the rights that enable him to perform it; but that he has such rights is not altogether without point. For, once again, there is a difference between having a duty and simply being made to do whatever is to be done. Turkeys have no duty to participate in the celebration of Thanksgiving, although the holiday would not be the same without them; nor have they a right not to attend.

In sum, although we often say that a person is (not) responsible without specifying precisely the bounds of his responsibility, the relevance of such a statement is limited to specific conduct or consequences and may be qualified further in various ways, except in the special case—more common in philosophic discussions than in everyday life—in which one means to affirm or deny that a being is or ever could be responsible (leaving for subsequent consideration, if the answer is affirmative, whether the being is responsible in a specific instance). If we say that a person has a right or not or that his right is honored or not, the statement refers to specific conduct in specific circumstances and may also be qualified further. Recognition of a person as a responsible being carries with it the ascription of a vast array of rights to which we ordinarily refer simply as liberty. It is scarcely necessary to mention such rights, for precisely that reason; without them there could be no responsibility, and in the absence of responsibility there are no rights. Our more ambiguous and imprecise way of referring to responsibility and rights is responsive to their features that ordinarily interest us most. If the implicit limits and qualifications are made explicit, responsibility and rights coincide.

The strongest objection to the conclusion that responsibility and rights fully coincide is also the most general. Although it is often highly contestable and may depend on judgment about what a person can be expected and ought to do, responsibility is a matter of fact, what is the case. Considering whether someone's involvement in an occurrence makes him responsible, we can only ask, "Is he responsible?" to which the response, however qualified or uncertain, can be only that he is or that he is not. It makes no sense to ask whether a person *ought* to be responsible. One might as easily ask whether in general chipmunks ought to be responsible. What could the question mean, unless it were somehow a comment on the Creation? We can, of course, ask whether a person ought to be *held* responsible; but that is a different question, and the answer to that as well depends in the first instance on whether he is responsible or not.[6] Rights, however, are normative; they have direct bearing on how persons ought to behave. Rights *ought* to be respected, and their most important practical consequence is the duties they impose. Indeed, they are commonly regarded as the bedrock of normative reasoning. How then can a statement that a person is (not) responsible be the equivalent of a statement about what rights he has?

This difficulty, however, is one that we have already observed about rights, not in connection with responsibility but considered by themselves. For, their normative significance notwithstanding, about rights also one can say only that a person has a right or does not. What would it mean to say that a person *ought* to have a right? One can say that since a person has a right, he ought to be treated in a certain way. But that is not at all the same as saying that he ought to have a right. (The reductionist urges that to say that a person has a right is equivalent to saying how he ought to be treated in some respect, thus not only disposing of the facticity of rights but eliminating them altogether. Throwing the baby out with the bathwater no more gets the baby clean in this instance than it does in others.) So also, one can say that a person ought to have a legal right or, less elliptically, that there ought to be a law establishing such a right. But that too leaves the facticity of rights as such unassailed.[7] It is just this "objective" aspect of rights that has led some philosophers to call them "moral facts" or, more evasively, to describe them as primary and unanalyzable. The point of such a description is simply that rights are not derivable from normative premises.

On the other hand, although we refer to responsibility insistently in the indicative mode, it too has direct normative consequences. For one's responsibility determines what one deserves: praise or blame, reward or punishment. The extent of individual responsibility has also some other practical significance. Only insofar as persons are responsible, for example, will certain kinds of incentives or deterrent measures be effective. And in some situations, other considerations may lead us to disregard a person's desert. But desert itself is normative, and hence responsibility, matter of fact or no, is—somehow—normative as well. In this respect also, responsibility and rights go together.

Constitutive Attributes and Circumstantial Attributes

The common ground from which responsibility and rights spring is individual desert: in the terms in which we usually speak of the former, what a person deserves, and in the terms in which we usually speak of the latter, what a person is due. They can be brought together in the following way. The internal distinction between responsibility and excuse may be said to draw a line between those of a person's attributes that are *constitutive* and those that are *circumstantial*. The former attributes constitute a person as the unique person that he is; taken all together, they are himself, or his self. Conduct traceable to them is, then, traceable to the person and, therefore, is conduct for which he is individually responsible. So also, constituting him as the person he is, such attributes (and their effects) are duly his, his by right or his rights. Circumstantial attributes describe a person as a natural being; they are his only circumstantially, that is, as a result of circumstances having nothing to do specifically with him- or his self at all. Conduct traceable to circumstantial attributes is explained as the consequence of other causes, circumstances that happened; it is conduct for which the person has an excuse and is not responsible. And since they are merely circumstantial, such attributes (and their effects) are not duly his, not his by right or his rights.

To say that some of a person's attributes are "constitutive" of his self and others merely "circumstantial" accidents or that some are his "rightfully" and others not seems deliberately paradoxical, or at any rate odd. Attributes, after all, are attributes of someone. They do not float around independently and attach, as it were, to this person or that—rightfully or otherwise. As Hume famously concluded, aside from "his attributes," there is no "he."[8] To refer to Roger Clemens is to refer to a great pitcher. That and that alone is why Roger Clemens rightfully has a place on the team. It makes no sense to say that he has a right to be a great pitcher or that his pitching ability is duly his, as if it were somehow in doubt. So, one may argue, even if it is comprehensible to speak of constitutive and circumstantial attributes to express a conclusion about a person's responsibility or excuse for a particular act, it is much clearer to speak directly of responsibility and excuse; reference to a person's attributes as himself or not himself has no general meaning outside that context. The color of Richard's hazel eyes, for example, is among his attributes, perhaps one that he prizes most. What does it mean to say that it is constitutive, his by right, or that it is circumstantial and not a matter of right at all? Can we say more than that it is his or, more simply, that Richard has hazel eyes?

So long as a person's attributes are noted only to describe him, there is no occasion to think of them as rights or not rights, any more than we think that way about attributes of any natural object: animals, plants, even rocks. If we only mention the color of Richard's eyes, we describe him as he is, not as he does. Suppose, however, that Richard's good looks made him fatally attractive and there were a fatality. We might then have to decide how far the color of his eyes is his responsibility and not merely a circumstance having causal significance without implicating his responsibility at all. Would it be up to him to wear dark glasses in public, lest another person succumb? Or would it be up to those who are unusually susceptible to hazel eyes to keep out of his way or to avert their eyes, because that was their responsibility? In view of what happened last time, the dons could hardly avoid considering such a question, were Zuleika Dobson to appear again at Oxford.[9] Does the potential child abuser have a responsibility to avoid situations in which he might be tempted, even if he must give up activities in which others engage and which he would enjoy, or are those whom he might harm simply the unfortunate victims of nature's indifference?[10]

Suppose the color of Richard's eyes accounted for his great success as a movie star and the seven-figure income that went with it. (Elizabeth Taylor is said to have violet eyes, which some might think contribute more to her cinematic appeal than her talent as an actress.) If it were thought socially useful to devote a portion of his large income to public purposes of which he did not personally approve, how much, if any, of his income is his by right and not to be taken against his will, and how much is available for the general good? No doubt we should not describe a decision to tax Richard's income as an appropriation of that portion of his eyes, whether they were his self or not.[11] Were the issue to arise, we should probably say that the success of his movies depends not only on his contribution—his good looks—but also on the whole social structure that makes the production and distribution of movies possible, or something like that. But, of course, the same sort of thing could be said of any responsible action for which a person individually is praised or blamed, the consequences of which depend not on the isolated action alone but on all the necessary attendant circumstances as well.

Suppose it were discovered that persons with hazel eyes were unusually susceptible to some disease or suppose they were (thought to be) unusually dull-witted. Would Richard justly have a claim—would he have a right—to public funding of research to find an antidote to the disease or to provide special education? Or is all of that his own responsibility? If he applied for admission to a university, how should his academic record be weighed against the superior record of someone with ordinary brown eyes, who must be rejected if he is admitted?

Although the color of one's eyes is not thought to have such large significance, all too obviously issues of just that kind are not only hypothetical. (For Richard's hazel eyes, substitute Clemens' eye-arm coordination.) Once the color of Richard's eyes is not regarded merely descriptively but is assessed as a potency, a source of what happens, we must decide whether their color is his *normatively*—that is to say, whether as *duly* constituted he would have those eyes and he therefore deserves them and their consequences, or not. If so, it is his responsibility; he may justly claim the benefits as his right and justly must suffer the burdens, also as of right. If not, he has no right to the benefits and likewise has a right not to suffer the burdens.

But doesn't the example of Richard's eyes indicate the limits of this way of thinking and show that, however closely related in some cases, responsibility and rights are nevertheless distinct? The excuses that we accept in avoidance of responsibility are, after all, quite limited; they extend only to unusual and rather clearly identified conditions and circumstances that place a person outside the broad range of the normal. Similarly, claims about rights rarely refer to one's ordinary personal characteristics; such claims arise within a limited range of conflicts of individual interests that are acknowledged to be subject to social determination. The typical payoff of a right is the duty it imposes on others. Whether they work to his advantage or not, most of a person's attributes are not so regarded. There is little point in asking whether Richard's eyes are his "rightfully" or "not rightfully" if, either way, they are his all the same.

The ordinary right to physical integrity would protect Richard against his eyes being taken from him, just as the government's ordinary power to tax would prevail over his claim to keep all the income that his eyes bring in. Yet even those rather obvious conclusions have to be qualified as for the time being. It is not so long since the income tax was challenged seriously as a violation of individual taxpayers' rights; although the legal question is now definitively resolved, the philosophical question evidently is not.[12] It may not be so long before our rapidly developing capacity to transfer body parts from one body to another puts in doubt one's unqualified ownership of his own body, after death or even during life. Already, state statutes provide for the routine "harvesting" of the corneas of a cadaver's eyes during an autopsy, for subsequent implantation in a living person.[13] In an age in which external and internal body parts are regularly removed, replaced, or altered, we should be cautious about basing much on bodily integrity.

Even if we agree that Richard's eyes are indeed his and likely to remain his, practical questions remain. If he were to be blinded in an accident or if he simply had very poor vision, would he have a right to some ameliorative provision for his handicap, if he could not provide for himself or even if he could? *Is* bad vision a handicap, or is it just the (bad) luck of the draw? Such questions do not apply only to physical attributes but extend over the whole range of human characteristics. Intellectual and emotional characteristics and character traits generally are alterable up to a point, sometimes by physical means like drugs but in any event by all the socially determined variables that compose one's environment. If the limits of human ingenuity of this kind are reached, there is little, or perhaps nothing, that itself or the consequences of which cannot be ameliorated or burdened indirectly. As the Wizard of Oz understood, we may not be able to give the scarecrow a brain; but we can give him a college degree, which will look good on the wall of his office and probably get him a better job. The cowardly lion may never be a hero; we can give him a medal and an honored place on the dais, all the same. And if we cannot deprive the Wicked Witch of the West of her powers, we can tax her profits. Whether they fully realized it or not, the most important insight of the "state of nature" theorists, which was really a rediscovery of Aristotle, is that there is no state of nature. The person we encounter is through and through a joint product of nature and the human community in which he lives.

Still, the argument may be, however he got to be the person he is and whatever the consequences of his being that person, Richard is one entity. There is not one Richard, with a lot of "circumstantial" attributes, hazel eyes and all the rest, and another Richard constituted normatively, with heaven knows what color eyes or anything else. It is the very same person whom we sometimes describe and whose actions we sometimes judge. When we affirm that Richard is responsible, that he has some rights and not others, we mean that very person whom we see before us, Richard as he is. A similar objection troubles Kant's argument that the freely acting, moral agent is a noumenal being, whose characteristics are in principle unknowable.

True enough. We do, however, routinely distinguish between Richard as autonomous agent, responsible for his actions and incurring desert, and Richard as a natural being, the determinate composite effect of natural causes, no more responsible for what happens to him than a hazelnut or a rock. That distinction, furthermore, does not depend on some phenomenon external to Richard himself, which, as Kant stated clearly, would be only another natural cause. It is rather a crucial distinction between Richard himself—whole and entire—on one hand constituted normatively, that is to say, as of right, and on the other hand, as he is only circumstantially, that is to say, as a matter of fact. Although it is unfamiliar and perhaps seems strange to speak in this way of a person's attributes as constitutive or circumstantial, it affirms nothing that is not contained implicitly in our ordinary patterns of speech and thought.

If that is indeed the case, one may ask finally what is gained by adopting so unusual and, on the face of it, puzzling a way of referring to matters that we understand well enough as it is? Describing responsibility and rights alike in terms of a distinction between constitutive and circumstantial attributes makes the connection between them explicit. It enables us to explain the connection as a response to the determinist challenge and, finally, to elucidate rights as the (human) resolution of the antinomy of freedom and cause. The transitions from responsibility to rights, as we now use those concepts, and from rights back to responsibility, in the deeper sense of freedom within a determinate causal order, are not proposed here to provide new explanations of our experience. Rather, they bring to the surface the deep structure of our experience as we, perforce, experience it.

What Rights Are

The human duality of autonomous self and determinate being is understood to be the great stumbling block to an adequate account of responsibility. The dependence of responsibility on freedom and the manner in which that duality challenges it was described briefly in Chapter Two. As there expressed: Unless a person's act is fully determined by the actual, determinate person that he is, in what sense is it *his* act? But unless the act is fully undetermined, in what sense is it *free*? All the great variety of responses to this puzzle have urged that one or the other side of the duality is overstated or can be overlooked. None of the responses succeeds, because each side taken by itself states what we know to be true or, at any rate, are unable to doubt. Freedom *is* a condition of responsibility. Every event, including human behavior, *has* a cause (and, in any case, indeterminacy also defeats responsibility).

Looking for a way out, one might speculate about a linguistic usage that made explicitly a radical distinction between the autonomous person and the nonautonomous thing, two entities housed, as it were, in the same physical matter and occupying the same space. One would say, for example, that "he (John) kicked the ball" but "it (John) tripped over the ladder"; "she (Ellen) picked up the pebble" but "it (Ellen) was hit by the rock"; "he (Tom) lied," but "it (Tom) made a slip of the tongue." The "point of view" approach of P. F. Strawson, Thomas Nagel, and others to the problem of free will, which asserts that there simply are a human, moral perspective and a scientific, causal perspective, comes very close to adopting this usage, in substance if not in form. Since it is central to this approach that there is no unified perspective, it hardly matters whether one refers to perspectives or to persons. There may also be traces of such a usage in some reflections about the soul and other disembodied human states of being. It is, however, not a linguistic happenstance that we do not refer to ourselves in that way. The autonomous, normatively constituted self and the determinate natural being are not two entities occupying one space even conceptually; they are one and the same.

The solution to the puzzle is *not* to separate these two ways of being human, even as distinct points of view; for although the moral and causal perspectives are indeed different, they are perspectives of a unitary human individual. The solution is found if, instead of attempting to banish this unity, we recognize it fully. More precisely, if we attend to the tight connection between responsibility and rights, the duality of autonomous self and determinate being does not stand in the way of an account of responsibility. It is, on the contrary, the essential, distinctively human characteristic on which the possibility of responsibility depends.

In a normatively ordered universe, constituted wholly according to the right, persons would have only the attributes—physical, intellectual, emotional capacities as well as character traits of every kind—that are rightfully theirs. So constituted, exercising their rightful capacities in accordance with their rightful traits, they could not but do what it is right that they do. Unable not to do what is right, they would lack freedom and personal responsibility in the distinctly human sense. They would in fact be a community of angels. So also, in a universe from which right was altogether absent, there would be no responsibility. Human beings, like other natural beings, would exercise the powers that they have in fact; but they would no more be personally responsible than a tiger or a tornado is personally responsible for the damage it does.[14] For there would be no basis on which to break the chain of natural causes at the individual human being, who—which—would be simply a locus of natural forces. Only in a human community, in which right is real but contingent, are there persons, free and responsible.

Responsibility, furthermore, is insistently individual. It requires that the act in question be *self*-determined, in the strong sense that it is the act of a fully constituted, unique individual differentiated from all others, whatever particular characteristics they may have in common. Were there no individual but only a generic collection of attributes, however detailed and complex, there could be only an impersonal (causal) connection between attributes and behavior, without personal responsibility. (Imagine that someone were held responsible for an act because, although he did not commit the act himself, he was "just like" the person who did. A police lookout bulletin indicates that *someone* who fits the description in the bulletin is the wanted person, not that everyone who fits the description is.) Human beings are, of course, concrete individuals differentiated from one another by their composite individual characteristics—height, eye-arm coordination, eye color, mathematical aptitude, ear for music, taste in films—as well as by unique spatial-temporal trajectories. So also, however, are elephants, hazelnuts, and rocks—everything. That differentiation as a matter of fact does not sustain the agency of human beings any more than it sustains the agency of other living beings or of nonliving things. For considered only descriptively, such characteristics are the effects of immediate or remote causes that we did not ourselves determine. They differentiate us as natural objects but not as responsible persons.

Human responsibility requires that one be a fully constituted, unique individual normatively as well as descriptively. It requires, moreover, as we have seen, that one's individual normative or, as I have called them, constitutive attributes and one's descriptive or circumstantial attributes not fully coincide. If persons always and inevitably had their due, responsibility would collapse into causal determination or causal determination into responsibility. More precisely, we should have no occasion to refer to either; and there would be no use for the concept of rights as well.[15] Yet, unless some of a person's attributes are constitutive, there is no basis for normative differentiation among persons at all. Were we all normatively alike, not only rights but also individual responsibility and the very notion of persons as individually responsible agents would have no application.[16] The differences among human beings as a matter of fact not only would explain the differences in their conduct but also, lacking normative significance, would constitute an excuse for their conduct, whatever it was. In sum, the contingency of right, without which there is no responsibility, is concretely the (incomplete) dependence of individual rights, by which persons are differentiated normatively, on the determinate circumstances of their being.

There are rights because there are persons. The starting point is our awareness of persons as autonomous beings, freely, hence responsibly, determining their ends and incurring desert. Such beings are constituted duly, as of right, lest responsibility have no purchase; but they are so constituted incompletely, lest freedom have no play. The paradox of persons differently constituted as a matter of fact nevertheless constituted normatively as a matter of right is the essential, unavoidable paradox of the human condition itself: freedom within a determinate natural order. Human subjection to cause does not defeat individual responsibility but makes it possible. That there are such beings is not a dictate of reason, which, confronting the antinomy of freedom and cause, can go no further. It is, nonetheless, a matter of fact, an aspect of reality given directly and incontrovertibly in experience.

Constitutive attributes are those that are a person's by right, because they constitute him as the unique, individual person he is. They and their fruits belong to the person himself, because normatively they are the person himself. He is not obligated to use them for the general good, because their disposition is a matter for his own (self-) determination. Nor, if they are deficient, does he have a right that they be supplemented or ameliorated. Just as the better-endowed person may employ the attribute as he determines, notwithstanding any conflicting considerations of the general good, the worse-endowed person must employ it as he can, notwithstanding his own relative or absolute lack of well-being. That is the practical significance of calling the attribute a matter of right.[17] Conduct traceable to such attributes is self-determined; it is, therefore, conduct for which the person is responsible.

Circumstantial attributes are those that are a person's only as a matter of fact, consequences of the causally determinate circumstances of his being. Although such attributes describe him as he is, from a normative point of view they are accidents having no essential connection with him as a person. Accordingly, he has no special right to determine their disposition and they may be claimed for the general good. So also, someone who is not well endowed may claim that his deficiency should be ameliorated to accord with what is his as of right. Just as the better-endowed person may be required to surrender the fruits of his circumstantial advantage, in a just society the disadvantage of the worse-endowed person will be alleviated. Conduct traceable to circumstantial attributes is not self-determined; it is conduct for which the person has an excuse.

This conception of rights has in some respects a broader or narrower range than their applications in common use, but it is consistent with our present, at least implicit understanding. Our everyday liberty includes the rights to exercise all those ordinary capacities by which we conduct our daily lives on our own, by and for ourselves. Although we seldom have need to speak of liberty that way generally, we do not hesitate to do so if it is circumscribed in some respect. So, for example, one would hardly have thought to mention the right to wear one's hair as he pleases—until the right was questioned.[18] On the other hand, we ordinarily refer to rights without mentioning a host of qualifications that are taken for granted. The right to own property is fundamental and unquestioned; but it is ringed with qualifications, like taxation and all the specific limitations on how particular property may be used. We may speak of the right to work without qualification; but it does not include a right to work at whatever one chooses: robbery, drug peddling, and so forth. Even the right to arrange one's hair as he pleases is not unqualified.

The most important departure from common use is that rights extend not only to attributes that we ordinarily think of as powers—intelligence, fine hazel eyes, eye-arm coordination—but also to dispositional traits that determine what we do with the powers we have. It will seem strange to regard diligence or anger as one's right, unless one perceives them as powers, to be exercised or not as one decides for himself. It is indeed a matter of right, and were it challenged we should immediately so regard it, that one is able to be diligent or even to be angry if that is one's disposition (though, again, not without qualification). Exercising one's rights is not equivalent to doing the right thing but to being responsible for what one does. Rights, that is to say, make us fit for moral judgment; they do not guarantee that we shall act morally. And, it is important to note, the dispositions that lead one person to act morally and another not, whatever their cause, are regarded as constitutive, not circumstantial, attributes, in all but the most extreme cases, when we speak not of immorality but of pathology. Only because they are constitutive—because we reject the claim "I [he] couldn't help it"—is praise or blame possible.

A person's rights may thus be regarded as establishing a boundary between the person himself as an autonomous, that is to say, responsible, being and his natural or circumstantial, that is to say, causally ordered, situation. The recognition of rights as arising within and dependent on a human community brings the *kosmos* of the Greeks and the Providence of Christian theology down to earth; but the speculative origins of all three are the same. Instead of supposing that the natural order itself sustains individual desert or that the absence of individual desert in our earthly existence is only an appearance that is corrected in the perspective of eternity, a program of rights "rectifies" the natural distribution of attributes by which one individual is distinguished from another, enhancing the capacities of some and diminishing the capacities of others. However we may be situated by the distributions of nature, nurture, and circumstance, rights afford us our due, whether by validating powers of those who happen to possess them or by conferring powers on those who happen not to possess them. In either case, the power that the right confirms is also a limitation on the power, actual or potential, of some other person(s). Insofar as a person's powers exceed his due, a program of rights invalidates them, thereby extending the powers of others. Whether a person's powers so rectified are more or less than his natural distribution, fully constituted as a possessor of rights he has neither more nor less than his due. He is an autonomous being, *self*-determined in the full sense that responsibility requires.

It is only by rectifying nature, by reconstituting ourselves as bearers of rights, that we make human responsibility intelligible. At the same time, it is striking how limited is the actual extent of such rectification. Although the fundamental premises are entirely unlike, there is less difference concretely between the conception of a normative natural order and our own sense of justice than one might have supposed. Oedipus and the young man at Fenway Park would not have difficulty recognizing each other.

If this account of rights as attributes constitutive of the autonomous self accords with our actual attribution of rights and responsibility, it is nevertheless subject to a fundamental objection that we have encountered before: that the very notion of constitutive individual attributes, normatively justified heteronomy, is incoherent. It supposes that differences among human beings for which they have no responsibility may yet be differences among them regarded as responsible persons. But such a supposition contradicts what we mean by responsibility and its corollary, desert. Having as one's due what one has not oneself responsibly incurred is no more acceptable conceptualized as rights, humanly determined within a social order, than it is conceptualized as the dispensation of nature. What difference does it make that Oedipus learned his fate from an oracle (no doubt mediated through human voices) and our young man learned his from the manager of the Red Sox, supported by the practices of the community? From an individual point of view, one is no more responsible for who he is than the other. Whether we refer to the cosmos or speak instead about rights, the objection to undeserved desert remains.

The conclusion to which this argument points is that outside of positive law (or some other posited normative order) there are no rights. There being no basis for differential individual rights, universal human rights (discussed in Chapter Seven) also fall. Although there might be some authoritative basis for a judgment about the right or the good, it is unconstrained by any independent claims of individuals. Nor does it provide a basis for individual moral judgment, except as a *façon de parler*. From our own vantage, our existence allows no place for desert, no more for what we do than for what we are.

The sufficient response to this conclusion is derived not from reason but from experience. There is no self-determination without responsibility, no responsibility without rights. Without self-determination, there are no persons, only things. Whether or not we are able adequately to defend the ascription of particular rights or even to explain fully the form that such an argument would take, we are aware of them. It makes no difference whether the direction of our thought is "If persons, then rights," or "If rights, then persons." The propositions are one and the same. And there are persons. We start from there.

"Well and good," one may say, "but where is there for us to go?" There must be rights, perhaps; but doesn't the argument thus far demonstrate that no specific rights can be validated? For the antinomy of freedom and cause persists unresolved. The specific rights that a community recognizes are only legal rights, instrumental to the society's vision of the good, whatever it may be. Clubs are trumps, even if they are not always used to beat the other players over the head; about the distribution of the deck, there is nothing to be said. Once again, however, the specification of rights emerges not from the abstract conceptions of reason but from our actual experience of the concrete individuals whom we identify as persons. How this happens is the subject of the succeeding chapters.

CHAPTER SIX

What Has Rights

T HE CONNECTION THAT WAS made in the previous chapter between responsibility and rights points toward an explanation of the long-standing, inconclusive debate about what kinds of beings and, possibly, nonliving entities are capable of possessing rights; and, if one attends to the grounds for literal and metaphoric extensions of the central case, it provides a way out. The conclusions that I reached there will not please defenders of animal rights. Nor will they be welcome to those who have special concern for rights of certain classes of human beings: the unborn, the senile, the comatose, and others who are temporarily or permanently incapable of acting for themselves. If rights attach only to autonomous beings, about whom it is sensible to speak of responsibility and desert, then animals have no rights; for whatever affection and regard we may have for them in other respects, animals are not responsible and incur no desert. Similarly, the rights of individual human beings who are conceded to lack responsibility are then problematic. Attribution of responsibility and desert being excluded from the start, rectification of the natural order in accordance with what is due, in order to accommodate individual responsibility, is beside the point.

Except for some analytic philosophers who may have an interest in the abstract issue, the question whether such entities have rights is bound up with concrete practical questions about what duties persons have toward them. So far as such duties themselves are concerned, the general resemblances between paradigmatic rights of responsible (human) beings and rights that are ascribed to nonresponsible beings are strong. There are other resemblances as well, which make it easy to extend the notion of rights far beyond the paradigm. As a matter of ordinary language, there is not much reason to prefer the narrower or broader view. Since the vocabulary of rights has great rhetorical power, it is unlikely that those whose personal morality includes strongly felt duties to some categories of nonresponsible entities and those whose political objective is to enforce such duties will be persuaded not to regard them as rights of the entities in question. All the same, although questions of rights and duties typically are linked, they are not necessarily so; and it may be possible to account fully for duties toward nonresponsible entities without defending their possession of concomitant rights.

To ask the question "What sorts of beings have rights?" without first giving an adequate account of what rights are, as so often is done, is to invite reliance on ordinary linguistic usage, which in this context is a malleable and suspect test. On that basis it is unsurprising that the outcome is a standoff between the two leading theories of what qualifies an entity to be a rights-possessor—responsibility or interests—with any number of ad hoc variations trailing along. I start here with the explanation of rights and why there are any, rooted in responsibility, that is given in the preceding chapters. My intention is first of all to show that all the features of ordinary language and especially all the moral and practical concerns that inform the issue about what beings have rights can be accommodated within that explanation. Because in addition the ascription of rights to nonresponsible beings and nonresponsible entities generally departs in essential respects from the standard case, I conclude—allowing an uncertain special exception for nonresponsible human beings—that neither animals nor any other kinds of nonresponsible entities are properly regarded as having rights. The duties that persons have with respect to such entities rest on other, more complex, but firmer grounds.

*   *   *

As far as the notion of responsibility itself can be extended beyond the straightforward case of ordinary responsible action, the ascription of rights readily goes along with it. In the easiest case, a person who expects to be unable temporarily to act for herself designates someone to act for her and indicates specifically how he is to act. Barring special, unforeseen circumstances, there is no difficulty in concluding that even while she is incapacitated, she has rights and exercises them, and that she is responsible for the outcome. Such situations are, indeed, not far removed in that respect from an ordinary bargain or contract, whereby we extend our capacities, including among other things the limitations of a single spatial-temporal trajectory.

From that small extension of the central case, the range of responsibility expands to include situations in which the period of incapacity is longer and the directions that are given do not fully determine the action to be taken: because they are not express or are imprecise, because the situation requiring action was not anticipated or other circumstances have intervened, or simply because the passage of time has weakened the directions' hold on the person who must act. In some situations, the incapacity may have been wholly unanticipated and no directions given; but the course of the person's ordinary conduct leaves no doubt what her directions would have been. In others, the most careful, precise planning may be undermined by unforeseen events. There is no clear line marking the limit of personal responsibility. All the variables having been weighed, the more it appears that someone else has acted "mechanically," as it were, to carry out the incapacitated person's actual or hypothetical intention, the more easily the action that is taken can be regarded as an exercise of the latter's rights and within her responsibility. Although she does not personally take any action at all, the person who acts "stands in her shoes" and functions as the instrument (or even tool) of her as a responsible person. The weaker the basis for a conclusion about the incapacitated person's intention, the weaker is the basis for ascribing rights and responsibility to her. But provided that the question that the actor asks is how the person herself would act, enough of the latter's responsibility may remain to regard the action taken as an exercise of her right. (The actor may, of course, ask that question but inexcusably get an entirely wrong answer. If so, his responsibility for his mistake will cut across the responsibility of the person for whom he acts.)

A line is crossed if there is no indication of how the incapacitated person would act or if, although there are indications, the person who acts ignores them and asks simply what would be the best thing for him to do, for the person or without any qualification at all. It is then no longer possible to regard the incapacitated person as responsible for the action taken (except insofar as she may be responsible for some of the data affecting the actor's decision) or as herself exercising any individual right at all, directly or indirectly. A right to do only the right thing, much less the best thing—even if it is what is best for oneself—is no right at all.

Although the ascription of actual responsibility and, therefore, rights comes to an end, there is another basis on which, without undue violence to the concept, one may regard an incapacitated person as possessing rights. Most often, such persons' interests are protected by laws imposing on others duties of care and designating an official or a private person as surrogate to enforce performance of the duty. Even though the incapacitated person has no actual responsibility for the action that is taken, the element of enforcement at the behest of the surrogate gives metaphoric content to the notion of exercise of a right; and since the surrogate acts in the interest of the incapacitated person and in her name, it is easy to ascribe the right to the latter and not to the surrogate himself. The right at stake, however, is distinctly a legal right, brought into being and confirmed by the element of enforcement. (And, in fact, the law provides generally that the incapacitated person's property, rather than the surrogate's, is at risk if things go wrong, thus associating the legal right and legal responsibility.)

If we rely in this way on surrogation to support the ascription of legal rights, there does not seem to be any reason to restrict them to human beings; for the same elements that compose the right in the latter case, an act by the surrogate in the interest of the other, may be present in particular or general provisions for the care of nonhuman beings. In the case of some animals, there may even be something akin to the actual, if rudimentary, exercise of a right. Suppose the owner of a champion dog leaves money in his will for the dog's care. Can we not regard the dog as having a legal right, enforceable by whomever the law designates as its surrogate in such circumstances: the will's executor, someone named as the dog's guardian, or a public official? Suppose further that the will provides specifically that the dog is to be allowed to run in the field whenever it wants. The dog in time learns that the gate to the field will be opened whenever it stands at the gate and barks. Unless one resists ascribing rights to dogs on some other distinct ground, the enforcement metaphor by which rights are ascribed to the incapacitated person seems no less applicable here; and it is perhaps aided a little by the dog's actual behavior.

Recognizing the dog's right will, of course, not trouble those who defend animals' rights generally. The argument, however, does not end there. Suppose a testator provides in her will that a special hybrid bean plant is to be given good care after she is gone and leaves a fund for that purpose. Or a rock, whatever good care means: cushioned on a velvet pillow in a climate-controlled case, dusted weekly, and so forth.[1] If the law has an arrangement for enforcement of such a provision, can we not say that the plant or the rock has a legal right to the care? (We might even describe the plant, climbing toward the light or sheltering behind a windbreak, as indicating its preference, much like the barking dog. As for the rock . . . well, imagination gives out.) Once we have relied on enforcement by a surrogate to sustain the notion of exercise of a right, there is not any insuperable linguistic barrier to ascribing rights to dogs, plants, and even rocks.

Although he believes that animals have rights, Joel Feinberg has said that "to ascribe rights to such things as . . . rocks, stones . . . and other 'mere things' is to commit a kind of 'category mistake.' . . . It is absurd to say that *rocks* can have rights . . . because rocks belong to a category of entities of whom rights cannot meaningfully be predicated."[2] His reason, with which others have agreed, for denying rocks the capacity to possess rights is that they do not have interests: "A mere thing, however valuable to others, has no good of its own."[3] He is, however, willing to apply to mere things concepts like "good repair," "preservation" and "decay," or "care" and "neglect," as if they are directly applicable to the thing itself and not only in relation to the function that some other has for them.[4] Although it is an extension of the usual case, it does not seem metaphorically extreme to explain such terms on the basis of a thing's "interests" or "good," especially if the surrogate's duty is to preserve or care for it without regard to any interest of his own or of anyone else: not obviously more so, at any rate, than referring to the interests of a dog, which presumably does not itself possess the concept. Whether one extends the notion of interests metaphorically to nonsentient things or extends the notion of rights metaphorically to things that lack interests, at least so far as legal rights are concerned, it does not seem altogether absurd to say that anything for the benefit of which a surrogate acts may have rights.

The ubiquity and practical importance of legal rights suggests them as a model of rights generally. Having entertained the extension of legal rights to all kinds of nonresponsible entities, the extension of nonlegal rights as well may seem but a small further step. There are, however, critical differences, the general nature of which was considered briefly in Chapter One. Nonlegal rights as such are not enforceable. Whatever weight is provided by the metaphor of enforcement as exercise of a legal right is, therefore, missing. A further difference, which goes to the heart of the matter, is that a legal right and legal duty arise together and depend alike on the rule establishing both. Outside the law, however, rights and duties are not necessarily so bound. Yet in the present context, that is just the way the argument typically runs. Many persons who agree that there are duties to animals and other nonresponsible entitles nevertheless deny that they possess rights; and the argument that they do have rights depends heavily on the agreed premise that persons have such duties.

The right of animals not to be treated cruelly, for example, typically builds on the common moral perception that it is wrong to treat animals in that fashion. If that perception is stated as a duty not to treat animals cruelly, as it commonly and unexceptionally is, one may suppose, by analogy to a great many duties, that it is grounded in some right, specifically a right of the entities that benefit from performance of the duty. Such an inference is circular, however, and explains neither the right nor the duty, unless the right rests on something other than the duty—some individual good of the entity in question, which is objectively valid and sufficiently strong to prevail over considerations of the general good, the qualities that we have observed in rights generally. If the duty is based on a normative proposition about what it is right for persons to do or, simply, what is right, it sustains no individual right, although the duty itself be accepted without question.

The moral objection to gratuitously cruel treatment of animals is intuitively so obvious that one may be disinclined to debate its basis. The moral issue is, indeed, largely settled by the description of the conduct as cruel. Closely examined, however, neither the moral principle nor the individual duty derived from it can easily be traced to a "good" intrinsic to animals' nature, as the theoretical argument for animal rights requires. The extreme cruelty of animals' predatory practices against one another and the harshness of other natural hazards to animals are sufficient evidence that animals are not in any sense "naturally" exempt from pain or even cruelty. The same might, of course, be said about the natural hazards, illness and injury and so forth, of a human life. One may fairly insist that the duty to refrain from cruelty has to do only with human conduct, since only persons are the subject of duties in the first place. In the case of animals, however, unlike humans, what counts as cruelty even restricted to human conduct depends heavily, if not entirely, on human perception of what else is at stake. Strong utilitarian arguments do not overcome the objection to cruel treatment of another human being. A common example is torture to discover, say, a crucial fact: where a bomb is hidden or where the enemy will launch an attack. Many, probably most, persons would conclude that even in such cases, torture is impermissible; but even if one were to conclude that torture was justified in some extreme circumstance, recognition of the right and regret at having to violate it would remain. All too obviously, utilitarian arguments powerfully affect what treatment of animals is regarded as permissible, whether one expresses the conclusion as a justification for cruel treatment or, more likely, a reason for not describing the treatment as cruel. The latter ambiguity explains why it is commonly said that only "gratuitous cruelty" to animals is forbidden; no such qualification is necessary or even appropriate with respect to human beings. Persons may agree that animals ought not to be treated cruelly but disagree greatly about what that duty prescribes. Hunting for sport, for example, is one of the activities most condemned by defenders of animal rights; but there is no reason to suppose that persons who hunt are indifferent to the treatment of animals generally or, for that matter, uniformly deny that animals have rights. If there is some ambiguity about what constitutes cruelty toward another person, it is not remotely comparable in degree.

The relevance of utilitarian considerations strikes directly at the argument that the duty is derived from the right of the animals themselves. Reference to a right purports to make the duty specific to the individual entity, which is precisely what such considerations contradict. Once that relevance is conceded, the asserted right has no theoretical significance, and it is apparent that the duty can be fully discussed and acknowledged without it. Indeed, the chief function of reference to a right is that it avoids the burden of explaining the duty. The so-called interest of animals, which is said to sustain their possession of rights and which plants and nonliving entities are said to lack, comes down to sentience, which itself comes down to little more than the capacity to feel pain. The argument "sentience, therefore interests, therefore rights" substitutes an unexamined intuition for the real argument that is needed. Accounting for the duty without the right is a more complex task; most likely it has to do with animals' instinctive avoidance of pain and our ability to comprehend their manifestations of pain, as well as the experience of the actor who deliberately causes pain to no other purpose. However difficult the task may be (and however strong the intuition that there is such a duty), reliance on a right does not make a case but only states a conclusion.

Defenders of animal rights may urge that the significance of ascribing rights is not only to emphasize the duties that the rights represent but also to acknowledge the dignity that attaches to a possessor of rights, as something valuable for its own sake, an "end in itself." To accord that dignity out of all the Creation only to human beings and not also to at least the higher animals, according to their capacity, is, it is sometimes said, nothing more than a form of species discrimination. So, for example, if one subscribed to Albert Schweitzer's philosophy of "reverence for life," it would provide a basis for recognizing rights of all living beings, from which flow our duties toward them.[5]

To insist that human beings alone possess rights may from a sufficiently olympian perspective seem merely anthropocentrism. In a universe of so many living kinds and so many other things, why should a single species be so honored? Yet rights are expressive of dignity only because we regard (human) moral autonomy as uniquely valuable. Ascribing a right and honoring it, we acknowledge and bring into play the responsibility, that is to say, the autonomous personhood, of the right-possessor. If the perspective is enlarged, there is no particular reason to regard the possession of rights as a preferred status rather than simply a human characteristic.[6] Angels have no rights. Nor do lilies of the field, which may nonetheless be of greater value in the cosmic order of things. Rights are special only from the distinctly human perspective. That is itself a reason for suspecting that only human beings possess rights.

The denial that animals and other categories of nonhuman beings and living things have rights does not in any respect diminish the obligation of humane treatment or any more particular duty that we may have toward them. Nor does the denial that inanimate entities have rights preclude the recognition of special reasons to preserve objects of special value: the Grand Canyon, the Lascaux cave, the Parthenon, or even a rock—the Rosetta stone. Whether the rubric of rights is used or not, the question that needs to be answered in each case is what duty we, as responsible human beings, have and on what basis. Provided that that is understood to be the question and that it is addressed directly, it perhaps does not matter a great deal practically if the answer is expressed in terms of a right. Still, one may conclude that the duties that there are will be more secure if their defense is not by way of a shortcut that avoids addressing substantial issues.

What, then, should be made of rights ascribed to human beings who are temporarily or permanently, idiosyncratically or typically, not responsible? According to the preceding argument, strictly speaking they have no rights, however extensive may be the duties of others to care for them. The law typically provides for their care, specifying who has such duties and who is authorized or empowered to enforce them. As noted previously, this surrogacy furnishes a metaphorical basis for ascribing at least legal rights to nonresponsible human beings. Such legal rights are themselves, however, commonly defended on the ground that the human beings in question have nonlegal rights, which the legal rights confirm and make effective. One way or another, it is evident that nonresponsible human beings are a special case, which needs to be explained if the general distinction that I have made between responsible and nonresponsible beings is to be preserved.

Rights originate in the concrete experience of agency, in oneself and in others. Although when to regard an individual or individuals generally as responsible is to a considerable extent an empirical question, the bounds of inquiry are not entirely open. The starting point, a structural aspect of our experience, is a categorial distinction between persons and things, according to which persons exercise self-determination and things do not. At the same time, inclusion in one category or the other is ordinarily settled by a single, uniform rule that the category of persons is coextensive with the class of human beings: All human beings are persons, and all persons are human beings. Whether a being is human or some other sort of being is settled in all but the rarest cases by obvious physical criteria, reducible finally to the single, decisive criterion of birth to a human mother.[7] Although the behavior of some primates and other animals in some respects approximates human behavior and may prompt us to treat them with sympathy and respect, they are not (regarded as) persons. Human beings, on the other hand, are (regarded as) persons while still infants, before they have acquired the capacity for self-determination, and continue to be (so regarded) even if they lose the capacity and are entirely under the care and control of others. So also, a human being who from birth never becomes self-determining is thought of as a person and not a thing, although his lack of responsibility is not in doubt.[8]

Theoretically, the equation of humanness and personhood might be challenged. The challenge would be unavoidable were we confronted by an extraterrestrial being who—which?—lacked most other human characteristics but exhibited what appeared to be self-determined action. In such a case, it is difficult to predict what we should conclude. The fact that the beings were extraterrestrial would make it easier for us to include them among persons, because the situation would be on unfamiliar terrain from the start; but suppose they looked just like some terrestrial creatures—apes, for example, or dogs.[9] One supposes that their capacity to communicate with us and to refer to themselves as self-determining would make a difference. Yet some animals have rudimentary capacities of this kind; and we do not entertain the question whether they may not be, at least a little, persons after all. Were we to conclude that the extraterrestrial beings were persons, we should have to rework a considerable portion of at least the Western human tradition—the Book of Genesis, for example, which regards human beings as unique, though part of the same Creation as everything else. While the issue is confined to life on Earth, the general equation of humanness and personhood is unassailable as a practical matter.

Since responsibility, as I have used that term, is the essential characteristic of personhood, considered by itself the qualification of all human beings as persons subsumes the proposition that all human beings have rights. That conclusion is, however, contradicted in specific instances by the individual human being's lack of responsibility. Although we do not disregard the actual facts as a practical matter, in a variety of formal ways, not altogether consistently, we affirm the categorial presumption. It would generally be regarded as incorrect and, still more, shockingly inhumane to refer to an incapacitated human being, even one in what is described as a "vegetative state," as not a person but a thing. On the other hand, it is conventionally proper to refer to an infant and perhaps even a very young child as "it," the neuter pronoun generally reserved for things. Yet a senile or incapacitated person is referred to as "he" or "she" even after the capacity for self-determination is permanently lost. The explanation, if there is any, is perhaps that the latter have a personal life history. We use the personal pronouns also to refer to adult human beings who, because of extreme disabilities, have never become responsible at all; but such cases are rare.[10] Since the contradiction between general presumption and specific facts as well as the inconsistencies in our habits of thought and speech must be absorbed in one place or another, one might as easily conclude that nonresponsible human beings have no rights, although they are persons, as conclude that being persons they have rights, although they are not responsible. What is important theoretically is to locate the source of the contradiction in the initial categorial distinction rather than in some aspect of rights that is detached in principle from responsibility.

There is a further aspect of human responsibility that makes the categorial distinction as such more comprehensible and at the same time makes it easier to suppose that, their categorial status aside, nonresponsible human beings have rights. It is the human condition that we are never fully and exclusively normative beings but are always bound within the causally determinate natural order. At all times, even when we are most fully in control, we have responsibility for only a portion of the occurrences in which we are involved. While awake and deliberating carefully, one may sneeze, or trip, or be affected in countless ways by occurrences for which he has no responsibility whatever. No separation between the responsible person and the nonresponsible being is possible; they are one and the same. So also, even a healthy adult is responsible at all only intermittently. Circumstances in which there is no present responsibility vary greatly: a brief, special loss of agency (anesthesia during an operation); a longer, utterly ordinary loss (sleep); a prolonged, terminable loss (curable physical or mental incapacity); an extended, terminable absence (infancy); an extended, permanent absence (senility); and all the gradations in between. In many such circumstances, the continuity of a human life justifies the ascription of rights because the person has made provision in advance. But even if that is not so, as sometimes must be the case, personhood, as we think of it, would be radically defective if it were interrupted whenever there was a total loss of responsibility. The persistence of the self as subject is intrinsic to our perception of an individual as one and the same person and human being, responsible or not.

Because the normative and the natural are so fully intertwined in us and the normative even as such is dependent on its conjunction with the natural, it is not so surprising that we adhere to the equation of humanness and personhood even in the limiting case in which normative attributes are completely and permanently absent. It has been suggested that the conclusive and dispositive presumption of personhood shields us against dangerous arguments that some groups of persons are inherently more worthy than others. That may be so; but the recognition of personhood has not always prevented the most horrifying crimes against—the term is instructive—humanity. It seems to me that in this case allowance of an a priori substantive proposition is more convincing than any instrumental explanation that treats the matter as one that we might even hypothetically have resolved differently.

If all human beings are persons, whether they individually have a capacity for responsibility or not, then one may say also that as persons, they have rights. All the same, the substance of the issue is not whether a human being in some nonresponsible state has a right—which perforce she will not exercise herself—but whether other human beings, who are responsible, have a duty regarding her. Such duties may be defended on utilitarian grounds; they may, for example, protect the rights of other human beings who are responsible against mistaken or deliberate violation. But more often they are regarded as ordinarily transcending utilitarian calculation. Whether we think of them simply in that way or as related specifically to rights is not finally of great significance. In either case, they attest the unique place of human beings within the Creation, the uniquely human condition.

CHAPTER SEVEN

Human Rights

F OR ALL ITS CURRENCY, the idea of human rights notably lacks specific meaning or content. Nations challenge other nations to meet a higher standard of human rights and accuse one another when, predictably, the challenge is not met. The import of the term "human rights" in that context is intended to be that the rights in question are not ones that may be qualified by national interest; they cross national boundaries and hence are appropriate matters of international concern, as ordinary domestic law is not. The invariable response to such challenges is that national circumstances or sensibilities do count, either making it impracticable for the time being to recognize some right or dictating a different array of rights (which the nation that issued the challenge fails to meet). The General Assembly of the United Nations adopted the Universal Declaration of Human Rights without a dissent in 1948. In thirty articles, the Declaration sets forth a list of rights that is universal only in the sense that it includes just about everything. No nation recognizes all the rights on the list or even acknowledges that it ought seriously to consider doing so. This international approach to human rights and the Universal Declaration in particular have not been without effect. The most skeptical observer is likely to conclude that the international and in most cases, often as a consequence, the domestic political attitude toward individuals' rights is far different from what it was fifty years ago. All the same, at least in international politics, where the term has had the most currency, it is evident that it is used, at best, only aspirationally, to refer to goals that ought to be pursued. Even so understood, human rights are contested and far from universal.

There remains a conviction among scholars and theorists as well as many politicians that whatever else our aspirations may include, there is a core of human rights that are incontestable; and the popular appeal of the idea of human rights supports the conviction. Although the term itself is relatively new in the history of ideas, human rights are not a recent discovery. They continue the long tradition of natural rights, which also claimed objectivity and universality, although any list of specific natural rights was hard to come by and any that was provided plainly lacked either. A way out of this impasse is to concede that no catalogue of specific rights can be shown to belong to all human beings in principle or in fact but to urge that certain rights are so closely related to ordinary ("natural") human desires and so widely acknowledged by persons of good will that, for practical purposes if not strictly theoretically, they are objectively valid and universal. But the uniformity and agreement on which this argument depends obtain only at the most general level and do not survive the effort to delineate specific rights in the actual circumstances of an ongoing community. One is left with a deep suspicion that in this instance, as in so many others, objectivity and universality are a function of ambiguity. So the question remains: Are there any rights that all human beings possess, simply as human beings? Or, closer to the older idiom: Are there any rights that all human beings possess because it is in the nature of being human to possess them?

The heart of the issue, and the central theoretical difficulty for defenders of human rights, is the connection that is made between humanness as a matter of fact and the possession of rights, which has normative significance. Many persons affirm strong views about our duties toward other human beings, on the basis of common human characteristics: rationality or the ability to feel pleasure and pain or, on another plane, possession of a soul or being made in God's image. Although such characteristics, if accepted as fact, together with some normative proposition(s) might commit one to a view about how human beings ought to be treated, they do not by themselves yield conclusions about human rights.[1] They are plainly insufficient as a basis for a plausible utilitarian argument about the general well-being. But even if such an argument could be made, the conclusion about human rights would not follow. For it is the very point of rights that they are individual and not derivative of the general good. A similar objection applies to any argument that derives human rights from a general normative proposition. The issue is not whether x is a human right because (all) human beings ought to be x, but whether human beings ought to be x because, as human beings, they have a right to x.

One may respond that that notion of a right is too stringent in this instance. All that can be intended by the notion of a human right is that it would be a desirable state of affairs (according to some criterion) if all human beings had what the right provided. But if that is so, it is not clear what the reference to a right adds to the latter proposition except an escape from the heavy burden of defending it on other grounds. If we were able to conclude that all human beings ought to be x, what need would there be for the further proposition that x is a human right? Unless the right is established independently of the normative proposition, which itself is essentially contestable, it seems impossible to establish the objectivity and universality of application that is at the heart of the claim of *human* rights. Unless, that is, a right follows simply from the fact of being human, all the differences among individual human beings as well as all the different circumstances of actual human communities are potentially barriers to its universal application. For the right to be sustained as a universal human right, it must be the case that a failure to recognize or honor it is a denial of the indubitable fact that one is human.

The connection between responsibility and rights provides the basis for such an argument, dependent only on the fact that all (and only) human beings are persons, exercising freedom and responsible. In some societies at some times, certain categories of human beings have been excluded from full personhood in practice. The instances of such exclusion caution that although the personhood of human beings is a matter of fact, it can be denied. There have, however, been few efforts to defend such exclusion theoretically, Aristotle's defense of slavery being the notable example. The most brutal oppressors usually have not sought to justify their oppression explicitly on the ground that their victims were not persons. That may suggest a stronger, straight-forwardly empirical basis for the equation of human beings and persons than can easily be articulated. But whatever its ultimate basis may be, the recognition of all human beings as persons provides the ground for a category of human rights. Which of a person's specific, differential attributes are constitutive and which circumstantial varies dramatically from one community to another and is contestable even with respect to a single community. There are, however, some general conditions of responsibility, lacking which a person could not be said to be responsible at all. Those conditions apply to all persons, that is, to all human beings; but since their fulfillment is not necessary but contingent, they are appropriately denominated human rights.

1. The right not to be subjected to constraints on autonomous action too great to be resisted. From a wholly abstract, olympian perspective, all limitations on human action may be viewed alike, whether they are part of the common human condition (our inability to fly) or one's individual circumstances (a lame person's inability to run, or most persons' inability to run a five-minute mile) or are imposed "from without" by another human being (one's inability to stroll in a park without paying protection money to the neighborhood gang). In each case, the uninhibited exercise of one's will is subject to a constraint, which we can imagine removed. There is no right to be free from any and all such limitations, which would amount to liberation from the natural causal order and be a denial rather than a fulfillment of specifically human nature. Nor does reference to personhood or responsibility resolve the opposition between competing liberties in a human community, which necessarily closes or inhibits some avenues for responsible action by protecting or encouraging others. Some aspects of life, like religious faith, have been singled out as necessarily within the domain of individual responsibility. In American constitutional law, freedom of expression is frequently so regarded. But although some forms of conduct can be undertaken only by a responsible actor, because it is understood to include an individual commitment, there does not seem to be any specific conduct failing which we should not be able to characterize a human being as a person. Insofar as the right to religious freedom, freedom of expression, and the like are founded on human personhood rather than on more parochial social values, what they signify is the need to preserve a capacity for the exercise of any responsibility at all rather than a requirement that it be exercised in a particular way.[2]

Human nature does not settle what specific aspects of our lives are properly self-determined. Is it "proper" for a wolf to kill its prey, "proper" for a person to be knocked over by the wind? Such questions have no significance for us except as elliptical references to what a responsible person might have done to prevent the occurrence. The Greeks could indeed ask such questions because they had a conception of normative natural order. The Erinyes were said to be guardians of the natural order. So, in book 19 of the *Iliad,* Achilles' horse is offended by his accusation that it deserted Patroclus on the battlefield, and it speaks up to defend itself. Restoring the natural order, the Erinyes silence it. Lacking a conception of nature generally as normative, we can ask what is proper or not proper only within the range of responsible action, that is, for persons, human beings constituted normatively.

Human rights themselves, therefore, do not determine a range of responsibility. All that can be regarded as a human right is: within the range of responsible action, a right to be free from constraints imposed by or reasonably avoidable by other human beings that are too great for ordinary human will to withstand. The right implicates more than bare physical possibility. It may be that there is no constraint short of a physical impediment that no human being will be able to withstand. Heroes and martyrs furnish abundant examples of extreme and unpredictable strength of will. Effective agency does not require that the better choice also be an easy one. Still, as a responsible person, one has a right that his autonomy not be overcome by pressure that experience teaches would deprive an ordinary human being of will that he otherwise possesses. The obvious example, which usually is recognized as a human right, is the right to be free from torture: the deliberate infliction of pain to induce one to take some action. The right not to be subjected to overpowering constraints includes ones that arise from nonhuman as well as human sources, insofar as they are reasonably within human control; there is no distinction for this purpose between action and omission.

2. The right to physical and mental well-being. It may be that one can always try. Nevertheless, a person must have some actual capacity in order to believe that it is worthwhile to exercise his will and try to make it effective. In addition to specific capacities that differentiate one human being from another, the capacity to act effectively at all depends on general well-being. Every person has a right to a level of well-being sufficient reasonably to prompt the exercise of will. The rights to food, clothing, and shelter fall under this rubric; they are collectively an expression of basic human physical needs. But physical health is not enough. Even if those needs are satisfied, one may experience psychological deprivation so severe that one is incapable of effective action. One has a right also to mental well-being. The right to well-being might be subsumed under the first, as a right not to be subjected to the constraint of general incapacity. Our usual habits of thought distinguish in most instances between personal incapacity and an external constraint.

3. The right to education. Effective agency is a matter of intellect as well as will. One has to perceive accurately a situation calling for action and understand the consequences of actions that one might take. This perception and understanding depend on having general information as well as a capacity to reflect, abstractly and concretely. Repeated failure to accomplish what one intends may reasonably prompt a conclusion that it is pointless to try. Every person has a right to education conducive to effective agency. That is not to say that responsibility depends on some absolute level of knowledge. Although a well-educated nobleman in the tenth century would not act effectively if he were removed to the twentieth—a knight of King Arthur's court in modern Connecticut—it would be absurd to suggest that no one was responsible for anything before, say, 1800. Similarly, a tribesman from the Amazon Basin would not act effectively in New York; nor, for that matter, would a New Yorker on the Amazon. But there is no reason to doubt that each is responsible at home. What counts as effective action is contextual. An informed intellect may be regarded as an aspect of general well-being and subsumed under the previous right; but it seems sufficiently distinct to be classified separately.

4. The right to moral consciousness. Although the subject has been much studied, we have rather limited understanding of how moral consciousness is acquired.[3] It seems reasonably beyond dispute that the propensity for and habit of moral decision are in large part learned. Human beings whose capacity for moral decision is undeveloped and whose exercise of responsibility is accordingly diminished are stunted as persons. Every person has a right to the development of moral consciousness. In a sense, every bad act betrays a lack of moral consciousness; but it is not the case, as occasionally is suggested, that only the good are free. Very bad acts in most circumstances are indicative of very bad people. Still, there is a difference between a person who chooses to do what she fully understands to be wrong and a person for whom the moral aspect of her act is obscure.[4]

5. The right to moral opportunities. Most of us probably regard an occasion calling for explicit moral decision as a burden rather than as an opportunity. Typically the decision that one is called on to make requires a choice between one's own preference and an outcome favorable to or favored by some other(s). Even so, the exercise of freedom is the uniquely human characteristic. One may fairly assert that the *telos,* or proper end, of a *human* being is to nurture the autonomous self. Not only must one have the capacity for responsible action when it is called for; it must be called for as an unexceptional incident of one's life. Opportunity for moral decision does not require that one run an ethical obstacle course; one need not perversely hope to be led into temptation. One does, however, have to be let decide. The path must not be so smoothed, desires satisfied, and obstacles removed that one is a passive recipient of an engineered environment. Nor must one be so educated or trained—like Rousseau's citizen or Winston in *1984*—that he invariably and automatically prefers the good, or what passes for the good.[5] Angels are not persons. There is a human right not to dwell in paradise.[6]

The rights that I have described are commensurate with the conditions in which it is meaningful to speak of a human being as a person. Their denial has the effect of diminishing responsibility for conduct to which the denial directly relates. Individual persons have found extraordinary resources of will in exceptional circumstances; so it may seem correct to regard the content of each right as the least that possibly satisfies those conditions. That least, tested by the most extreme actual cases, is not much. There is no reason, however, to make what, significantly, we call "superhuman" efforts the measure of what is human. What is at stake is the descriptive category of persons, which calls for reference to the standard, or normal, case.

These rights seem to me all that can be said to arise directly from our nature as human beings. None of them affords a litmus of responsibility, still less a catalogue of precisely what is permitted or not. There is no reason to expect that they would or, in view of the multiformity of human experience, to regret that they do not. They are stated somewhat differently from those most frequently identified as universally valid human rights, although it is evident that my list has a great deal in common with them. Their particular enumeration and formulation have no special importance. What is crucial is that each can be explained and defended as a human right, without additional assumptions or special pleading. As I have stated them, they may seem too weak and indefinite for the work they have to do, which is to protect persons against oppression in the name of their particular communities' perceptions of the good. But human rights do not exhaust the catalogue of rights. Within a community, the general conditions of responsibility as such are amplified and made specific. The bounds of personhood thus defined give rise to a full complement of rights for persons in that community. How that is accomplished is the subject of the next chapter.

Three other rights are often proposed, in one form or another, for inclusion in a catalogue of human rights:

The right to what one has. The assertion of a right based simply on a notion of ownership or property—"It's mine!"—has strong intuitive appeal. Typically, the claim of ownership is substantiated by reference to the provisions of positive law, which sustains bundles of rights by the designation of material (or immaterial) things as private property. Often enough, however, the argument loops back and uses ownership, regarded now as a matter of fact, as the premise of a claim that, the property being one's own, its owner has rights with respect to it that the law is bound to respect. The short response to that argument is, of course, that if ownership is established by the law, then the rights of ownership extend only so far as the law itself prescribes and, in any event, are only as valid as the law itself.

A richer notion of property as a natural right is defended by Locke in the famous fifth chapter of the *Second Treatise of Government* and by some contemporary philosophers, among whom Robert Nozick is prominent. Locke's argument starts from the premise that one's body is her property, from which he reasons that the fruits of one's labor are her property and also, therefore, anything to which her labor is joined. The argument is notoriously weak, if for no other reason (and there are others) than that it depends on the assumption that one person's appropriation of goods leaves "enough, and as good . . . in common for others"[7] at any point in time, including the indefinite future. Nozick makes a similar argument about owning one's labor and its fruits, which founders simply on the weakness of his assumptions about what are the "fruits" of one's labor so understood.[8] The "enough, and as good" argument enabled Locke to conclude that anything to which one's labor is joined is the fruit of her labor. Nozick sensibly does not adopt that argument; but without it, his parallel conclusion has no mooring and is not even superficially plausible.

The strong ground for a natural right to property, which is the substantial core of Nozick's argument, is that personhood is actual and concrete in individual persons, constituted as individuals by their particular attributes. "What one has" might be regarded as an oblique reference to personal attributes that one rightly has, those that constitute her normatively as the person she is and no other. So understood, the right to "what one has" is a compelling response to any program that regards all one's individual attributes as part of a common stock, available for the general good. Nozick uses it in that way against John Rawls's argument that in principle none of a person's abilities or their lack is deserved.[9] Just as certainly, however, it is unavailing to establish a right to everything that one has, or any particular amount, portion, or aspect of what one has. An undifferentiated claim to what one has simply because one has it substitutes power for right or asserts that power, in whatever form, is—or makes—right. Unless one explains specifically how or why what one has is one's due, having is only a contingent fact and not the basis of a right. Nozick, like every other extreme defender of a right to what one has, makes this equation of power and right plausible by adding a marginal qualification. There is always imposed protection against appropriation by force. Such a qualification seems to follow from, rather than to contradict, the right to property; unless one has such protection, what right is there? That is, of course, true. But it only highlights the inadequacy of the general argument that having is itself the ground of having by right. After all, one way to have is to take. Evidently, some of one's powers are rights, but not all. Unsurprisingly, writers on the subject tend to protect intellectual capacities more than physical ones.

Still, the argument contains an important truth. Some of a person's attributes must be hers normatively—as of right—if there is to be a distinct person at all. Such attributes, which I have described as the normative constituents of a person, are she, and they cannot be appropriated or used against her will without depriving her of the autonomy that is hers as a person. A crude distinction between attributes of the physical being and everything else has strong intuitive appeal and is frequently serviceable.[10] The autonomous will requires physical means to make itself effective, which the body provides in the first instance. If the claim to one's body were challenged, it might be a question whether the more apt response was "It's I," or "It's mine." But since personal identity persists despite all kinds of displacement and substitution of internal and external body parts, as an original matter there is no reason to insist that everything physically contained within the borders of the human body is normatively constitutive or, on the other hand, that everything that is normatively constitutive is so contained. One may well conclude that a person requires tools or material equipment in addition to her body to make her will effective; but there is no evident basis for a presumption about what specific equipment is included. When one moves beyond the body to things that are not one's self even linguistically, the automatic equation of power and right (and absence of power with absence of right) is not even superficially plausible.

The right to equal dignity and respect. A human right to equal dignity and respect has been attractive to many philosophers, who have, however, been considerably unclear about what they have in mind. On one hand, the relevance of equality to the matter of human rights seems critical and obvious. For if they attach to all persons simply as such, there seems to be no ground for differentiating among their possessors.[11] On the other hand, there are no individuals to possess any rights at all unless individual differences are recognized and protected. A central element of the asserted right evidently is that one's interests and ends are to be taken into account with no premium or discount because of the particular person whose interests they are. Without further specification, however, being taken into account guarantees little. Although being left out of account may be an assault on one's dignity and a particularly overt manifestation of lack of respect, we are also, more frequently, affronted by finding that our interests have been weighed in the balance and valued, as we believe, too lightly. In any case, the inequalities that trouble us need not refer to particular persons. Smith's opponent may say to the assembly, "Pay no attention to Smith. She doesn't count." He is, however, much more likely to say, "Only those who have paid their dues [Smith being the only one who has not] can vote." With a little ingenuity, the requirement that one not be left out of account can be met and swallowed up in the accounting that is made. Of course, some accounting rules are more acceptable than others; but a standard of equality does not say which.

Ronald Dworkin, who uses the term "equal concern and respect," urges that it means that calculations of the general good should include only personal preferences, having to do with how one lives oneself, and not external preferences, having to do with how others live. To count the latter, he argues, would give undue weight to preferences of the dominant group, which would, in effect, be counted twice. In that way, he traces specific civil rights to the principle of equal concern and respect. Such rights, he says, protect the polity against improper consideration of external preferences in circumstances in which experience teaches they are likely to be found.[12]

One of Dworkin's examples is racism, belief "that a black man is to count for less and a white man therefore to count for more than one."[13] If that is what he means by an "external preference," his point may be conceded, because the so-called preference does not refer to any specific interest and refers to individual characteristics (black and white) only to identify the individuals who possess them. It is as if the proposition were that Smith and Jones and O'Neill and . . . [all other black persons, individually named] don't count, not that such and such interests are unavailing or that persons who have such and such characteristics are not preferred in this instance. Dworkin's way of stating the racist belief straddles both forms of expression. The significant point is that it fails to mention *any* interest as a justification of the preference that it affirms, in a manner that suggests that no justification is needed. Smith and Jones and O'Neill and all the rest are, for aught that appears, excluded simply as individuals, not as members of a relevant class. That being the case, it is difficult to see on what basis it could be claimed that the interests of black persons had been taken into account at all.

Discrimination need not be, and nowadays rarely is, stated so baldly. Neighborhood schools may have the foreseeable consequence of racial segregation, which some people may count among their merits; others, however, may prefer neighborhood schools for different reasons, despite their segregative effect and not because of it. They may believe that local control improves education, that children thrive most in a sheltered, familiar environment, or that they ought not to travel long distances getting to and from school. One may regard a preference based on such reasons as not very weighty in view of the reasons why some persons, black persons in particular, prefer integrated schools. If so, then the latter will prevail. But the simple proposition that only personal preferences count does not dictate that result.

Some of Dworkin's other examples seem more to his point. He mentions objections on moral grounds to "homosexuality, or contraception, or pornography, or expressions of adherence to the Communist party."[14] If persons' "external preference" that not only they themselves but also others not engage in such activities is taken into account, he argues, those who prefer to engage in the activities are denied equal concern and respect, because their single affirmative preference has to compete against the dual affirmative and negative preferences of others (those who prefer homosexual sex for themselves presumably having no preference that others not engage in heterosexual sex, and so forth). The calculus works as Dworkin suggests only if one assumes or has concluded antecedently that the conduct in question, which the disfavored group prefers and the favored group does not, is, in John Stuart Mill's formulation, self-regarding conduct: that is, it has to do only with how one lives one's own life and not with how others live theirs. That being so, the only way to state the favored group's "negative" preference is as a preference about how other people behave. But although *some* conduct must be (treated as) self-regarding if there is to be any scope for personal autonomy at all, whether any specific conduct is self-regarding or other-regarding is deeply problematic.[15] In view of the broad opposition to homosexual practices, pornography, and, it may be, contraception, it is, to say the least, not obvious that those activities are self-regarding. The "Communist menace" may never have been as threatening as once was thought. But to declare that supporting the Communist Party was self-regarding conduct, at any rate in the period after World War II when fear of communism was at its height, seems merely to substitute assertion for argument. And if conduct is not self-regarding, a preference concerning whether others engage in it can be stated no less easily as a personal preference, having to do with one's own liberty, than as an external preference, restricting the liberty of others. Once the assumptions about which conduct is self-regarding are exposed and set aside, "preferences" are simply competing liberties. Since one or the other must be given precedence, which prevails is not by itself an indication of equal concern and respect or its lack.

Dworkin's argument is instructive because, more than most, he has tried to give the abstract right substance independent of contentious evaluations of specific differential individual attributes. If that were possible, then "taking into account" would have the significance ascribed to it. Sometimes it is suggested that dignity and respect are themselves the "goods" to be distributed, separate and aside from any more specific accounting, and that the point of the right is to distribute both equally, notwithstanding the differential attributes that make one person able to claim a larger share of society's rewards than another. It has proved difficult indeed to describe what dignity and respect are on those terms. All too likely, they resemble the attitude of the walrus and the carpenter to the oysters whom they met on the beach.[16]

As a practical matter, the right to equal dignity and respect has meant that certain shared characteristics—notably race and gender but also ethnic background, national origin, and religion—are not as such (ordinarily) to be taken into account. Historically, those characteristics have been the basis for weighing the interests of members of one group so identified less than the same interests of members of another group, without a well-founded belief that the differential characteristics that define the groups are specifically relevant.[17] The explicit exclusion of such classifications from consideration is historically justified because it was the persons merely as members of the groups rather than a weighing of their respective interests that mattered. But precisely the same interests might be outweighed and disfavored on other grounds. The child who would formerly have been denied admission to the college of her choice because she is black may be denied admission because she is not able enough or because her parents are not alumni or cannot afford the tuition. If she is admitted, the interest of another child who satisfies those criteria is denied. The elimination of invidious discrimination affords dignity and respect to those of the previously disfavored group. Beyond that, the task of affording dignity and respect to each while preserving the dignity and respect of all is a complex, many-faceted problem the solution to which eludes any general formulation.[18]

If the individual attributes and interests that are the basis of differential treatment are left aside, what remains is personhood itself. Each has the rights associated with being a person, equally with all other persons. The basis of the rights is not an equality with others, but simply that one is a person, to whom individually those rights attach. Nothing is gained, and the true basis of the rights is obscured if they are described as a matter of equality.

The right to life. The question whether there is a right to life brings the puzzle of personal meaning to a narrow focus, in the context of temporally limited human existence. There is—supernatural theories aside—no agency without life. Personhood and the agency that it implies are confined to living human beings. Mortality is part of the human condition, and personhood is limited by it. Just as there is no right to be freed altogether from the natural human condition while one is alive, there is no right to immortality. If, then, there is a right to life, it demarcates a line that separates the unavoidable condition of mortality from avoidable death. It is, more precisely, a right not to be killed or, perhaps, in some circumstances not to be let die.

If there is such a right, it stands on a different footing from the others, which depend on the initial assumption that the possessor of the right is a person and, as such, a responsible being. Rights follow from this assumption because they are conditions of responsibility, which cannot consistently with it be denied. In this case, however, violation of the asserted right has the effect not of contradicting the assumption but of falsifying it; as a matter of fact, a dead human being is not responsible. What was, then, a responsible being possessing rights is a responsible being no longer. The right to life is the right to be a (living) responsible person—to have rights. But if only such beings have rights in the first place, such a right is otiose.

Strictly speaking, life is a condition of having rights; and there is not a right to life as such. From the human point of view, the value of (human) life does not inhere in life itself, but arises from autonomous humanity as the source of all value. One may believe that there is a higher, supernatural source of value, which dictates the value of human life. In that case, the latter value and the duty to preserve it would be qualified, as the story of Abraham and Isaac suggests. In the absence of such a supernatural reference, autonomous humanity must itself be the ultimate source of value; human beings alone being self-determining, they alone have a capacity to value at all. (The goal-directed behavior of animals and the tropisms of lower animal life and vegetable life may be said to reflect values of the animals or vegetables themselves only in an attenuated sense, since the values are not chosen but are given, as part of their nature. If one supposes a purposive *natural* order, of course, they reflect values immanent in nature.) Only on this basis can it be said that the value of life extends equally to all human life without distinction. The deliberate taking of human life to satisfy a personal aim is the supreme wrong, not because it violates an individual right to life, but because it implicates a rejection of all moral values.

That is not to say that the deliberate sacrifice of human life is always wrong. There are many special circumstances, qualified in various ways, in which the loss of a particular life or lives or of a predictable number of unknown lives is thought to be justified by some value preserved for other human beings.[19] We need not examine such cases generally here. The cases that concern us are those in which the presumptive value of life is problematic because the personhood of a living human being is in doubt. On that basis, it may be argued, the value of autonomous humanity is absent, and the taking of life need not be justified by extraordinary circumstances peculiar to the individual case; rather, a category of cases in which the taking of life is subject to ordinary consequential calculation can be specified in advance. The cases debated most often are (i) the fetus and the permanently unconscious, and (ii) the condemned criminal.

No one—literally no one—urges that a fetus be held accountable: for the discomfort it causes its mother, for the expenditure of resources to sustain its health, for the offense it gives another small child in the family. No one—literally no one—urges that the comatose patient be held accountable: for the grief of others, for the expenditure of medical resources, and so forth. If the patient's own act is the cause of his condition, one may hold him, as he then was, responsible, just as one may hold him responsible, as he then was, for other harm that he did. But that raises entirely different questions. Perhaps it is conceivable to speak of his present condition as a deserved consequence of his prior conduct. (But see the discussion of capital punishment below.) Nevertheless, his conduct now is not a basis for holding him responsible for its consequences. Nor does the fetus or the patient merit praise if such consequences are avoided. Far from affirming their individual responsibility, the ascription of rights to the fetus and the comatose patient is intended to impose responsibility on others to act in their behalf and provide for them what they cannot provide for themselves. Were that all, the conclusion that neither the fetus nor the patient has rights would follow directly.

It was observed in Chapter Six that the categorial distinction between persons and things is applied generally by an a priori assumption that all human beings are persons. The inclusion of the fetus and the comatose patient among human beings is itself not beyond dispute. The fetus is in some respects not (yet) a distinct being but an appendage of the mother. Although that point is usually made to challenge the characterization of the fetus as a *person,* it contradicts more precisely its characterization as *a* (human) *being* at all. (The challenge to personhood is thus made indirectly, by reference to the a priori assumption.) It seems harder to argue that a comatose patient is not a human being; and those who favor terminating life do not, so far as I am aware, argue in those terms. (Here again, use of the neuter pronoun for a fetus but not for a comatose patient may be suggestive; but in the former case, one does not ordinarily know which of the personal pronouns to use.) The argument is, however, not far removed from what is asserted about the fetus. Although the patient is not attached physically to a specific person, he is as little capable of existence as an independent being as the fetus. One might urge, only a little metaphorically, that he too is not a distinct being.

Although one may question whether the fetus or patient is a "being" in the full sense, there is no question that it, she or he, is human. Both cases, furthermore, shade insensibly into other, less extreme cases—infants and senile persons also are incapable of sustaining life independently—and from those into ones in which status as a human being is not remotely in doubt. In addition, the notion of a surrogate exercising rights for another individual is easily applied, since the individual himself will be responsible in the future or was responsible in the past. Lacking any more precise criterion of what counts as a human being that is dispositive for these cases, one is thrown back on the simple equation of human beings with persons. It is that equation, however, that raises the issue in the first place. If all that is at stake is the abstract question whether the fetus and the patient have any rights at all, one may be inclined to disregard any doubts about their status as human beings and to rely on the equation's certain application to other cases in which responsibility is imperfect, and let it go at that. But if the question is concretely whether the life of this or that fetus or patient should be protected, at considerable cost to another specific individual or to the community, it cannot be disposed of so easily.

Whatever their view of the right to life as such, most persons agree that while the fetus or patient remains alive, she or he ought to be treated with some care. In the case of the patient, at least, that is certain. Even those who favor terminating life do not suggest as an alternative that comatose patients be "warehoused" in conditions calculated to preserve life at a minimum cost (and, it may be supposed, without pain). Likewise, it is generally conceded that a live fetus ought not be abused or injured, although whether that is prompted by regard for the fetus or regard for the person it will become is perhaps not clear. One may characterize these claims as "shadow rights" or "quasi-rights."[20] But although such a qualified label has a point, it leaves unanswered the question it purports to address: Do these claims— "shadow-rights"—have the status of rights or not?

Another way out of the difficulty is to avoid referring to rights and speak only of the duties that others may have, which is the usual payoff of rights anyway. If we agree that there is a duty of care, what difference does it make whether there is or is not a concomitant (shadow) right? But that also does not seem adequate. For the duty surely does not rest only on utilitarian considerations of the general good; it reflects at least in part, and probably in large part, the felt sense that rights attached to personhood are involved somehow, even if problematically and incompletely. If one puts that unelaborated sense of the matter aside, considerations of the general well-being are likely to point in both directions. Those who disagree with the outcome may well suspect that the considerations that prevail merely bolster a conclusion reached on another, undisclosed basis. In fact, usually what is opposed to the fetus' right to life is the pregnant woman's right to control the use of her body, in ordinary circumstances an especially strong particularization of the general right to liberty. If all that opposed that right were non-rights-based duties, themselves dependent on an uncertain weighing of consequences, the woman's right would surely prevail—allowing the strictly theoretical possibility of a rare exception if a particular fetus were predicted to become someone whose life would result in great general good.[21] But if the status of the fetus as a person is acknowledged at all, on any basis, then the woman's right does not automatically prevail; it is unavoidably in conflict with the autonomous humanity that is reflected in a human life, which is not merely a component in the calculation of the general good.

There may appear to be little difference between how a right to life or autonomous humanity as reflected in a human life is weighed in this context. If it were the former, however, one would have to regard it from the perspective of the right-possessor, who (unless, in the case of the patient, there had been directions to the contrary) must be presumed to choose to remain alive. If, on the other hand, one is concerned not with an individual right but with the source of the value of human life, one might regard it as relevant that the circumstances are so close to the moment when life begins or the moment when life ends. In the case of the fetus, the circumstances in which life was created may be thought to make a difference—the process of creation is itself an aspect of the human condition that we cannot altogether escape—or, in the case of the patient, the absence of any present or future possibility that the life of this individual would itself concretely reflect autonomous humanity.

No one will suppose that reflections of this kind will have much bearing on the outcome of the political debate about the legal right to have an abortion. (The controversy about terminating the life of a comatose patient is no less intractable and is a source of great anguish for those who are directly involved. Their number is, however, far smaller than the number of those who seek an abortion, and the public has not become involved in the same way.) In the first place, on one side of the controversy, the issue is settled for many people by belief that there is an authoritative proscription against abortion, which is not accessible to reasoned argument on different premises. On the other side, the issue is bound up with women's assertion of selfhood against a multitude of restrictions on the realization of one's self, which have only recently been generally acknowledged not to have their source in "nature" but to be socially imposed. In that concrete context, indecisive abstractions about what counts as a person or, indeed, what counts as human or as a being, are not likely to be heard.

One may conclude that in our public life we are about where we should be. The Supreme Court's opinion in *Roe v. Wade*[22] is frequently criticized for purporting to decide the question whether there is a constitutional right to have an abortion on the basis of whether a fetus is a person and, further, for making arbitrary distinctions according to the age of the fetus. Both criticisms seem to me misplaced. Like it or not, the personhood of the fetus is at the very center of the issue; and although the particular lines that the Supreme Court drew are indeed arbitrary, the closer the fetus comes to having the full characteristics of a human being, the more easily one may conclude that she or he is a person. (Whether or not *Roe v. Wade* was good constitutional law is a different question.) It would be idle to deny that the failure to reach a definitive resolution is the cause of great social tension and individual distress on both sides. But it is doubtful, for the time being, that the tension can be avoided or that the sum total of distress would be less if it were all on one side. (That is not necessarily to say that one weighs the consequences for those on each side alike.) In the end, one can only ask for sympathetic recognition that practically and theoretically the issue goes to the heart of what it is to be human.

In the matter of capital punishment, the issue is reversed. The premise of a sentence of death or, indeed, of any criminal punishment is not only that the condemned person was responsible when he committed the crime but also that he is responsible when the punishment is carried out.[23] His execution falsifies that premise. The very act of punishment at the same time makes the application of punishment invalid. The question, then, is whether the nature of a criminal's act can signal the absence of the personhood that makes punishment appropriate at all or, perhaps, deprive him of it. Can a human being, by deliberate conduct, put himself outside the category of persons, so that we can dispose of him merely as a (human) being? Can responsible conduct ever be so far outside the range of what is morally acceptable that it demonstrates not simply immorality but a lack of moral capacity altogether?

In the last years of the twentieth century, one may feel compelled, however unwillingly, to conclude that there is no moral boundary of that kind. Too many acts of unspeakable iniquity were committed within living memory by human beings who exhibited all the characteristics of persons elsewhere in their lives. To conclude that, having so acted, they were not persons is to confuse moral condemnation of the act with characterization of the actor. Indeed, although it enables us to dispose of the actor for reasons of the general good, without the special consideration and extraordinary justification that personhood demands, it disables us from precisely the moral qualification that it is most important to preserve. We appear sometimes to impose capital punishment on just such a basis, simply as instrumental social policy. On deeper reflection, however, our attitude is otherwise; we accept the burden of justification and assert that the person deserves to die.[24]

Yet may a person not deserve capital punishment precisely because he is responsible, just as one may deservedly be punished by the loss of legal or nonlegal rights? The forfeiture of none of the rights invoked by other criminal punishments calls into question personhood itself. Even a person condemned to death is not regarded as without rights; the conditions of detention of a condemned person are not infrequently attacked as violative of basic human rights. To make the argument that capital punishment is deserved strictly intelligible, it is necessary to conceive as the punishment not the deprivation of life but whatever pain or other injury attends the circumstances prior to execution, including the anticipation of death and awareness of opportunities lost, and the execution itself. Having been executed, a human being is no longer a person and not amenable to punishment at all. His death could be regarded only as the unavoidable, incidental consequence of the deserved punishment. In fact we do not regard capital punishment that way. The punishment is loss of life; we take strenuous measures to mitigate so far as we can the incidental physical and other kinds of pain that attend it.

The rejection of capital punishment does not depend on the criminal's right to life but on the overriding importance of autonomous humanity, which, so long as the criminal is a person, inheres in him individually. All but invariably, it is his violation of just that value that calls for extreme punishment; the taking of his life for reasons of general social policy, like the supposed (but altogether unproved) deterrent effect of capital punishment or the public cost of the traffic in illegal drugs, is strictly inconsistent with the condemnation that is its basis. This conclusion does not settle definitively the question whether capital punishment ought ever to be imposed. In this context as in others, one may urge that extraordinary circumstances in the particular case justify the taking of life on utilitarian grounds. Kant, insisting on the autonomy of a person after he has been (justly) condemned to death, argued that no utilitarian consideration could ever justify *not* executing him.[25] He would have objected all the more strongly to the imposition of capital punishment on such a basis. Although cosmic justice, with which Kant was concerned, admits of no exceptions, human justice is not so absolute. Nevertheless, the taking of human life is a rejection of autonomous humanity in the particular case and represents the most extreme and absolute departure from the normative order that gives meaning to our own existence. If the practice of capital punishment cannot be ruled out absolutely, therefore, the current tendency judicially and administratively to regard it as not altogether exceptional is a mistake.[26] Capital punishment can be justified, if at all, only by the clear and convincing demonstration of an overriding good that cannot be postponed or replaced, which preserves intact our claim to be acting morally at all.

CHAPTER EIGHT

Civil Rights

I N CHAPTER FIVE, the puzzle of freedom and responsibility was brought to ground as the duality of autonomous self and heteronymous ("natural") being. That duality is the essential, distinguishing characteristic of human beings, in virtue of which they and only they are persons, exercising freedom and responsible. Heteronymy, furthermore, is not merely the dictates of what we think of as "nature"—bare causal necessity. Just as the autonomous self acts within the natural constraints of the determinate being—one may run or one may walk, as he determines; but one cannot (unaided) fly, whatever he determines—it is subject also to constraints imposed by other persons—one may run or one may walk, as she determines, unless her way is blocked, or she is hobbled, or the law effectively prohibits running. And just as the autonomous self may be constrained by the actions of other persons, so also actions of other persons may free the autonomous self from natural constraints—one may run or one may walk; and, if he has the price of an airplane ticket, he may fly. Although we react very differently to one kind of constraint or another, from a certain point of view natural and human constraints are alike simply manifestations of heteronymy, aspects of the individual for which he is not personally responsible.

Chapter Seven identified a category of human rights: attributes that are conditions of any responsible action whatever and attach, therefore, to all human beings, simply as persons. Nevertheless, they are not guaranteed by the determinate nature of our being. They are contingent; and, more particularly, they are ordinarily dependent on the actions of other persons, by way either of noninterference or of provision. One can say of them generally, therefore, only that they are rights, which *ought* to be respected and, so far as other persons' actions are concerned, realized concretely. Nevertheless, as rights they are a matter of fact; they attach not in virtue of some further normative proposition but solely in virtue of the fact that the possessor, as a human being, is a person.

Although human rights satisfy the general conditions of responsibility, because they attach universally to all persons they are insufficient by themselves to sustain personal autonomy. As elaborated in Chapter Five, responsibility is individual. It is predicated only of a fully constituted individual, differentiated from others. Every human being, no less than any other kind of being, is a concrete individual; but from that point of view, our differential attributes are merely circumstantial, the determinate consequences of causes beyond our control. As responsible persons, we must be differentiated not descriptively but normatively, each having the attributes that are uniquely his due. So regarded, as what I have called normatively constituted individuals, our actions are *self*-determined, and we are responsible.

We have now to confront directly the puzzle that was presented at the end of Chapter Five. As a responsible person, each of us must have, in addition to the universal human rights, differential individual rights. Yet nothing differentiates one person from another normatively except individual desert, which attaches only in virtue of the very responsibility that requires that we be normatively constituted. How can differences among human beings for which they as individuals have no responsibility and which are, therefore, not deserved nevertheless be differences among them as responsible persons?

Left to itself, reason confronts without resolution the paradox of the human condition: Having one's due is both a condition of responsible freedom and consequent on its exercise. No genuinely equivalent restatement of those abstract propositions or ratiocination about them overcomes that flat contradiction. Our awareness of responsibility, however, is not a product of reason; it is neither a deduction from abstract principles nor an induction from the data of experience. Rather, as I described it in Chapter Two, responsibility is a structural fact, inherent in the organization and order of our experience as the ground of the distinction between persons and things. The direction of our thought is from concrete particulars to the abstract and general. All the same, the basis for a specific attribution of responsibility cannot be wholly a matter of observable natural qualities, which individuate descriptively but not normatively. Our apprehension of responsibility requires that our experience contain within it non-natural grounds for the conclusion that a person has her due and is responsible in a particular respect. That is to say, the source of the specific rights that differentiate us one from another must be found in experience itself.

The Origin of Rights

Pursued as an idea of reason, a solution to the problem of what a person is due is typically cast as a theory of justice, and more particularly as the constitutive principles of a just human community. The principal difference between formulation of the problem as the conditions of responsibility and its formulation as the principles of justice is that the former focuses attention on the normatively constitutive attributes of persons who individually are the subject of desert and the latter on the uniform standard by which desert universally is assessed. The fundamental issue, however, is the same: How can individuals, differently endowed by circumstances beyond their control, have their due and nevertheless remain individuals? What objective basis can there be for justice, between the unacceptable extremes of all other-determined differences being nonconstitutive, which eliminates individual responsibility (and therefore desert) as we understand it, and all such differences being constitutive, which eliminates individual desert (and therefore responsibility) as we understand it?

The most important answer to that question in recent philosophy is John Rawls's theory of justice.[1] Rawls posits an agreement among parties in an "original position," a crucial feature of which is that none of them knows his individual characteristics. Although all know that they are differentiated individuals, none knows whether he is more or less powerful in any particular respect than the others. In that situation, Rawls asserts, the parties would agree to certain principles, which are, therefore, fair and define a just community.

A number of distinct objections to Rawls's theory can be reduced to the observation that he validates his principles on the basis of the supposed initial agreement, but there is simply no one there to agree or to agree with. The parties in the original position are without any attributes that would lead them to take different positions from one another and, therefore, require, or even permit, an agreement. Indeed, they are not really individuals—not really *persons*—at all. All their differences being hidden behind a "veil of ignorance," they are effectively identical. Although they know that they are different, what they all make of this knowledge and how they react to it are perforce the same. To overcome this and to reach an "agreed" resolution, Rawls is required to exclude some alternatives. The parties are made to choose the "maximin" outcome, in which the position of the worst off cannot be improved by any other distributive principles. That condition being fulfilled, Rawls asserts, a person's "envy" of someone else who is better off is irrational and can be disregarded. Rawls's critics have been quick to point out that such a restriction of the original position cannot be supposed to reflect a universal preference of actual human beings. Not every person would choose to minimize risk, and many persons do envy others' good fortune for no reason other than that it is better than their own. (Rawls's criterion of rationality in this respect seems arbitrary; but even if it is not, it is difficult to see the relevance of rationality to the specific issue, since what is at stake is the validity of an agreement, which depends on the voluntary assent of the parties and not the reasonableness of its terms.) In his later writings, Rawls does not contend otherwise and acknowledges that this restriction and other such qualifications of the original position are adopted precisely to ensure that its results are those he has in mind. Hence, in subsequent restatements of his theory he has described it not as a theory of justice unqualified but as an effort to elucidate the principles of justice immanent in the western liberal, democratic tradition.[2]

If that is the nature of the theory, however, anyone, making different assumptions, may propound a different theory of justice, as Robert Nozick famously has done.[3] Nozick opposes Rawls's initial hypothesis that the contracting parties are normatively alike with the hypothesis that they are normatively unlike. They approach the bargaining table richly endowed with individuating characteristics that are rightly theirs; the rights of all commanding equal respect, neither the characteristics themselves nor their effects can be appropriated from a person without his consent.[4] All that the better endowed persons would consent to give up is the minimum that protects their rights generally from the more violent kinds of aggression. The outcome for Nozick is a much more libertarian view of justice. He, like Rawls, defends his conclusions as a version of western liberalism.

A different kind of response to Rawls's theory is offered by "communitarians," of whom Alasdair MacIntyre and Michael Sandel are exemplary.[5] They also argue that Rawls's parties in the original position are too thinly constituted to stand in for real persons. Nozick's persons, on the other hand, are far too thickly constituted; they come with all their rights, derived only Nozick knows how, already in place. Thus, they argue, we cannot begin to think about justice or, properly more broadly, a full conception of the right and the good unless we imagine real persons, living in a community and endowed not merely with differential attributes but also with personal identities—that is to say, with rights—validated by that community. Only from such a starting position can we work toward adequate normative principles, because only such persons have any need for them. Strong as the communitarian critique of more particular theories of justice has been, their affirmative program has proved to be very feeble. At worst, it has seemed to validate any community's norms as definitive for that community. Although they plainly do not intend that result, they have not succeeded in avoiding it. Because they do not explain on what basis a community's practices are, or ought to be, accepted, they have no general recommendation about when or on what basis they ought to be rejected.

For all the difference of their respective conclusions, the methodological starting point of all these theories, and of others like them, is the same. Without quite saying so explicitly, they agree that a standard of justice (or the communitarians' broader normative conception, incorporating such a standard) originates in will rather than in reason. That is the significance of Rawls's and Nozick's reliance on consent, even though both are obliged to insert arbitrary nonconsensual elements to complete their theory; and it is the evident import of the communitarians' reference to the established norms of a particular community. Thus also the contractarian theories of rights, mentioned in Chapter One, which make it a test of the validity of a right that no one could reasonably withhold his consent to be bound by a system because such a right was incorporated within it. Although such theories rely heavily on the presumed dictates of reason, it is the act of will that is dispositive; as it were, reason proposes and will disposes. The explanation for this common, reluctantly acknowledged starting point is not far to seek; it is simply the failure of reason confronting the puzzle of normative heteronymy, undeserved desert. The "trick," as the deficiencies of all of the theories illustrate, is to find a basis for a universal voluntary agreement among real persons, who are differently constituted individuals. If reason on its own is inadequate, however, it fares no better when it is put at the service of will. The basis for such an agreement has to be sought in another way.

Suppose there were only one human being. Living alone, she learns that sometimes good or bad things happen to her that she can repeat or prevent from being repeated, whereas other good or bad things happen to her no matter what she does. If she puts seeds in the ground in a certain way, plants, which she can eat later, grow in the same place. But sometimes they die. Pouring water onto the ground where the plants are growing keeps them alive. But just when they are ready to be picked, they turn black and die after a night when it is cold. If she covers them during the night, some survive. But animals eat them . . . She thus becomes aware of her own causal agency. Over time she extends her agency and explores its limits. Also, observing that the behavior of other beings and things is variably opposed to her own, she attributes concrete causal agency to them and supposes that they, like herself, are trying to obtain outcomes favorable to themselves. Perhaps, insofar as she identifies specific reactions like anger, pleasure, or pain in herself, she projects them also onto other supposed agents. Stretching all that as far as it will go, she envisions what happens around her as a contest of wills in which sometimes she and sometimes they gain the upper hand.[6] But there is no basis on which she can contemplate an evaluation not according to her own or others' specific purposes. Any conception of normative order that she might have would be limited to a particular point of view. Insofar as she possessed conceptions of "good" and "bad," they would be the equivalent of "I am happy," or "I am not happy," or "It is happy" or "It is not happy."

Now add to her universe another human being. If she and he were unable to communicate beyond giving signals of something about to happen and she contemplated him only as another causal agency, the actions of which affected and were affected by her behavior, nothing would be changed. So far as his actions were concerned, she would still conceptualize "good" and "bad," if at all, only in terms of her will or his. Suppose, however, that she and he are able to communicate with each other in some form that allows them to be aware of one another's purposes, not only as reflected in what happens but independently, as possibilities or projects entertained but unrealized. As before, they are both aware that some occurrences are good for one and bad for the other, and vice versa. If the agency of neither can affect such an occurrence, that is an end of the matter, each perceiving it as the case may be. But if the agency of both, or even one, can alter the outcome in a way more favorable to one or the other, they will now be able jointly to entertain that possibility. Thinking only in terms of causal agency, they will eventually become aware that they can adjust their various efforts in a way that makes the eventual outcomes taken all together more favorable to both. Each using her and his respective advantages and taking account of the other, there will be some equilibrium that is better for each than she or he could achieve alone. The leap from individual purposive action to cooperative action for a joint purpose would be a large one; but if there is communication between them, it need not be radically different from using other objects as tools to achieve one's own purpose. (The notion of a mutually advantageous equilibrium describes even some animal behavior, as, for example, when two animals of a species encounter each other and the weaker signals submission to the stronger in order to avoid combat.) If such an accommodation is reached, it will establish a new vantage from which to assess outcomes and the conduct of each. Still having in mind only their respective agencies, one way that they might think about the accommodation is that the agreed outcome is not good *for one* or *for the other* but is simply good. Although they would retain those distinct perspectives for other purposes, so far as the agreed position is concerned, both regarding it as, in the circumstances, preferable from both their respective points of view and there being no other point of view to consider, no reference to any point of view need be made.[7]

In some such way, a distinction between subjective and objective good might arise. The latter, reflecting only the actual accommodation between the two persons, would of course reflect their subjective preferences; but there is no reason why that should occur to them at all or, if it did, why it should have the least significance. From their individual points of view, in comparison with their individual preferences, the position of accommodation would be objective, in the only sense that term could have for them. In time, a true normative order might come into being, insofar as the two persons themselves were concerned. They would gradually develop a mutual understanding of what was within their respective powers, for their accommodation could extend no further than that. As its value became clear, it would be extended to the full range of their mutual power. Whether it remained a tacit accommodation or, as might be expected, eventually became an explicit agreement between them, it would specify the conduct of each, whether provision or only forbearance from interference, as a duty and the enhanced power of the other as a right. Living up to its terms, they would do what is right, and departing from it, what is wrong. Within its terms, each could do whatever she or he wished to advance her or his individual interests. And whatever happened to either that was not within its terms would simply be a natural occurrence, the determinate causal order.

With the acceptance of a common standard against which the behavior of each was measured, the ideas of rights and responsibility also would develop. The mutual understanding would to some extent redistribute the powers of each, confirming some and enhancing or restricting others. So also, it would provide a measure for evaluation of individual action that was distinct from causal efficacy. The "rights" and "responsibility" so established would initially refer only to the terms of the understanding; but lacking any more objective standard or indeed any other conception of either rights or responsibility, the two persons would have no reason to attend to that as a qualification. Further, since whatever accommodation was finally reached would be to their mutual advantage, a failure to honor it by one person would predictably lead to a response by the other, without which the departure from its terms would in effect constitute a new accommodation. If the departure were favorable to the other person, it would effectively constitute an offer for a new accommodation, acceptance of which would be signaled by a favorable response; if it were rejected, either the original accommodation would be reinstated or, the rejecting party having greater power in the circumstances, the departure would become stabilized and a new accommodation more favorable to the rejecting party would be reached. The predictability of a response whenever the accommodation was violated would attach to the idea of responsibility a rudimentary notion of desert, which itself would establish a bridge between responsibility and rights by the fact that the departure and response might be isolated and nonrecurring or become the basis of a new accommodation.

It is not difficult to imagine how an established agreement might eventually take on a life of its own and its original basis in the self-interested will of the parties be forgotten. Additional persons would become parties to the agreement "naturally," as it were, because it was in place and working; and anyone who did not accept it voluntarily might be made to do so because that was in the interest of the rest. In this way, the terms of the agreement, which were originally dependent on nothing but will, the available preferences of particular individuals, would come to seem the product of reason or, at any rate, to be regarded as independent of particular wills. Within our own experience, there are abundant examples of such a phenomenon; practices that were adopted for instrumental reasons gradually acquire the force of custom and at last seem to be "in the nature of things." Once that happens, particular terms of the agreement will be subject to challenge as inconsistent with the objective standard of reason manifest in the rest. Similarly, the ideas of rights and responsibility would acquire independent objectivity and, as the response to departures from the now public understanding became institutionalized, the idea of desert as well.

The preceding account suggests how an objective conception of what a person is due might arise not as an idea of reason but concretely, as the product of experience, more particularly experience of individual causal agency and the exercise of will. The conception would inform distinct concepts of rights, responsibility, and desert, initially tied to the specific circumstances in which they originated—and, therefore, from our point of view rudimentary and imperfect—but gradually, without losing their grounding in matters of fact, acquiring objectivity. All that needs to be assumed is that there are individuals with different attributes who are aware of their own causal agency and the causal agency of others, with whom they are able to communicate. Such persons, differentiated concretely from one another, are neither too thinly constituted for an actual agreement, like Rawls's persons in the original position; nor, having no rights at the start, are they too thickly constituted prior to any agreement. What drives them together is their awareness of a possibility of mutual advantage and ability to communicate about it; their actual agreement, rather than any independent conception of fairness or rights, is dispositive. Nevertheless, over time the terms of the agreement—the community's practices—furnish a normative standard, no longer dependent on individual will. The standard is quite literally constitutive of the community, and the community of it.

Having the rights so conferred, persons are also responsible to the extent of their rights. Their responsibility is not confined to causal efficacy to accomplish their own or others' will but has now an objective normative standard against which to be measured. So also, with that standard fully in place, fully dissociated from its subjective origins, the idea of justice is born. One can imagine, furthermore, how that idea, combined with affection and empathy, might be enlarged and give rise to conceptions of morality and virtue. Without rights and responsibility, there is no charity or mercy, no gratitude, generosity, or courage; for without rights and responsibility, all that one gives and receives, all that one does and is, is only a matter of fact, the determinate effect of causes other than oneself, and neither one's due nor one's self at all. If justice, as we think of it, is not the highest virtue, it is nevertheless the underpinning of all the rest, because it is the vehicle for rights, which constitute the self.[8]

The account given here is Hobbesian in its essential features. Hobbes spoke of the sovereign's power to impose order, which has led to the charge that he confused might and right. But the "war of every man, against every man" is a theoretical construct, not a call to battle.[9] Hobbes was as aware as anyone that the so-called war takes many forms and that victor and vanquished are both relative positions. Although in the end clubs are trumps, there are other winning cards in the deck; no one is so powerful that he is immune to a conspiracy, and even the most powerful must depend on an accord. However unequal its terms, the compact between sovereign and subject that brings the community into being is a product of will, justified only by the fact that it is the best that is available in the circumstances.[10] What was critical, Hobbes believed, and the point of departure for the whole theory is that no independent conception of rights or justice be smuggled into the result. In that, he was entirely correct. All the same (as, it seems to me, one way or another Hobbes also understood) once the community is established, the normative order that constitutes it is no longer a matter of will alone. For it is contained within persons' actual experience of what there is.

The circumstances of a human community are vastly different from and more complex than those of an imaginary Eden or, as it were, a deserted island on which persons wash ashore one by one. For the present purpose, the most important difference is that the fact that human beings, oneself and others, are persons, exercising responsibility, is never in doubt. What I have described in the simplest terms as originally only an agreement between individuals for limited purposes, which develops finally into an apprehension of responsibility and rights generally, is fully in place from the start. The stages of that hypothetical scenario suggest, however, how the specific content of the abstract concept of a right is derived.

Rights arise directly out of the recognition of persons as persons. Among any group of mutually dependent individuals interacting with one another as a community, common understandings pervasively and unexceptionally reflected in public and private practices of every kind establish generally the bounds of individual responsibility and, therefore, what rights there are. Without that much, even the distinction between persons and things would be problematic. Our attention is drawn to situations in which responsibility is uncertain and controversial; but they are of interest only because throughout our lives, most of the time there is no question whatever. To test the matter, imagine how one would go about persuading someone of his mistake if he were to argue seriously, without disagreeing about any of the relevant data, that a tree was individually responsible for dropping its leaves and ought to be called to account. Or imagine how one would reason with someone who argued seriously that it was simply irrelevant whether a person was responsible for an occurrence in consequence of which he was to be punished in some way. All the same, responsibility is not an observable quality that inheres in human beings considered as natural objects. And although the distinction between persons and things in general is not contestable, particular attributions of responsibility are. Not only may one challenge a specific attribution or nonattribution; one may also challenge the general premises about kinds of conduct on the basis of which specific attributions are ordinarily made.

Unsurprisingly, our understandings about responsibility in general as well as our specific judgments about a person's responsibility in a concrete situation elude simple classification. The usual categories have no place for propositions that are empirically verifiable as a matter of fact but contain more than can be verified by observation and remain essentially contestable or that, viewed from another perspective, have descriptive content but normative significance. And so it has seemed that we can refer only disjunctively to the practices of a community, however well settled, and the normative principles that establish rights. On that basis, the only possible relation between practice and principles is that they do or do not coincide, or that they ought or, possibly in some exceptional circumstance, ought not to coincide. In this respect, our conceptual ordering differs from that of classical Greece. The contrast is instructive. For the Greeks, the human was not necessarily less valid objectively than the natural, nor was there a strict separation between fact and value. The critical distinction was made elsewhere, between *physis,* the permanent and unalterable normative order of nature, and *nomos,* the normative order of the community, no less real but of human origin and, therefore, alterable over time and variable from one community to another.[11]

Adapted to a modern idiom, the term *"nomos"* aptly refers to the community-based source of the bounds of personhood, formulated in terms of the individual as responsibility or rights and in terms of the community as justice. So understood, the *nomos* of a community is expressed in laws, rules, and practices that have to do directly or indirectly with retributive or distributive justice: reward and punishment, praise and blame, liability and excuse, as well as when a person is, as it were, on his own and must (or may) utilize the resources that are at his command and when he may claim resources from or must surrender resources to the community. But a community's *nomos* will be expressed still more generally and pervasively in the patterns of thought and speech that organize and describe experience as, on one hand, the exercise of freedom and responsibility and, on the other, natural circumstance. Not every enacted law or actual practice will be so included, for *nomos* is not merely descriptive but also normative, and neither enactment nor adherence guarantees conformity with it. If the members of a community adopt legislation or take other measures that conflict with its own well-established understandings, the latter are not simply overthrown and a new *nomos* come into being. On the contrary, even though such legislation be followed, it will be subject to challenge on the ground that, violating the *nomos* of the community, it is unjust.

Nothing except its *nomos* determines what counts as a community for this purpose. Within a national state, some persons who generally adhere to the nation's laws may nevertheless compose a smaller community constituted by a distinct *nomos;* insofar as they are disfavored by the larger community, they will experience the conflict as injustice. That is not to say that every combination of persons is a community or every conscientious deviation from a prevailing normative standard a manifestation of a distinct *nomos.* There are communities, but there are also individuals with individual moral judgment.

The content of *nomos* is conventional, in the sense that it is humanly determined. The concrete measures and practices in which it is expressed may be adopted more or less deliberately, and even those that arise and become established without deliberate effort may be called in question and confirmed or rejected by individuals or by the community collectively. It may change over time and is not uniform in different communities. Nevertheless, *nomos* is altogether unlike social conventions of etiquette, dress, and the like, which one may dismiss as "merely conventional" and disregard with impunity (not least to show that one is unconventional). It includes the weightiest aspects of a community's shared way of life, which most members of the community will ordinarily regard as beyond question and requiring no justification.

Although *"nomos"* may be appropriated from the Greek for this purpose, it is not a familiar term, and the conjoint descriptive and normative concept that it expresses is from our point of view deeply problematic. The idea of civil rights, which is prominent in political discourse, is, however, closely analogous; not, evidently, coincidentally it refers explicitly to the community as the source of the rights in question. Civil rights are usually regarded as superior to plain legal rights; in some sense, which is seldom fully articulated, they are prior to and independent of positive law. Laws are enacted to protect civil rights; failing enactment, the law is said to deny them. All agree that it is a principal task of government to protect civil rights, so much so that a failure to protect them is usually regarded as outweighing substantial achievements of other kinds. They seem, therefore, to depend on law not for their existence, but only for recognition. On the other hand, we think about civil rights with regard to a specific community and do not automatically transfer a conclusion about civil rights from one community to another. It would be distinctly odd to ask what a person's civil rights are without indicating where he comes from or to speak of "universal civil rights" as we speak of human rights.

This ambiguous status of civil rights as objectively valid norms against which a community's positive law is measured and at the same time a reflection of a community's particular values typically is passed over, because they are contested within a community and understood to be so limited. But unless it is accounted for, debate about them cannot be joined, because it floats freely between reference to positive law at one extreme and an assertion of rights unmoored to any objective standard at all at the other. In United States jurisprudence, this is most evident in debate about the meaning of constitutional provisions in the Bill of Rights and elsewhere, which have the formal character of positive law but are regarded as incorporating "fundamental" civil rights. The concept of a right itself incorporates the same descriptive/normative duality that is present in *nomos* and is explained in this instance by the origin of civil rights in the community's actual way of life, which gives content to the notion of responsibility.

Ordinarily when we speak of civil rights, we refer to those potentially vulnerable entitlements that are peculiarly within the protection of the law: the right to vote, the right to education, rights specified in the

Bill of Rights, and so forth. But there is also that vast array of rights that we take for granted as the most ordinary and obvious liberty, or simply one's ordinary responsibility as a person. Although many such rights are of the greatest importance—whom we marry, what work we do, whether to have children—and would widely (but not universally) be recognized as civil rights were they called in question, others are in themselves unimportant, even trivial. Together, they delimit the range of self-determined action. Such rights, though embedded deep in the fabric of the community, are not given incontrovertibly by nature. Nevertheless, at any time a very large range of rights must be regarded as settled. We must, without controversy, regard persons as constituted normatively, if we are to regard them as persons at all. Without that much, consideration of individual responsibility in particular circumstances and of further, contested rights could not even begin. The source of these normative facts is the community itself.

How a community's *nomos* develops and changes, how it is communicated to individuals within it, how they acquire it and incorporate it within their own experience or reject it are the subjects of the human sciences—anthropology, sociology, psychology—and lie beyond our immediate interest. All that needs to be stressed is that a community's *nomos* provides specific content for the structural fact of human responsibility. So doing, it gives content to the concept of a person, possessing rights and distinguished thereby from things. Rights so derived, factually grounded in the actual practices of a community, objectively valid but mutable and variable from one community to another, conform to what we mean by civil rights.

In any human community, therefore, there are civil rights. Otherwise, as Hobbes stated most clearly, it would be inaccurate to speak of a (human) community at all. The *nomos* of a harmonious, well-ordered community will be relatively broad, coherent, and widely accepted. Its laws, public and private practices, and general normative outlook will be perceived to be consistent. A disordered community may recognize the same or different legal rights; but there will be less coherence, and the sense of rights as objectively valid rather than as a transitory disposition of power will be less strong. If a community is undergoing a revolution or disintegrating, it may be difficult to speak of its *nomos* at all. But some rights must remain (even if they are not faithfully honored), unless the sense of justice itself be lost, so that individuals feel themselves to be situated in a world in which power is distributed arbitrarily and one uses the powers that one has without responsibility. At any time some claims, recognized as legal rights or not, may be struggling toward recognition as civil rights, and some civil rights may be losing general recognition. Examples of this process in contemporary American society are discussed in the next chapter. Not everyone will perceive every claim alike, although much will be largely beyond dispute, one way or the other. A healthy community's attitude toward civil rights falls somewhere between the two extremes: neither so rigid and unassailable an acceptance of the status quo that their humanly contingent nature is forgotten nor so complete a rejection of it that they lose their relevance.

The terms in which civil rights are usually debated are not those that I have used in the preceding discussion. It is hardly surprising, after all, that we should suppress the paradox of human freedom by containing it in suspension, as it were, within concepts that appear to look in another direction and do not display explicitly the failure of reason. Ordinarily the issues presented here as responsibility and rights are debated in normative terms, as matters of justice, liberty, and equality. The issues cannot be resolved in those terms, and the outcome is either a normative abstraction without specific content or a standard that has its roots, as I have indicated, in *nomos*.

The defenders of a right typically characterize their claim as a demand for justice. Justice as an abstract ideal, however, has little explanatory force; it qualifies a claim as a claim of right, based on objective, independently valid grounds, without describing the content of the claim further or indicating its specific grounds. Such explanation is not necessary if what is at stake is retributive justice and the claim is straightforwardly based on a denial (or affirmation) of responsibility; for responsibility is the sole ground of retributive justice. So, the convicted criminal may claim that her punishment is unjust because she "didn't do it"; and if she establishes the fact of her innocence, the justice of her claim follows as of course. The same is true of a claim that one is responsible and deserves accordingly. The hero who saves his city from destruction may simply claim (somewhat redundantly, to be sure) his "just deserts." Since, however, responsibility establishes only *that* one deserves and not *what* one deserves, the latter claim is incomplete. The absence of responsibility, in contrast, establishes an absence of desert, and there is nothing more to be determined. One is, however, responsible only insofar as he is duly constituted—has his due with respect to the matter at hand. A claim of retributive justice may, therefore, implicitly raise a question of distributive justice—that is to say, rights—because the claimant's denial or affirmation of responsibility is itself contentious.

Usually, unless a claimed right is acknowledged to be a debatable matter of social policy or referred to principles or practices the validity of which is not in doubt (the U.S. Constitution or, more narrowly, positive law), it is referred to the political ideal of liberty or of equality, both of which purport both to convey the substance of the claim and to explain why it is just. Examined more closely, both ideals can be recast as a resolution of the fundamental issue of responsibility and have definite content only as an expression of the community's *nomos*.

Liberty is the rubric that regards differential individual characteristics as normatively constitutive. One asserts his liberty to do what he is able to do without hindrance, to keep what he has without obligation to others or, more particularly, surrendering it to the state. Confirming a power as a right, liberty affords opportunities precisely because it validates difference. The person whose attributes are more favorable in the circumstances prevails; and his success is hailed as fulfilling the ideal of liberty and, therefore, just. Equality is the rubric that regards differential individual characteristics as not normatively constitutive but circumstantial. One asserts a right to equality in some respect with another person who is better endowed, on the ground that normatively—as deserving persons—both are alike. Eliminating a difference in power, equality denies opportunities to those whom the difference would favor. The person whose attributes are more favorable does not prevail, because his advantage is eliminated; and denying him his success is hailed as fulfilling the ideal of equality and, therefore, just. In either case, the differential characteristic that is validated or invalidated may be regarded as natural or as wholly or partly a social product. One may claim as his right the liberty to use his intelligence or good looks and keep its rewards or the liberty to keep and use his inherited wealth. So also, although one does not claim a right to "be as intelligent as" some other person, he may claim a right to special education or to weighted scoring on tests or to any of the benefits that his lesser intelligence would otherwise deny him. Whether natural or social, the opportunity that is at stake is found only within a community that includes others who are not fully alike in the relevant respect.

Significant rights confirm or alter the distribution of powers by imposing duties elsewhere. Consequently, the assertion of a right to liberty or equality might from another point of view be characterized differently. One's liberty to use her differential advantage is another person's individual responsibility for his differential disadvantage. The latter's claim to equality with the former might also be characterized as the former's lack of right to more than the latter has. From the neutral perspective of justice, there is no difference. But since liberty confers only an opportunity and not a duty to use one's power to her own advantage, it would be otiose and peculiar to claim the liberty to have less. And except to sustain the equality of the disadvantaged, there is scarcely reason to reduce the power of the advantaged. Similarly, a claim to liberty might be opposed as a denial of a right to equality, not because it fails to deny the claimant's power but because it fails to increase the power of someone else, which increase would impose duties on the better endowed person. And a claim to equality might be opposed because the duty it imposed on others was a denial of their liberty.

As abstract ideals liberty and equality are without specific content, because they are mutually opposed and interchangeable. They suppose a point of view. Each addresses the fact that human beings are differently endowed and asserts that a particular distribution of powers, conforming more or less to the actual difference, is normatively correct. But without more to go on, the assertion is altogether bare of argument. Differences in fact are only that. Abstractly, no normative principle of distribution commends itself more than others. For the paradox of human freedom and responsibility—undeserved desert—applies alike to any individual characteristics whatever. None of our differences as mere beings, removed from the context of any particular community, is more or less normatively constitutive of us as persons than any other. Abstractly, we are in the situation of an isolated being communicating with no other and conscious only of agency. Encountering other human beings and aware of our differential powers, we are aware also of the common understanding that constitutes us as persons and becomes definitive of the right for the time being. Liberty and equality, that is to say, acquire their content as substantive political ideals, confirming some rights and rejecting others, from the *nomos* of the community.

CHAPTER NINE

Applications

T HE FOREGOING ACCOUNT of rights does not by itself answer questions about the scope of specific rights or, indeed, whether a claim of right is properly so regarded at all. It is a central part of the argument that such questions cannot be answered by reason alone, as a deduction from first principles. On the contrary, answers emerge only from consideration of a community's way of life—what I have called its *nomos*—manifested in actual understandings and practices that constitute it as a community; and accordingly the answers are valid only for that community. Within any community, over a very broad range rights are directly derivative of noncontroversial matters of fact that define personal responsibility, others are likely to be sharply contested, and all are in principle contestable.[1]

The argument discloses, however, a number of general implications for practical discussion of concrete rights. First, although we commonly speak of rights as attaching and belonging to a person without limitation to any particular context, the application of a right is limited to the range of conduct it affects; its only direct significance is whether or not the person is (properly) responsible for conduct within that range. Honoring a right does not increase a person's responsibility in other respects; nor does denying it furnish an excuse for conduct that the right does not reach. So also, the duty of others that usually is the most important practical implication of a right is material only insofar as the person having the right engages in or contemplates engaging in conduct within its range. One may have a right and others may have a concomitant duty; but asserting the right only in order to exact the duty has about it a quality of meanness and waste. Narrowing the focus of the inquiry in this way may help us to avoid a sense that when rights are involved, nothing less than the whole person, her dignity and self-respect, is at stake and to replace the stridency of abstract rhetoric with manageable concrete proposals. But it is true as well that the denial of specific rights, without which one is unable to exercise responsibility in ways that the community regards as measures or indicators of worth, will diminish her stature as a person, no matter what other rights she may have. And if a person is thus diminished, we should not expect that her exercise of responsibility generally will be unaffected.

Second, no abstract principle, whether of justice or of liberty or equality, by itself sustains any right whatever. On the contrary, rights, independently derived, give content to such principles. The idea of justice affirms that persons deserve and, therefore that they have rights and are responsible; but it does not say how far desert is reflected in our individual circumstances as they are and how they are to be rectified. Liberty and equality are both presumed to be good. Yet every liberty is opposed by another and opposes equality in some respect; every equality denies some liberty and increases the significance of the liberties—inequalities—that remain.

The claims that are most vigorously asserted as rights nowadays are usually those of persons who are relatively less well off. Opposition to such claims is strong; but, except for a group that is commonly described as the "extreme right," it is as likely to be manifested by indifference or by expressions of social policy as by articulation of an opposing right. Consequently rights may appear to be mostly the currency of those who are without, in the name of equality. But while a community persists, from any point of view or position on the political spectrum there are rights. The question is not whether there are rights or "how many," but whose and what rights there are.

Third, it may seem tactically sound to cast one's interests in the vocabulary of rights. But making every contested issue a matter of right may impede social change that would be generally beneficial. The absence of a right does not conclude a political or social argument against those whose interest the right would favor, and the assertion of a claim as a right may press the issue theoretically further than it can go. In a vital community there is abundant space for accommodation of conflicting interests, not as a matter of right but as social policy responsive to a felt sense of the common good. The recent shift away from communism in some countries implicated a rejection of some kinds of interests as rights and their inclusion within more fluid social policies. Some other interests have been recognized or strengthened as rights. From the western liberal point of view, both shifts were beneficial to the inhabitants of those countries.

On the other hand, some recent objections to the defense of rights in general, on the ground that they favor individuals and impede a social resolution of social problems, are misplaced. Insistence on one's own rights despite the needs of others may be profoundly selfish. All the same, to speak of communitarian values as if they were generally superior to the rights of individuals and warranted disregard of those rights is to lose sight of the source of those very values. It may be that a harmonious community functioning at its best is more than the sum of its parts. Even so—and putting aside reservations about the actual functioning of actual communities—considered as an entity apart from the individuals who compose it, the community is nothing. Even altruism, after all, is a responsible act, not enforced tribute. Disengaged from the rights of the persons who are affected, social policy becomes social engineering: the manipulation of persons as things toward ends not their own, which others have chosen for them. Once again, it is a matter of whose rights and what they are.

Finally, useful discussion about specific rights proceeds not by deductive reasoning but by analogy, not proof but persuasion. From one's own point of view, another person's disagreement usually should be characterized not as an error but as a different perception. If one is inclined to say, "Don't you just see . . .?" (or, that failing, "You must be blind!"), the style of the challenge, if not the manner of expressing it, is quite likely correct. Resting on our experience of ourselves and others as responsible persons, rights (and what is not a matter of right) accumulate from concrete particular to particular, the certainty of one conclusion supporting another according to perceived relevant similarities and differences. Generalizations about what rights there are merely collect such particulars and are not principles from which they can be deduced. The only general test is the coherence of the whole, which is also a matter of relevant similarity and difference. One is more likely to persuade, therefore, not by insisting on an abstract proposition that, even if he accepts it, will leave the other person unconvinced, but rather by attempting in the first instance to perceive the issue as he does, to elicit the examples that he finds persuasive and why he does, and then to offer examples that illustrate one's own point of view. It ought not to dismay persons on either side of a controversy about specific rights that there are no knockdown-dragout arguments. Few concrete issues of substantive practical importance are resolved without similar reliance expressly or implicitly on the persuasiveness, without proof, of analogical arguments.

It is hardly surprising that a theory of rights does not go beyond broad, general recommendations of this kind. At this late date, after so much sustained interest and effort, it is not to be expected that we shall come upon a certain catalogue of what rights there are. At the same time, the practical payoff of a theory is its bearing on the hard issues. Furthermore, the "fit" of a theory of rights with the way in which we talk and think about rights in our ordinary lives is itself a test, albeit not a conclusive one, of the soundness of the theory. Rights originate in the human condition, and we must apprehend them from our own, human perspective. In the remainder of this chapter I consider three of the most contentious current issues as both an illustration and a test: rights of the handicapped, gay rights, and rights of minorities to affirmative action.

Rights of the Handicapped

Persons confined to a wheelchair have a right of access to public buildings.

Deaf children have a right to attend public schools and to be taught in sign.

A blind person has a right to have books available in braille.

All the preceding claims and a great many others like them have been asserted forcefully in the last several decades. Although the claims as stated are ambiguous whether the right in question is one of permission (not to be prohibited), protection (not to be hindered by others), or provision (to be enabled), neither permission nor protection is ordinarily in doubt; and it is evident that what is asserted is a right to be provided individually with a capacity that one otherwise lacks. The claims are specifications of a general argument that persons with certain kinds of disabilities, mostly but not invariably attributable to a specific physical condition, have a right to a social provision that functionally eliminates or ameliorates the disability. More often than not, such rights are not opposed on theoretical grounds; it is, after all, unappealing to make a stand on principle against benefiting persons who are palpably deprived of something of great value, which most others have without effort and take utterly for granted. Rather, opposition is passive and consists simply in denying the claimed relief. Since the denial is not accompanied by acknowledgment of any injustice, denial of the relief is effectively denial of the right. From that practical perspective, whether there are special rights of the handicapped and, if so, their extent is sharply contested.

Although the usual objective of proponents of such rights is the enactment of legislation or other similar legal action, the claim of right is not itself a claim of *legal* right. There is in fact a broad array of legal rights, contained in legislation or administrative regulations and the like.[2] The application of such rights in a particular case may be contested; but if so, the issue is resolved in the usual way in a court of law or in some other legal proceeding. Broad propositions about rights of the handicapped like those stated above are concerned not to validate a specific legal claim but to secure enactment of a law that will support such a claim. Such law might be defended on grounds of social policy alone; it might be argued, for example, that assisting the handicapped serves the general good, by contributing to a more productive or harmonious community. But in view of the disregard of other persons who, without being handicapped, are similarly unproductive or unfortunate, such an argument is hard to sustain. Claims that the handicapped have rights are claims that there *ought* to be a law establishing the legal right in question, because there *is* a nonlegal right. We need first to consider what the specific content of such a claim is and how it relates to the responsibility of the handicapped. The asserted right of wheelchair access to public buildings will serve as an example.

Whether or not there is a right of wheelchair access, most persons, who do not use a wheelchair, will have access. Their access will be regulated in some respects: buildings will ordinarily be open during regular working hours, some offices will not be open to the public, and so forth. Access to some buildings will be denied altogether or limited to a small portion of the public, which has "official business" there. As a practical matter, many persons will have more restricted access than the public generally for some reason peculiar to their own circumstances: because they live far from where the buildings are located, are unable to leave their home or job when most buildings are open, or do not have appropriate clothing.

Suppose now that there is not a right of wheelchair access. Nevertheless, many persons who are confined to a wheelchair will have access on the same terms as others. They will obtain the means of access by hiring someone to help them get through revolving doors, up and down stairs, and so forth; or someone will help them because of an individual attachment or relationship. But many persons, lacking such resources, will not have access. Whether, constituted as they are and confined to a wheelchair, they have access is their own responsibility; it depends on what provision they can make and, if they can, what provision they choose to make for themselves directly or indirectly. Although we might feel sympathy and should not generally blame someone who was unable to provide for himself for the consequences of a specific lack of access (say, inability to obtain employment), neither should we feel moral regret, a sense that what ought to be is not, about such consequences. And if he has clear means to provide for himself and does not, we might, despite feeling sympathy for him on account of his disability, look critically on his failure to do so.

Smith, who is confined to a wheelchair, applies for a job at a state agency. With his brother's help, he comes to the agency's office for an interview. At the end of the interview, the official tells him that he is the most qualified applicant and offers him the job. Smith accepts gladly. When Smith asks the official to let his brother know that he is ready to leave, the official remarks, " I suppose he will help you to get to and from the office each day."

"No," Smith replies, "He took this morning off from his job; but he cannot do that regularly. I shall have to ask the agency to send someone to pick me up at my house in the morning and take me there at night."

At that point the official may decide that Smith will be so valuable an employee that it is worthwhile to provide the help he needs. But if not, he will tell Smith that no one is available and that employees are simply expected to be in the office at nine o'clock (and to leave at five o'clock). In that respect, Smith is not different from another highly qualified applicant who can work only half a day because there is no one to look after her children in the afternoon. He is not so different, generally speaking, from an applicant who has all the necessary job skills but makes an unfavorable impression at the interview. If Smith is not able to get himself to the office, he is not the most qualified applicant after all, and someone else will get the job.

Suppose, on the other hand, there is a right of wheelchair access. The individual situation of most people will be unchanged. Those who do not use a wheelchair will continue to act as they did. Those who do use a wheelchair and have adequate resources to provide for themselves will still be able to do so, and probably many will. But if the right is honored, the situation will change for those who cannot provide for themselves. If Smith fails to apply for a position with the state agency and explains that he is confined to a wheelchair, he may be reminded that he has a right to access or, more simply, that there are a ramp and a special elevator in the building. If he still does not apply, we shall regard his unemployment as his own doing, for which he is himself responsible; and, insofar as it has consequences for others—his brother, who must support him—we may blame him for not applying. Just as before, when he had no such right, whether or not he is employed is his own responsibility, because then as now, with respect to the matter at hand, he had his rights. Now, however, he having a right to access and his natural lack of power having been rectified, he is responsible not only distributively but also retributively. On the other hand, if the right is not honored, not only shall we excuse Smith from the consequences for others of his unemployment; we shall excuse him also from the consequences for himself. The responsibility is not his, but attaches to those who failed to honor his right. Even if a ramp for wheelchairs was not completed because of an unforeseeable fiscal crisis, which, we believe, justifies disregarding the right—"Everyone has to give up something until the crisis is past"—we shall feel some moral regret because Smith, rightly, ought to have access and, given his qualifications, ought to have the job. On the other hand, when Smith, perceiving our discomfort, adds to his catalogue of woes that he has no chance to compete in a road race and win the prize, we shall not feel the same kind of regret, although we may sympathize with him and urge the organizers of the race to have a wheelchair class of entrants. Nor shall we feel the same regret if he laments that he loves Betty, who will not marry him because he is confined to a wheelchair or, simply, because she loves someone else. As to those matters, no rectification is necessary; he has his rights, and the matters are his own responsibility.

In sum, the substance of a right of access is not an abstract generalization about human beings. It is complexly related to specific judgments about one's responsibility for a particular aspect of his life, in this case what someone who is confined to a wheelchair can expect to do and be expected to do inside public buildings. Affirmation of the right implicates duties of other persons directly or indirectly and, therefore, qualifies some rights of theirs. That will often be its primary practical significance. But the right as such concerns the range of responsibility of the person whose right it is as a self-determining individual. It rectifies the actual distribution of powers by substituting or compensating for the handicap, which is his attribute only circumstantially, and in that respect constitutes him duly.

How then do we decide whether there is a right of wheelchair access to public buildings?

Although some level of physical well-being is a human right, its basis is that responsibility of any kind requires enough capacity to make it worthwhile to exercise one's will and take responsibility. Persons who are confined to a wheelchair lack a substantial capacity that most others have, which may reasonably be regarded as a natural human capacity. Nevertheless, persons so confined retain a vast range of ordinary capacities; and no one, I think, would assert that they are in some sense not fully human. There are other reasons why one might effectively lack access to public buildings, which would not remotely call one's humanness into question. Being kept out of public buildings would at most be an incidental consequence of the altogether different, pervasive kind of oppression that does affect human rights.

No abstract principle of justice, liberty, or equality substantiates such a right. A reference to justice requires a prior conception of what is due; but from where might such a conception come? Mere difference does not sustain an argument that anything is due to whoever is less well off. The most likely source is the fact that most people have the use of their legs. The right claims only as much access as they have, which may reasonably be regarded as due on that basis. The comparison with other persons (including ourselves) may arouse our sympathy; we may respond strongly and attribute the response to a sense of fairness. But whatever action we may be inclined to take for other reasons, the core of the comparison as an argument for justice is that there is a right to wheelchair access, which, being a right, is due to those who require it. Unless one can convincingly make the case for such a right, the argument from justice has no foundation.

The liberty of (some) persons in wheelchairs would be increased by provision of access; but necessarily, the liberty of those who would be obligated to make the provision directly or indirectly would be decreased. Absence of a right preserves their right to use their resources as they choose and leaves them at liberty to make provision or not. Some kinds of provision cannot be made privately even if one has the material resources to do so. Without at least the permission of the government, one can hardly bring in a construction crew to build a ramp onto a public building. Theoretically, one might use one's resources to provide access in another way: say, hiring persons to give assistance to whoever needs it. But that is not likely to be a practical possibility. In any case, the argument that the government must be ready to provide access in order to protect the liberty of private individuals to do so bases the asserted right on the liberty of others rather than on the liberty of those who need wheelchair access. That surely cannot be correct.

Equality would be served, insofar as the power of those who have access on their own and the power of those who do not would be more nearly equal in that respect. But that would merely shift the unequal distribution of powers in another direction. If there is a right (and the right is honored), Smith's superior qualifications win him the job. If there is no right and Smith cannot provide for himself, he is unqualified, however superior his qualifications in other respects; and someone else, who is otherwise less qualified, will get the job. Without more to go on, a bare reference to equality as easily supports the latter person's claim to amelioration of his limited intellectual capacity or inability to make a favorable impression at an interview or even his lack of diligence. The same indeterminacy applies to more specific equalities. Most persons in the United States would probably subscribe to the proposition that everyone should have an equal opportunity to work, to approach the government, or to participate in the governmental process. Although wheelchair access would facilitate all those activities for persons confined to wheelchairs, none of those propositions entails that there is such a right. The elimination of some inequalities evidently is implied; but it is intended that some remain, for there are to be opportunities, taken by some and not by others. For aught that abstract "equal opportunity" tells us, physical capacity rather than intellectual capacity or good work habits may be a proper source of opportunity. (It is in Fenway Park.) Whether it is general or specific, equality as an ideal does not dictate what power(s) in particular are to be equalized. More particular goals might yield more particular conclusions; but without the support of some principle that differentiates normatively among individuals, the conclusion in this case would be only that wheelchair access is an apt means to contestable ends.

In light of the above, one may be satisfied that our question has been answered. There being no human right and no abstract principle that establishes a right to wheelchair access superior to other claims, there is no right of that kind. Whether or not there should be such access (as a legal right or not) is strictly a matter of social policy, informed, perhaps, by sympathy for those who are confined to wheelchairs, but a matter of policy nonetheless. That conclusion has its own difficulties. The arguments above do not contradict a right of access (except as a human right); rather, they fail to support the right. But it is not so clear where the burden of proof lies. Countless rights that are aspects of our ordinary liberty are simply taken for granted. If the burden of proof is on those who assert a right, the preceding arguments contradict all rights except the few very general ones that count as human rights; for the arguments apply alike to all. Some people have indeed concluded that except for a narrow range of indefinite human rights and an unlimited range of potential positive legal rights, rights are a type of political or social ideal and can be regarded only as an expression of what their proponents believe persons ought to have or to be, according to a conception of the good that either is accepted as authoritative but is beyond rational discussion or invites discussion but only about debatable ends and the means for achieving them. Neither of those ways of thinking about rights captures the nature of rights claims or the manner in which they are debated.

An actual discussion about a right of wheelchair access, in which the proponent of the right did not preempt disagreement by referring to a (deemed-to-be) incontestable authority and the opponent accepted the possibility of genuine (nonlegal) rights, might begin in a variety of ways. The proponent might point out that access would enable persons confined to a wheelchair to do something that other persons do as a matter of course and would thereby contribute to their individual liberty and to their equality with others. Or she might make an implicit reference to justice: "It is not their fault that they need special access." Reliance on such abstract ideals will not carry the discussion very far, however; the reference to justice, for example, without specification of which differential attributes are one's own responsibility, might be met in kind: "Lots of people can't do just what they want to do." One way or another, if the parties pursue the discussion seriously, they will begin to compare the asserted right with other specific claims that are regarded unexceptionally as rights or not rights, either for the persuasiveness of the comparison itself or because it qualifies and gives content to a general principle. Some rather simple and obvious criteria of relevance are likely to dictate the initial comparisons. But the range and direction of the examples used on either side need conform to no pattern and are not predictable in advance; they depend simply on what occurs to the parties to the discussion.

So, the proponent might point to the community's unexceptional provisions for persons with other physical disabilities: special educational facilities for blind and deaf children, audible traffic signals for blind pedestrians, airline safety instructions in sign for deaf passengers. Or she might take a different tack. Emphasizing the importance of access and the liberty it confers, she might mention all the individual and public activities (job applications, educational programs, voting, trials, town meetings) that are carried out in public buildings and the measures that help and encourage people to participate in them. To each such example there is a variety of responses, again not dictated by a prescribed pattern. The opponent of wheelchair access might point to some distinguishing feature of the examples and deny their relevance: "Being blind is one thing; using a wheelchair is another." Or he may offer counterexamples of his own and implicitly suggest a different criterion of relevance: "A guy in a wheelchair can't play in the major leagues, no matter how much he wants to. No one makes him send another guy's kid to college."

The longer the discussion continues, the further it will extend to practices and understandings that are not closely related, as the parties look for common ground about what similarities and differences are relevant. At some point it will probably shift from physical disabilities to other kinds of comparative weakness and the community's attitude of greater or less social responsibility for the welfare of weaker persons: the elderly, the young, the unemployed, and so forth. It may range broadly among activities more or less similar to those that take place in public buildings and the community's shared attitudes about the importance of participation in them. There may be still broader consideration of how the community conceives personhood generally: How far does a leveling philosophy that equalizes individuals' opportunities prevail, and how far an individualist philosophy that regards persons, for better or worse, as "on their own"? When the discussion takes that turn, if not sooner, the community's attitude toward other kinds of differential capacities and their attendant responsibilities will have to be considered, for provision of wheelchair access must directly or indirectly affect the power of others to use their own capacities as they choose.

The participants in such a discussion may find that they agree about the community's actual practices and yet disagree about their significance. If the community provides wheelchairs to those who need them, is that a recognition of their right or is it a social policy of which they incidentally are beneficiaries? If the community does not provide wheelchairs, is that because it regards that as a person's own responsibility or because, although it acknowledges the right, there are overriding considerations of social policy the other way? One might suppose that unless there is a right to have a wheelchair in the first instance, there can hardly be a right to wheelchair access; but that is not self-evident, for one might be deemed responsible for his means of locomotion generally and not responsible for being able to use it for the particular purpose of access to public buildings. The community's reasons for its practices may be expressed explicitly in legislative history or public statements of one kind or another, which command general approval. Or they too may have to be worked out by consideration of concrete examples that, provided they are accepted as relevant, point one way or the other. And finally, even if agreement is reached about what the community does and why it does it, it may be urged that it is not dispositive, because the conventions of other communities, not relevantly dissimilar, or another kind of normative standard entirely dictates another, better outcome.

There is no prescribed formal structure to debate about rights. There are no general principles, factual or normative, which can themselves be demonstrated and from which conclusions about specific rights follow. Relying necessarily on analogy to provide the content for abstract propositions, an argument is only as strong as the relevance and weight of its examples make it. Nevertheless, it is possible to reason about rights and, sometimes, to state confidently a conclusion about what rights there are. Unsurprisingly, most contested issues do not yield a definite conclusion. It is easy to suppose, therefore, that there are no definite conclusions of any kind and, fixing on deductive reasoning as the only model, to attribute the lack to the absence of verifiable normative principles from which rights can be deduced. So to argue is to lose sight of the array of rights within a community that are essentially uncontested and underlie statements about individual responsibility that are asserted and generally accepted as a matter of fact. The pattern that (serious) discussions about rights take reflects their source in the *nomos* of the community, the actual conventions according to which persons are recognized as responsible for some conduct and not other, usually unexceptionally and without any special notice being taken. All there is finally to go on is the fact of responsibility, which acknowledges us as unique individuals differentially endowed and regards our differences as constitutive attributes, or rights, on one hand and circumstantial attributes on the other.

In the United States at the end of the twentieth century, it is not surprising that the question whether persons have a right to (some) amelioration of (some) physical handicaps cannot be answered definitively. The very notion of "handicap" raises difficult, contentious issues. Any differential disadvantage might be so regarded. But the larger the range of disadvantages that count as handicaps, the fewer persons are likely to support the general proposition that handicapped persons have a right to amelioration of their handicap. Is obesity, for example, or extreme obesity a handicap? Or is it simply a personal characteristic?[3] There is in fact very broad provision of various kinds of assistance (including wheelchair access) by the community itself and by numerous other more or less public agencies. The legal right to such assistance is extensive and in many respects well settled and unlikely to be diminished by legislation or judicial decision. At the

same time, the general notion of differential merit—individual differences of capacity that validate differences of result—is very strong. Just
how strong is indicated by the virtually universal acceptance of "equality of opportunity" as a fundamental principle of American life, as if
we can somehow reconcile our affection for equality with extreme
differences in individual well-being. A general social responsibility for
individual welfare is not widely acknowledged. There are, however,
some specific exceptions, among the strongest of which is provision
for the handicapped. The strength of the idea of individual merit
challenges disregard of palpable, idiosyncratic disabilities that cannot
by any account be regarded as *self*-determined.[4]

Answering my own question, I should say that handicapped persons
do have rights in connection with their handicap. The specific content
of such rights is highly controversial; it is certainly less than the advocates of rights for the handicapped assert and more than some members of the public think correct. There is, however, a base of such rights
that is largely uncontested, on which the debate about their full extent
builds. Practices intended to ameliorate the limitations of a handicap
are increasingly common. They include large public commitments, like
special education programs and building design, as well as smaller
measures, like designated parking spaces, that unobtrusively become
familiar and are taken for granted. Whether a right of wheelchair access
specifically is presently among the rights of the handicapped is uncertain. Substantial measures have been taken to provide access, more in
recognition of a right than as a matter of the general public good; but
access is far from complete, and were there persuasive arguments
against its recognition in particular circumstances, the right would, I
think, give way. Probably the most accurate conclusion is that there is
a right of wheelchair access, not yet fully settled, which is coming into
being along with other rights of the handicapped.

Gay Rights

What have come to be called "gay rights" include first of all permission
to engage in homosexual sexual conduct: the claim that the govern-

ment may not prohibit such conduct simply as such. Whether the government may prohibit homosexual sexual acts in public places, with a person below a certain age, and so forth are separate questions. The gay rights position with respect to such questions generally is that the conduct can be prohibited, if at all, only on the same terms as heterosexual sexual conduct. In addition, claimed gay rights include protection against indirect use of the government's powers in ways that inhibit homosexual sexual conduct or simply deny homosexuals opportunities or advantages that others have. On that basis are challenged laws that exclude homosexuals from the military or other public employment, do not allow them to adopt children, or restrict marriage and the legal benefits that flow from marriage (having to do with such matters as property and inheritance) to heterosexual couples. The claimed protection may extend beyond governmental action to discrimination against homosexuals by private persons and organizations with respect to activities that have a substantial public aspect. A distinct right of provision is not often included among gay rights, if only because no special provision is necessary to enable one to engage in homosexual sex. Something akin to provision is involved in claims that the government is required to open wholly private channels that are closed to homosexuals by private action. Laws that prohibit verbal abuse of homosexuals or any form of "gay-bashing" are similarly a kind of provision; but they are typically embraced within more general legislation pertaining to offensive conduct directed at other persons more broadly.

In a strict sense, laws that prohibit homosexual sexual conduct or discriminate against persons who engage in it do not deny the right to do so or the responsibility. Such laws are well understood on both sides of the issue to deny a legal right. But although they impose a burden on the conduct, persons remain free to engage in it, subject to that burden or not; and it is because they are (deemed to be) responsible for doing so that the burden is part of their legally imposed desert. The distinction between prohibition of conduct and its direct prevention is not insignificant, especially in this instance, inasmuch as the prohibition—if not the discrimination—is for most practical purposes disregarded. That having been said, legal prohibition and discrimination interfere with exercise of the right by deliberately altering the possible personal consequences of such conduct; and as indirect, however limited, modes of prevention, we may regard them for those whose conduct is affected as a denial not only of the legal right but of the right altogether.

The central issue was brought into focus in 1986 by the Supreme Court's decision in *Bowers v. Hardwick*.[5] A five–four majority of the Court ruled that states are not constitutionally barred from prohibiting homosexual sexual conduct, sodomy in this case.[6] Although the courts have decided other questions since, sometimes in favor of the gay community, the *Hardwick* decision remains fundamental; for if homosexual sex can be prohibited altogether, most claims for protection and provision must also fall as a matter of (constitutional) right, even though state or federal legislation may provide a legal right for other reasons.[7]

Arguments are occasionally made that the entire controversy is a matter of social policy and that the decision whether to prohibit homosexual sexual conduct is to be made on consequential grounds alone, there being no question of rights either way. The most sustained argument of that kind was made by Patrick Devlin in *The Enforcement of Morals*.[8] Lord Devlin urged particularly that a community properly exercises its authority to promote a common social identity among its members, for its own preservation and well-being. As others pointed out, even if that general premise is allowed, the gap between it and the prohibition of homosexual sexual conduct specifically is a large one, which Devlin's argument did not fill. Whether such a prohibition does significantly promote social cohesion in a way that generates public good needs to be proved.[9] The Supreme Court in *Hardwick* did not rely on consequential arguments of this kind, except perhaps indirectly. Rather, the opinion urged that statutes prohibiting sodomy are deeply rooted in American law and our legal and moral traditions and thus do not violate a fundamental right within the meaning of the constitutional requirement of due process. In the last few years, the AIDS epidemic has furnished a new consequential argument; but it would be difficult to sustain a prohibition of homosexual sexual conduct generally on that basis. Not only would a general prohibition of that sort sweep much more broadly than the social purpose requires; in view of the private efforts of homosexuals to avoid the spread of AIDS and the other ways in which AIDS is spread, it would also be curiously selective.[10]

Almost everyone recognizes that consequential arguments of this kind are makeweights. Even if the arguments are allowed some force, which many persons do not concede, they can scarcely be thought to overcome a valid claim of individual right to the contrary. The issue is, and is generally acknowledged to be, one of rights. As it is usually framed, the proponents of gay rights assert that there is a right to engage in homosexual sexual conduct, and the opponents deny that there is such a right, either independently or as an aspect of liberty. The Supreme Court made much of the latter distinction, the majority observing that a "right of homosexuals to engage in acts of sodomy" could not by any stretch of the imagination be found in the Constitution, and the dissent insisting that a right to liberty is found there and that that is enough.[11] Each side was, of course, correct about what the text of the Constitution contains; but since neither explained very clearly why its textual analysis and not the other ought to prevail, the impact of the distinction in both opinions was largely rhetorical. It points, however, to two arguments, one on each side, which go to the heart of the matter.

The dissenters' reference to liberty invoked John Stuart Mill's "very simple principle" that conduct that affects no one except the actor himself ought not to be regulated by the government.[12] That principle is the basis of the argument on which proponents of gay rights most often rely. They urge that private sexual conduct (one of the few pleasurable activities that satisfies Locke's proviso that "enough, and as good" be left for everyone else) is self-regarding if anything is and, therefore, that the general constitutional protection of liberty in the Fifth and Fourteenth Amendments applies. At the very least, they argue, the government has the burden of proving that it is not self-regarding and that its prohibition serves a significant public good. Even if one agrees, however, that the public policy arguments for prohibition are trumped up, the conclusion that homosexual sexual conduct is self-regarding does not follow. Persons who are offended by homosexuality may, and many of them do, claim that they are injured by it. One may, of course, dismiss such offense or "psychic harm" as different in kind from physical injury or other sorts of "material" harm and assert that it does not count as other-regarding conduct. But that is far from obvious. There are some forms of psychic harm, like the deliberate infliction of fear or disgust, that all would regard as other-regarding. The fact that the harm is deliberately inflicted may make a difference, but not on the basis of the nature of the harm. So long as we live as a community bound together by affective relationships, the characterization of conduct as self-regarding depends on normative judgment and not merely on observation. We cannot, after all, insist on those relationships when they serve our preferred values and deny that they exist when they do not. One may believe that those who favor prohibition ought not to be affected or even that they are not affected as they say they are; but neither of those propositions is self-evident. The force of Mill's principle depends very much on its application's being self-evident in the circumstances.

The majority's characterization of the issue as a claimed constitutional right to engage in homosexual sexual conduct points beyond a rejection of the application of Mill's principle. It misrepresents the argument of those who favor prohibition to say that their whole reason for opposing other persons' private homosexual sexual conduct is that they are offended by it. At bottom, and of fundamental importance, they urge that there is a specific duty applicable to all human beings not to engage in such conduct. (The other side's insistence that that amounts to a claim of offense manifests an unwillingness even to entertain an argument that does not subscribe to Mill's principle.) Accordingly, the law's prohibition does not restrict liberty at all, even if other persons are not affected, because it merely enforces a limitation on responsible conduct that would prevail whatever the law.

The source of this duty, according to those who perceive it, is various. For many persons, it has the authority of incontestable religious doctrine. For a great many others, it is not, at least not exclusively, a matter of religion. Rather it is a deep, albeit often inarticulate, sense of what is "natural." It is evident that from the perspective taken in this book about human rights, there is no such basis for a human duty. Although the description of homosexual sexual acts, sodomy in particular, as unnatural is common in the arguments favoring prohibition, the distinction between what is natural and what is not, religious doctrines aside, is altogether unexplained. That may be enough to defeat the claim of duty for those who reject it. But however shaky an appeal to "intuition" or some such thing is to those who believe differently, those who oppose homosexuality are not alone in relying on it. Proponents of gay rights dismiss talk about what is natural as inaccurate as a matter of fact, if it refers to what is found in nature, and the enthroning of ignorance and prejudice. It may be all those things. Nevertheless, to suppose that all that opposes gay rights is weak consequential arguments or prejudice is wide of the mark. Whatever its source, for many people what is at stake is a duty that defines the scope of human liberty as fully as do rights. For those people, unless that position is acknowledged and addressed on its own terms, the central issue is not joined.

Proponents of gay rights have made a good deal of the fact that many persons do not choose to be homosexual any more than others choose to be heterosexual; whether the explanation is genetic or social or some combination of both, one simply is homosexual, as the great majority of people simply are heterosexual. The general principle of the criminal law that one is not criminally liable and cannot be punished for conduct unless he is responsible in the ordinary sense and able to act otherwise is said to preclude declaring homosexual conduct a crime, at least for persons in that category. Abstractly the argument has force. It is, however, a specification of the determinist stop, which precludes any responsibility whatever. No evidence suggests that homosexuality is any more a compulsion or pathological than other dispositional states—including, incidentally, heterosexuality. It is, indeed, the homosexual community itself that insists most strongly that homosexuality is not in any sense "abnormal," but is rather part of the endless variety of the normal. If one "cannot help" being homosexual, that is so only in the sense that none of us can help being who she or he is. The criminal law recognizes no such defense.[13]

There is, finally, no plausible basis for defending the right to engage in homosexual sexual conduct as a human right. Even if the right is stated generally, as a right to engage in sexual conduct or to engage in the kind of sexual conduct that one chooses, too many human institutions have restricted that right for the claim to be made that one is not otherwise fully human. Although such restrictions are some-times involuntarily imposed, as in the army in some circumstances or in prison, they are also often undertaken voluntarily. Whether volun-tary or not, a brief or prolonged or even permanent interruption of sexual relations is well within the range of human experience. Indeed, although human beings vary greatly in this respect, it is a characteristic feature of the human life cycle. One may believe that a sexual life is an element of a richly fulfilled life; but that is another matter. A person's life may be unfulfilled for a variety of reasons, without putting his humanity at stake. So also, although many persons regard the sexual aspect of their lives as peculiarly central to their sense of self, the general right to liberty does not on that basis alone sustain a specific right of this kind. Without liberty—rights—there is no person; but the forms that such liberty takes are not specified in advance.

No abstract argument settles the issue either way. Even if one could conclusively overcome consequential arguments against gay rights, the more fundamental nonconsequential argument that there is a human duty not to engage in homosexual sex remains. That argument is not itself conclusive, for the existence of any such duty is sharply contested. Nevertheless, it does make it inadequate to urge simply that in the absence of convincing consequential arguments, individual liberty pre-vails. Discussion does not, however, end there.

Beginning at some point after World War II, probably around the end of the 1950s, the public American attitude toward homosexuality underwent a profound change, the extent of which the now familiar phrase "coming out of the closet" scarcely suggests. What had been regarded generally as altogether private and to be concealed as something regrettable if not shameful (and often that as well) became an unexceptional matter of fact. Not only do a very large number of men and women acknowledge their homosexuality; in all sorts of ways that attract no special notice, the community as a whole acknowledges that homosexuality is within the mainstream of ordinary life, even if not the widest current in the stream. In the 1990s it is not especially remarkable for persons of the same sex to live together as lovers, for a public figure to announce that he is homosexual, for homosexual groups to participate in public events with official sanction, for newspapers and magazines to discuss homosexuality and homosexual sexual practices in clinical detail, for advertisements to be directed at the gay community, for characters in books, movies, and plays to be homosexual, and so forth. The prevalence of homosexual sex in prisons, institutions of the state where persons are confined against their will, is incontestable; no one anymore pretends otherwise, and in some institutions condoms are freely available for protection against AIDS. There is still a great difference between the public perceptions of homosexuality and heterosexuality. One does not need to consider at all the impact of a public avowal that one is heterosexual; indeed, there is nothing to avow. Nevertheless, although individual attitudes toward homosexuality vary widely, it has become an unremarkable feature of our common life, one more respect in which persons differ from one another.

The change in the attitude toward homosexuality has been part of, or at least accompanied by, a broader change. The sexual aspect of human life generally has come into the open. Once again, plenty of ambivalence and ambiguity remains. But there is no longer a need to pretend that sex is not a central element of human experience. And, in particular, although the variety of heterosexual practices has presumably not changed, there is much greater public awareness and acknowledgment of how various they are. The range of the "normal" has increased to include the usual and the unusual without special mention; and the range of the "abnormal" has correspondingly shrunk.

The persistence of criminal laws prohibiting behavior that is so widely and openly practiced is curiously hollow. Laws prohibiting homosexual sexual conduct are virtually never enforced (although laws prohibiting homosexual or heterosexual sexual conduct involving an additional element of public nuisance or imposition on a minor, and so forth, may be). What is at stake is not merely nonenforcement, for practical reasons, of a law that is generally in accord with community sentiment. Scarcely anyone, including even those who believe that homosexual sex is wrong, expects laws that prohibit it altogether to be enforced or believes that they ought to be enforced. (In *Hardwick* the county attorney declined to prosecute although the facts constituting the offense were not in question.[14]) In that posture, such laws are all but entirely ineffective to restrict the conduct they purport to prohibit. No one believes that the laws themselves much restrain persons who do not refrain from homosexual sex for other reasons. They remain "in force," therefore, as a kind of official pronouncement that it is bad, and nothing more.

One may conclude that prohibitory laws give something to both sides. They square nicely with the belief that there is a duty not to engage in homosexual sexual conduct, which, however, as a public matter remains wholly abstract for practical purposes.[15] Those who have such a belief are given a formal nod, and others may do as they like. (One might regard the situation as parallel to the darker earlier situation, with the considerable difference that the automatic stigma and reasons for concealment of one's homosexuality are largely eliminated and a person can decide for herself how private a matter it is.) There is, however, a peculiar indignity to being told that one's conduct, albeit ordinary and unexceptional, is officially bad. If the conduct is permitted as a practical matter, indicating that arguments about harm are not seriously entertained, those who engage in it may resent the indignity all the more because it is gratuitous. Furthermore, the general principle that the government ought not to pronounce about morality as such is broadly accepted in the United States, unlike some other communities. Wide public recognition that for most people sexual identity is part of one's own definition of self, present actively or latently in most parts of one's life, and close to the center argues strongly that in this context especially the law ought to prefer the right to act as one chooses to the asserted duty to act as others believe one ought.

Such considerations function at the level of legal right as a matter of social policy, having to do not with supposed harmful consequences of homosexual sexual conduct but with how best to resolve a straight-forward moral disagreement, on both sides of which feelings run high. The combination of open inclusion of homosexuality within the pattern of American life and recognition of the crucial and unique role of sexuality in one's definition of self indicates more fundamentally that the right to engage in such conduct is among the constitutive attributes, as part of a person's responsibility and rights. That conclusion is independent of the question whether homosexuality is voluntarily chosen or not; for the determinist stop applies to all human conduct alike. Rather it depends on the perception that for most persons, sexual identity is not just one of the countless, nonessential elements of personal identity comprised generally within liberty but has distinct, irreplaceable significance of its own, and on the fact that homosexuality is not (regarded as) pathological or aberrant or even a particularly unusual form of sexual identity. The conclusion that there is a right does not follow inevitably; for the ways in which personal identity are implicated are different. But we cannot well ignore what being a person is when we consider what persons ought to be. Not only practical concerns but also respect for the human individual dictate otherwise.

It is an indication of the convoluted public attitude toward homosexuality that it should be accepted as one's own responsibility in so many ways and not carry legal recognition of the right along with it. The policy concerning homosexuals in the military that was announced in July 1993 illustrates the current situation. After its announcement, persons on both sides of the issue tried to resolve the policy's unconcealed ambiguities by posing hypothetical cases, which those responsible for the policy as well as those who will be responsible for implementing it wisely resisted. As an explicit formula, "Don't ask, don't tell" is as bad as its critics said. Inexplicitly, however, the policy instructs military personnel to pull back from efforts (already less than arduous or consistent) to eliminate homosexuals from the military and, so long as conduct is not called too forcibly to official notice, to let it alone. If that policy is fully carried out, military life will largely replicate civilian life in places where homosexual sexual conduct is formally prohibited and accepted in practice.[16]

Almost certainly, were the question not whether to repeal laws or regulations prohibiting homosexual sexual conduct but whether to enact them in the first instance, the answer in today's community would be no.[17] Much of the current controversy depends on the need for an affirmative vote for repeal, which tends to legitimate the status quo. Legislative and executive inaction in the face of controversy is not unusual and may indicate less about the community generally than about its politics. Putting it all together, I should say that notwithstanding the ongoing moral debate about homosexuality as an abstraction, the *nomos* of the community supports the conclusion, without qualification, that private sexual conduct that inflicts no harm is one's own business, that is to say, one's responsibility and one's right. (I do not think that the community's *nomos* presently supports the full equivalence of homosexuality and heterosexuality with respect to such matters as marriage and parenthood. Those institutions have socially defined meanings that do not necessarily change in tandem with a change in the attitude toward homosexuality as such.[18]) But for the persistence on the books of laws to the contrary, one's own responsibility for his sexual identity and the public obligation to respect it would be regarded as civil rights, among the rights embraced within liberty generally.

Affirmative Action

Few issues in contemporary American life have been so much discussed philosophically and politically and have so eluded theoretical and practical solutions as affirmative action or, less approvingly described, reverse discrimination: the advancement of members of a disfavored group identified by race, ethnicity, or gender over other persons, because of their membership in that group. Controversy about affirmative action is hardly surprising. The individuals who are directly affected for better or worse have a large stake in the outcome, which concerns aspects of life that count the most for individual achievement and satisfaction. But the explanation for our failure to reach substantial consensus is not just conflicts of self-interest. Persons who are not themselves at risk also take strong positions; and those who are affected do not think of themselves as, nor do they sound like, merely winners and losers in a contest. The losers protest not against a loss but against a wrong: that they are done an injustice. And the winners do not assert only that their gain is theirs to keep; they assert that it is their due. On both sides of the controversy there is a sense that, in addition to the concrete, practical consequences, one's stature as a person is involved.

There has on the whole been little resistance to measures designed to correct specific instances of past discrimination when both the person discriminated against and the beneficiary of the discrimination are identified. Measures of that kind, if not wholly uncontroversial, are usually perceived to satisfy ordinary considerations of corrective justice. To describe action in the past as "discriminatory" itself conveys that it was contrary to the appropriate norm, even though it may have conformed to common practices at that time. Since, however, discrimination was practiced against groups, its specific impact on individuals is not so easily proved; for the denial of some opportunity or advantage to a specific individual might have been justified as well on nondiscriminatory grounds. The difficulty is greatly compounded if one or more generations intervene between the supposed cause and its effect(s); other causes, including the affected individuals' own actions, might have produced the same outcome had there been no discrimination at all.[19] We may be certain that affirmative action favorable to members of the previously disfavored group will in many instances remedy an actual injustice; but whether it does so in a particular instance is speculative. Similarly, although discrimination gives some individuals in the favored group a benefit that is not their due, that may not be so in any particular case; the individual might have obtained the same advantage on nondiscriminatory grounds. Affirmative action is so easily labeled "reverse discrimination" because, even if its premises are fully accepted, in an unknown number of cases it may be just that.

Few persons now believe that the discrimination of the past was correct, at least with regard to racial and ethnic distinctions. Somewhat more persons probably believe that gender-based distinctions are appropriate or "natural," although they would no doubt disclaim belief that the distinctions reflect individual merit. Such classifications are believed to have only descriptive significance, and not so much of that. They neither confer worth of themselves nor are significant indicators of attributes that confer worth. Many persons, however, believe that the same principles that reject past discrimination require that remedial discrimination in the present also be rejected. They urge that so far as race, ethnicity, and gender are concerned, the only right is a right to equal treatment as a person, meaning specifically that those aspects of one's being *not* be taken into account. Even if past discrimination may have affected persons' present qualifications, in the absence of specific provable harm a person stands before us now as the person she is. From that individual perspective, someone in the previously disfavored group is not different from anyone else whose relative lack of appropriate qualifications is attributable to circumstances beyond her control. It makes no difference that in this case the circumstances happened to be social rather than natural (unfortunate genetic makeup) or idiosyncratic (neglectful parents). And if, on the other side, someone has benefited, he is nevertheless the person that he is and no less deserving on that account than someone who is born with a high I.Q. or good eye-arm coordination or whose parents sent him to music camp instead of out on the streets.

Proponents of affirmative action do not respond that race, ethnicity, or gender is a criterion of or indicative of individual worth but that discriminatory practices of the past had the wrong end up. They do not assert abstractly that black persons are more worthy and are accordingly due more than whites. Nevertheless, they argue, in the concrete circumstances of contemporary American life, being a member of the previously disfavored group is a ground for preferment and being a member of the previously favored group a ground for not being preferred. Their position has appeal because it responds explicitly to an acknowledged deep injustice. Yet it has proved powerfully difficult to elaborate the argument.

The simplest defense of affirmative action passes over the lack of proof of specific individual harm or benefit. Discrimination having been practiced against groups rather than against individuals, it is the group that has a right to a remedy; and its right is vindicated in the only way it can be, by preferring individuals on the basis of their membership in the group, as its representatives. Since membership in the groups in question is not regarded as indicative of worth and in a world without discrimination would be a statistically insignificant factor for the distributions that are the subject of affirmative action, such preferences work to correct the imbalance among groups that discrimination brought about.

It is, however, a mistake to speak of the groups in question as having a right to, or as due, anything, except as a collective reference to the individuals within the groups. The groups represent the individuals, not the other way around. In some instances we may speak of the responsibility and rights of a collective entity, like a club or corporation, which have a bearing on the responsibility and rights of individual members in virtue of their participation in the collective activity. Here, however, it is the very premise of affirmative action that there is no relevant collective entity; nor is there any "participation" that would justify transference of some assumed responsibility or rights of the group to the individual. The wrong in the past was the denial to individuals within the group of what was individually their due. It is precisely our inability to prove such individual wrongs to specific persons now that makes affirmative action problematic.

Caught between the objection to group rights on one hand and the practical inability to prove violations of specific individuals' rights on the other, many proponents of affirmative action have sought to remove it from the realm of rights altogether and to defend it not as a matter of corrective justice but simply as sound social policy. Giving a preference to minority applicants for admission to university, for example, may be justified as a policy of diversity that enhances the education of all the students who are admitted. Or, more generally, it may be urged that affirmative action in education and employment now is the best way to achieve an integral community, in which racial and ethnic classifications are irrelevant. Such arguments explain the need for affirmative action by reference to past discrimination; but its justification is not that the individuals who benefit have unjustly been deprived. Rather, they are incidental beneficiaries of a practice that serves the common good. Ronald Dworkin, for example, has said: "Affirmative action programs seem to encourage . . . a popular misunderstanding, which is that they assume that racial or ethnic groups are entitled to proportionate shares of opportunities, so that Italian or Polish ethnic minorities are, in theory, as entitled to their proportionate shares as blacks or Chicanos or American Indians are entitled to the shares the present programs give them. That is a plain mistake: the programs are not based on the idea that those who are aided are entitled to aid, but only on the strategic hypothesis that helping them is now an effective way of attacking a national problem."[20]

Arguments of this kind, which have appealed to the courts and to many commentators, are not as narrowly conceived as Dworkin suggests. Not only do they eschew a claim that the members of previously disfavored groups are "entitled to aid." Much more important, they depend on the proposition that no one, whether a member of the previously disfavored or previously favored group, is entitled to a preference on *any* basis that interferes with implementation of the "strategic hypothesis." Whatever his qualifications, it is asserted, a person has no right to be admitted to a university.[21] That being the case, it is permissible to admit or reject on instrumental or "strategic" grounds alone. Provided that the factors that determine admission are convincingly, or at any rate plausibly, related to the goal of the strategy and the goal is one that the society generally approves (or, if private action is involved, accepts), it is no more or less permissible to base admission to a university on race than to base it on scholarly aptitude, academic achievement, or any of the other factors that have traditionally been considered, likewise, it is assumed, in pursuit of some social or institutional goal. Certainly it is no less permissible than to base admission on athletic ability, geographic diversity, or whether one's parent went to the university. Similarly, although ordinarily one's ability to do the work effectively is all that counts in an application for employment, the best worker has no right to be hired; if the goal of a diverse work force outweighs production goals, another, minority applicant who is less able may be hired in his place. The rejection generally of race as a criterion, constitutionally and otherwise, is overcome in this instance by the importance of the specific social goal.

The argument that nothing more is at stake than the good of the community as a whole has been so attractive, not least to courts, because it offers a way out of the intractable opposition of rights asserted on both sides and allows flexibility and compromise by the application of different strategic hypotheses; if the ultimate goal is typically stated too generally and abstractly to allow much dissent, nevertheless the appropriate means for achieving it is something about which reasonable persons may disagree. Some proponents of affirmative action may believe, however, that even on its own terms the argument proves too much. For unless one dismisses certain conceptions of the social good and how to achieve it out of hand, which would require just the sort of rights-based principle that the argument wants to avoid, the argument is capable of legitimating the discriminatory practices of the past as well as those of the present. Even if one is prepared to reject past practices as certainly wrong from a utilitarian perspective on the basis of our present knowledge, it would be much more difficult to dismiss them from that perspective on the basis of what was believed to be true when the practices were adopted. We might then have to allow that the practices were permissible or even correct at that time, a concession that few will want to make. So also, even if we confine our attention to the present, the argument might legitimate discriminatory practices that one strongly disapproves. Social policies and the ways to achieve them are not readily cabined in advance. Suppose, for example, there were strong statistical evidence that race or gender was statistically linked to the choice of a medical specialty and the social need for practitioners of some specialties were much greater than the need for practitioners of others. One might then conclude that the need justified a discriminatory admissions policy. Others, of course, might conclude that despite the need, the society would be better served by a nondiscriminatory policy. Many people, however, will believe that neither of those instrumental conclusions is to the point and that although applicants' career plans might be considered, each has a right to be considered as an individual and not as a member of a group identified on one of the statistically relevant, discriminatory bases; that is, they have rights as persons and are not merely means for the accomplishment of ends not their own.[22]

It is, after all, because we believe that the discrimination of the past was wrong, a denial of the rights of those who were discriminated against, and not merely a mistake that we are so concerned to find a remedy now. We cannot readily affirm that belief and at the same time assert that discrimination now, albeit to achieve a desirable social goal, implicates no one's rights at all. Sometimes, it is true, an unusually weighty public good may be allowed to prevail over a claim of right. In a human community, the social pursuit of justice need not be absolute or else fail altogether. But the occasions when rights are not trumps must be special and idiosyncratic if they are to count as rights and not merely as another limited good weighed in the balance. Although the need for affirmative action is traced to specific social practices in the past, it is not conceived as isolated departures from what is right, to be applied in exceptional cases. On the contrary, it is proposed as a systemic response to a broad social problem; in order to succeed, it must be a general practice, routinely applied to enough cases to have a perceptible effect. Nor can its impact on the individuals who are disfavored by affirmative action be dismissed as too slight to undermine whatever rights they may have. Itself a consequential argument, the defense of affirmative action as social policy can hardly assert that it does not disregard rights because, after all, its effects are not very significant.

The social policy argument rarely addresses directly claims of rights that it rejects. Indeed, although affirmative action displaces in some measure qualifications that usually sustain a claim of right, like aptitude and achievement, they remain otherwise fully in effect. The more able black candidate is preferred to the less able black candidate, the more able white candidate to the less able. And so forth. Only, up to a point, the less able black candidate is preferred to the more able white candidate. When candidates are members of the same group, affirmative action is not an issue; so there is no reason on that account why the other criteria should not apply. And even if they are not members of the same group, affirmative action as an instrument of social policy is not applied exclusively, without any consideration of other social goals. No one suggests, for example, that the preference given to members of the previously deprived group extends so far that candidates' very competence to fill the position in question should be ignored.

Although one might suppose, therefore, that other, potentially conflicting social goals would explain the limited reach of affirmative action, such an explanation has not been forthcoming except in the vaguest terms, theoretically or practically. In practice, affirmative action invariably is limited to some more or less clearly understood proportion of the places to be filled, most often the proportion of members of the group that it benefits to the whole relevant population. But there is very little to connect that with the instrumental argument that is said to justify affirmative action in the first place. It may be urged that it is impossible actually to calculate how far the goal of affirmative action should prevail over other social goals and, that being so, that it is sensible to make a reasonable guess; if group membership would be statistically insignificant in a world without discrimination, proportions of the whole population is a reasonable guess. But a reasonable guess about what end result is desirable is not necessarily a good indicator of how the desired result is to be achieved. In any case, there is hardly ever a serious effort to justify or even to explain the actual decisions that are made. Rather, individuals and institutions that practice affirmative action avoid the burden of justification by not applying an explicit formula and insisting that each decision is an individual one. That approach fools scarcely anyone. Individual or not, what is the basis for the decisions? And how is it that year after year, the number of persons favored by affirmative action is about the same or follows a consistent trajectory, conforming in most cases to the standard of proportionality? Too obviously, the appeal of that standard is not that it is believed to approximate the best accommodation of multiple social goals, but that it appears to give every group a share to which it is rightfully entitled, putative social goods (whether those promoted by affirmative action or others) notwithstanding. In this manner, even when it is ostensibly based on the general good and not on rights, either of the individuals or of the groups that benefit, affirmative action tends to endorse the latter. It is for just that reason that affirmative action has been unable to shake off the objection that it establishes quotas, that is to say, entitlements justified neither by social policy nor as of right.

Even if affirmative action predictably advances widely shared social goals, it must ultimately be defended as a matter of right because it contradicts what is widely perceived as the merit of those whom it disfavors: merit constituted by desert, in consequence of their responsible acts, or by rights, the normatively constitutive attributes in virtue of which one is a responsible person. Nothing that is said about the injustice of past discrimination establishes that it is incorrect generally to regard as merit a person's achievements or the individual attributes of aptitude and character that account for them and to consider both in the distribution of benefits and opportunities, like admission to a university and employment. It is not odd, self-interested, or unworthy to insist that superiority in these respects ought to count, for it does count mightily throughout our lives, not least in the areas in which affirmative action is applied. In a society that recognizes and rewards individual merit as pervasively and fully as ours, the effort to subordinate it to social policy in important areas of some individuals' lives is bound to be perceived as injustice by those who are the losers. For not only what they have learned and experienced in the past but also what palpably remains true—a simple matter of fact—in the present over most of their lives argues so strongly to the contrary.

The great, great puzzle of affirmative action is how to make the effects of past discrimination not normatively constitutive of those who have suffered them, without at the same time making other attributes, the effects of other causes, not normatively constitutive as well. How, that is, without specific grounds for application of corrective justice, can we acknowledge the injustice of the past and undo its effects, and still regard persons as responsible, for better or worse, for their selves? The argument of opponents of affirmative action that persons now ought not to pay a penalty for the wrongdoing of others in the past is precise. They argue that the wrongs that were done are not their responsibility and ought not, therefore, to count against them. Even if their selves as now constituted may in some way be among the effects of those wrongs, from their individual perspective such attributes are not different from any others, which also are the determinate effects of causes beyond the individual's control. They have no normative self stripped of those effects; and to deny them their rights, their due in consequence of those attributes, is to that extent to deny that they are responsible at all, to regard them not as persons but as things.

Those who support affirmative action stand that argument on its head, with no less force. Whatever may be true of other sources of our selves, the conceded injustice of past discrimination unfits attributes that are its effects to be normatively constitutive. Even though persons living now are not individually responsible for the discrimination, such attributes are not their due and, therefore, not constitutive of them as responsible persons. To regard such attributes as the ground of rights undermines the notion of responsibility at its core and to that extent obliterates the distinction between persons and things.

Setting one argument against the other may seem to lead back to affirmative action as a matter of social policy, since no coherent account of rights stands in the way. But in the absence of responsibility and rights, there is no common good to pursue. Social policy to what ends? For whose purposes? In that situation, the strongest pressure toward a solution may be felt in the direction of equality. All of us, as human beings, having the essential feature of responsibility in common and past discrimination barring the differences among us from being normatively constitutive, we ought to share equally and alike in life's benefits and burdens. But that solution cannot be sustained, for it deprives us of the individual normative selves without which the question of what is our due does not arise at all. How indeed would a policy of "equality" be carried out? Is it thinkable that opportunities for education or employment be distributed by a lottery, the only truly "equal" process of selection among persons differently constituted and competing for the same position? Although there is something like a lottery—the determinate natural order—at work in all our lives, the recognition of responsibility and rights is an affirmation that justice finally prevails. Were we deliberately to adopt such a practice in the most important aspects of our lives, it would undermine the very sense of justice that leads us to consider it in the first place.[23]

We should not expect that disagreement and confusion about affirmative action will be resolved even over a long period of time. The community may come to regard long-standing practices as an acceptable political solution or simply as "the law." But no solution will be incorporated within the community's *nomos* as just, because the terms of the controversy preclude a consistent understanding of responsibility and rights. Comparison with the issue of rights of handicapped persons is instructive. Abstractly, there is no reason why the relative lack of qualification of members of the groups against which discrimination was practiced should not be considered a handicap, comparable to a person's inability to enter a building without special provision. In the former case as much as in the latter, the person's individual attributes are limited in some respect that makes him less qualified for the position in question (as is also, of course, our old friend who wants to play for the Red Sox). The critical difference is that in the context of affirmative action, we are not prepared to affirm generally that the attributes in question, many of which are accepted criteria of merit, are not normatively constitutive or even to entertain the possibility that they are not. On the contrary, proponents of affirmative action themselves insist that those attributes are normatively constitutive. The heart of their claim is precisely that members of the disfavored groups were denied their due on the basis of just such individual attributes; the relatively deficient attributes of (some) members of those groups now are not normatively constitutive only because they are determined by the past injustice. So far as anyone else is concerned, the manager of the Red Sox says all that needs to be said about the less qualified person's failure to be admitted to university or to be hired, by the Red Sox or by anyone else.

No policy can coherently incorporate nonspecific injustice as a circumstance making the attributes of some persons but not others not normatively constitutive, because, without a basis for corrective justice in favor of specific individuals, the injustice is simply another cause. Responsibility and rights, grounded in desert, do not distinguish among the types of cause, whether natural, social, or idiosyncratic, that determine us to be the persons we are, but only among attributes, as constitutive or circumstantial. Affirmative action is unlike rights of the handicapped in this respect. The latter issue asks whether we regard the attributes themselves, whatever their cause, as constitutive or circumstantial. A coherent resolution of the issue, affirming that they are or are not among one's rights, is, therefore, achievable.

Recognition that there is not a just solution to the problem of past discrimination or, even in principle, an approach to a just solution provides some practical guidance. In the first place, we can acknowledge frankly that the scope and duration of affirmative action are political questions, answers to which will inevitably depend on the shifting relative political powers of the relevant groups. Procedurally, within the American system of governance, that means that the questions ought to be answered legislatively from time to time and not constitutionally and (more or less) permanently. This conclusion will not sit comfortably with persons who believe that fundamental considerations of justice or of liberty and equality are at stake. Persons on both sides of the issue may reach that conclusion, however; and the course of constitutional decisions by the Supreme Court in the last several decades cautions against assuming that one's own side must inevitably prevail.

Substantively, affirmative action programs should shift as much as is practicable from measures that are directly and overtly competitive to ones that are not. Instead of preferential selection of applicants for a limited number of places, programs should be designed to enhance the capabilities of members of groups that suffered the effects of past discrimination, who should then compete without preference for the available places. To some extent, that is already being done. There are scattered enrichment programs for some minorities. But they are far too limited to alter significantly the pattern of nonpreferential admissions to university, employment, and so forth. No program of enhancement on any but a very large scale has a hope of success on its own terms, for members of the previously favored groups will not abandon their own efforts to provide for the rising generation. Unless such programs demonstrate their effectiveness by securing competitive success without preference, they will, correctly, be dismissed as tokens that do not respond to the injustice of the past.

Enhancement programs are not without cost, which must be met by the diversion of public funds from elsewhere or by increased taxation of private funds. The increase of power of those who benefit is matched by reduced power of those who are obliged to support the programs. But the right to keep one's property free from taxation is not widely asserted any more; and the tradeoff of rights of those who benefit from taxation and those who are burdened is much less keenly felt. There are not specific winners and losers, as there are if persons compete directly for positions.

In the current political climate in the United States, the kind of program that is required will not easily be adopted. There is not much evidence of a deep commitment to helping others to help themselves. The belief is strong that success itself sufficiently demonstrates that it is deserved. There are also indications, however, that the appeal of direct affirmative action programs is diminishing. If they are discarded, we shall have to find some other means of responding to injustices that were once part of our way of life and are historically part of what defines us as a community. Not only those who benefit from affirmative action must come to terms with that; for it affects the stature as persons of all alike. Having no firm foundation for rights one way or the other, we shall have to rely on the sympathy and good will that also are the fruits of community to get us through.

Committed proponents and, probably, committed opponents of the rights considered in this chapter may not be satisfied with conclusions that are avowedly tentative and uncertain. Nothing less than whole-hearted commitment may seem adequate to the claim of right and the weight of the interests at stake. Yet, firm convictions on one side of these issues are matched by no less firm convictions on the other side. The questions in each case whether there is a right and, if so, what is its specific content are so important because so many rights are un-hesitatingly accepted as rights, with all that that implies. Our inability to answer those questions definitively now does not mean that these issues and others like them are not and never will be appropriate for resolution as a matter of right. Indeed, with respect to rights of the handicapped and gay rights, it seems to me that the *nomos* of the community presently supports a range of specific rights, less than the most militant proponents claim but substantial nonetheless. Further-more, although prediction is hazardous, it seems likely that the core of gay rights, the autonomy of one's sexual identity, will be accepted as a simple matter of fact in the United States in the foreseeable future. If that occurs, most collateral rights having to do with public discrimi-nation against homosexuals will fall into place. So also, some specific rights of handicapped persons will become a matter of course. The general issue will remain; but the controversy will shift, recognition of some rights giving weight to claims of others. Affirmative action is another story. The outcomes of affirmative action itself so closely replicate the antinomy of reason that gives rise to rights as the foun-dation of justice that no resolution in those terms is to be anticipated. Affirmative action as a specific response to acknowledged injustice will cease to be an issue only when we can conscientiously assert that the consequences of the injustice have been eliminated.

In all of this, the source of rights in the human condition and the nature of rights as a profoundly human response are evident. William James observed that the religious impulse springs from "a sense that there is *something wrong about us* as we naturally stand."[24] Although that is not, I think, far from the truth, it proceeds from the premise that the human condition is in some way an imperfect, qualified version of another, transcendent reality. From a wholly human perspective, one might say that only as we naturally stand, possessed of rights and recognizing rights of others, are we distinctly *human* beings at all.

Notes

INTRODUCTION

1. Bentham was referring specifically to "natural rights." Jeremy Bentham, *Anarchical Fallacies,* in *The Works of Jeremy Bentham,* ed. John Bowring, 11 vols. (Edinburgh: William Tait, 1838–1843) II, 501. Elsewhere he called them "the natural, pre-adamitical, ante-legal, and anti-legal rights of man." Ibid., p. 524. See H. L. A. Hart, *Essays on Bentham* (Oxford: Clarendon Press, 1982), pp. 79–83.

2. A declaration adopted at Smokepeace 90, "the first international smokers' conference," stated: "Smoking is a human right and should be respected according to the Declaration of Human Rights of the United Nations." *Boston Globe,* Oct. 27, 1990, p. 2. As for lobsters, see "What to Put in the Pot: Cooks Face Challenge over Animal Rights," *New York Times,* Aug. 8, 1990, p. C1.

3. Judith Jarvis Thomson, *Rights, Restitution, and Risk* (Cambridge, Mass.: Harvard University Press, 1986), p. 251.

4. Ibid., p. 253. Her discussion of what rights there are is mainly in Judith Jarvis Thomson, *The Realm of Rights* (Cambridge, Mass.: Harvard University Press, 1990).

5. H. L. A. Hart, "Between Utility and Rights," *Columbia Law Review* 79 (1979):828.

6. L. W. Sumner, *The Moral Foundation of Rights* (Oxford: Clarendon Press, 1987), p. 11.

7. See generally T. M. Scanlon, "Contractualism and Utilitarianism," in Amartya Sen and Bernard Williams, eds., *Utilitarianism and Beyond* (Cambridge: Cambridge University Press, 1982), pp. 104–110.

8. The usual reference, if one is needed, is to David Hume, *A Treatise of Human Nature,* ed. L. A. Selby-Bigge (Oxford: Clarendon Press, 1888), bk. 3, pt. 1, §1, p. 469.

ONE. PERSISTENT PUZZLES

1. Compare Rousseau's shrewd observation: "The power that comes from the people's love is no doubt the greatest; but it is precarious and conditional, and princes will never be content with it. The best kings want to be able to be wicked if they please, without ceasing to be master." Jean-Jacques Rousseau, *Du Contrat Social,* bk. 3, chap. 6, in *Oeuvres Complètes,* 4 vols. to date (Paris: Pléiade, 1959–1969) III (1964), 409 (my translation).
2. This aspect of a right underlies the principle in American constitutional law that certain fundamental rights, such as those protected by the First Amendment, cannot be overridden on grounds of public policy alone but only for a "compelling state interest." See, e.g., Simon & Schuster, Inc. v. Members of the New York State Crime Victims Board, 112 S.Ct. 501 (1991), holding invalid the New York State "Son of Sam" law, which made a criminal's income from a work describing his crime available to victims of crime and other creditors, because it burdened the criminal's First Amendment rights without a compelling state interest.
3. See Judith Jarvis Thomson, *Rights, Restitution, and Risk* (Cambridge, Mass.: Harvard University Press, 1986), p. 253; idem, *The Realm of Rights* (Cambridge, Mass.: Harvard University Press, 1990), pp. 84–96.
4. Although the term "inalienable right" is familiar in political rhetoric and its intended meaning tolerably clear in that context, it is elliptic and superficially misleading. A duty may be imposed because one has a particular status, which itself is regarded as honorable and desirable. Those who are exempt from the duty may resent the exemption because it signifies that they lack the necessary status and are not regarded as worthy of the duty or, more particularly, as responsible in that respect. In such a situation, the duty may become emblematic of the status, and a claim that one is entitled to that status may be expressed as a right to the duty. The opportunity to serve one's country in the military has commonly been regarded as a right or privilege reserved for a certain group. That way of thinking about military service survived even the draft, to which some women's groups objected on the ground that women were excluded. Someone who is called to serve on a jury is likely to say that he has been summoned to "jury duty," although as a constitutional matter we still speak of a right to serve on a jury. In some countries a citizen's right to vote carries with it a legal duty to vote. On the other hand, when a

duty is imposed on persons of lower status and persons of higher status are exempt, the duty is not regarded by either as a right; on the contrary, those on whom the duty is imposed may claim a right to be relieved of the duty. Any duty contains, usually without requiring mention, a right to act as the duty requires. The description of a duty as a mandatory or inalienable right emphasizes the dignity accorded one who has the duty as responsible in that respect.

5. A right the exercise of which is not even potentially obstructed or assisted by others may seem to have no purchase, so that the question whether a person has a right collapses into the question whether it is right for her so to act. That is true only in the special case in which both questions are answered in the negative, on the same nonconsequential ground. It makes no difference whether one says that Adam had no right to eat the apple or that it was not right for him to do so, because the apple was forbidden fruit quite aside from any consideration of what the consequences of his eating it might be. In other situations, the questions whether one has a right and whether, if one has it, one ought to exercise it are distinct and may be answered differently.

6. Sumner regards the characterization of such goals as rights as "conceptual drift." L. W. Sumner, *The Moral Foundation of Rights* (Oxford: Clarendon Press, 1987), p. 17. There is some drift; but it is not without direction.

7. In some circumstances, the law gives a person standing to sue to enforce the duty of another even though the person himself will not benefit directly. For example, a private person may have standing to enforce a charitable foundation's duty to distribute its income. Quite commonly, a public official has the responsibility to enforce such duties; and private persons who have standing to sue for enforcement are frequently characterized as "private attorneys-general." Although we may speak of such persons as having a legal right, it consists only in the power to initiate enforcement; it is not a right to the substance of the duty that is performed.

8. Stanley I. Benn and Richard S. Peters, *Social Principles and the Democratic State* (London: George Allen & Unwin, 1959), pp. 88–89.

9. Sumner, *The Moral Foundation of Rights*, p. 199.

10. Although that simple account satisfies most practical (and professional) concerns, it is notoriously unsatisfactory at another, deeper level. Is *any* enforceable outcome, however immoral, a legal *right*? If so, legal rights are a matter of fact; but what distinguishes them from bare force? If not, legal rights appear to be at least partly prescriptive; but how does law incorporate this moral content? Those questions demarcate the militarized zone between legal positivism and natural law.

11. Wesley N. Hohfeld, "Some Fundamental Legal Conceptions as Applied in Judicial Reasoning," *Yale Law Journal* 23 (1913):28–59, reprinted in idem, *Fundamental Legal Conceptions* (New Haven: Yale University Press, 1923), pp. 35–64.

12. The categories of human rights and civil rights are discussed in Chapters Seven and Eight. The term "moral rights" is often used as a generic reference to rights that are not based on some posited system of rules. E.g., R. G. Frey, *Interests and Rights* (Oxford: Clarendon Press, 1980), pp. 4–17. The term suggests that the ground of such rights is a moral principle. Frey, for example, arguing that there are no moral rights, takes that position for granted. He says: "if we challenge the claim that women have . . . a right [to abortion on demand], what we find ourselves arguing about with the feminist is the moral principle which is alleged by her to be the ground of this right; and what ends up being in dispute between us is the acceptability of this principle. Its acceptability is everything: you are only going to accept that women have a moral right to abortion on demand if you accept the moral principle which is alleged to confer this right upon them." Ibid., p. 10. Since I do not believe that the rights that are in question are grounded on moral principle, at least not the sort of principle that Frey has in mind, I shall generally avoid the term "moral rights." That leaves only the generic "nonlegal rights," which is not so felicitous itself; but I see no alternative.

13. See, for example, the discussion of Joel Feinberg's account of rights later in this chapter.

14. This highly abbreviated description of legal reasoning is not an endorsement of "mechanical jurisprudence"—the view that the law is a deductive system, in which all the significant premises and their application are ascertainable with exactitude. Likewise, although I think that it is generally accurate to describe law as a system of rules, I do not intend to take a position about the distinctions among rules, principles, and standards.

15. Dworkin and others have argued persuasively that in order to answer the question of what the law is, one has to consider the question—in one form or another—of what the law ought to be. There is nevertheless a fundamental difference between asking the latter question en route to an answer to the former and asking it for its own sake. Compare, for example, Dworkin's discussion of law as "integrity" and his discussion of "law beyond law." Ronald Dworkin, *Law's Empire* (Cambridge, Mass.: Harvard University Press, 1986), pp. 225–275, 400–410.

16. This is the classic problem of legal positivism. Without a normative justification, the assumed validity of a legal system seems to depend only on the fact that it is effective. Hans Kelsen and H. L. A. Hart provide examples of

positivists' heroic efforts to throw a bridge over the modal divide. See Hans Kelsen, *Introduction to the Problems of Legal Theory*, trans. Bonnie Litschewski Paulson and Stanley L. Paulson (Oxford: Clarendon Press, 1992), pp. 55–65 (basic norm); H. L. A. Hart, *The Concept of Law* (Oxford: Clarendon Press: Oxford, 1961), pp. 92–93, 97–107 (rule of recognition). See generally Lloyd L. Weinreb, "Law as Order," *Harvard Law Review* 91 (1978):922–935.

17. H. J. McCloskey, "Rights—Some Conceptual Issues," *Australasian Journal of Philosophy* 54 (1976):99–115. See also idem, "Respect for Human Moral Rights versus Maximizing Good," in R. G. Frey, ed., *Utility and Rights* (Oxford: Basic Blackwell, 1985), pp. 124–125.

18. Responding to the objection that the classification of rights as entitlements is "unilluminating and uninformative," McCloskey says only that "the whole discussion of this paper spells out what is meant by an entitlement." McCloskey, "Rights—Some Conceptual Issues," p. 105.

19. Joel Feinberg, "Duties, Rights, and Claims," *American Philosophical Quarterly* 3 (1966):137–144; idem, "The Nature and Value of Rights," *Journal of Value Inquiry* 4 (1970):243–257. Both articles are reprinted in idem, *Rights, Justice, and the Bounds of Liberty* (Princeton: Princeton University Press, 1980), pp. 130–142, 143–155.

20. Feinberg, "The Nature and Value of Rights," p. 250.

21. In one respect, both McCloskey and Feinberg perhaps understate the descriptive content of their respective characterizations. "Entitlement" and "valid claim" are alike strongly suggestive of a legal right as the exemplar of rights generally.

22. Feinberg, "The Nature and Value of Rights," p. 255.

23. That is just the point that Frey makes to reject the notion of moral rights. See note 12 above.

24. Feinberg, "The Nature and Value of Rights," p. 252.

25. McCloskey, "Rights—Some Conceptual Issues," pp. 100, 104.

26. Feinberg, "The Nature and Value of Rights," p. 252.

27. Joel Feinberg, "The Rights of Animals and Unborn Generations," in William T. Blackstone, ed., *Philosophy and Environmental Crisis* (Athens: University of Georgia Press, 1974), pp. 49–50. See also Joel Feinberg, "Human Duties and Animal Rights," in Richard Knowles Morris and Michael W. Fox, eds., *On the Fifth Day* (Washington, D.C.: Acropolis Books, 1978), pp. 45–69. Both articles are reprinted in Feinberg, *Rights, Justice, and the Bounds of Liberty*, pp. 159–184, 185–206.

28. Feinberg, "The Rights of Animals and Unborn Generations," p. 50.

29. McCloskey, "Rights—Some Conceptual Issues," p. 115.

30. H. J. McCloskey, "Rights," *Philosophical Quarterly* 15 (1965):126–127.

31. Feinberg, "The Nature and Value of Rights," p. 250.

32. See Ronald Dworkin, "Rights as Trumps," in Jeremy Waldron, ed., *Theories of Rights* (Oxford: Oxford University Press, 1984). "Individual rights are political trumps held by individuals." Ronald Dworkin, *Taking Rights Seriously* (Cambridge, Mass.: Harvard University Press, 1977), p. xi.

33. Dworkin, *Taking Rights Seriously*, p. 92.

34. John Finnis, *Natural Law and Natural Rights* (Oxford: Clarendon Press, 1980). See especially pp. 111–125.

35. For an illustration of this point in the specific context of affirmative action, see Chapter Nine.

36. See Rex Martin and James W. Nickel, "Recent Work on the Concept of Rights," *American Philosophical Quarterly* 17 (1980):173–174.

37. See note 3 above.

38. Finnis, *Natural Law and Natural Rights*, pp. 118–125.

39. Dworkin, *Taking Rights Seriously*, p. 172.

40. John Rawls, *A Theory of Justice* (Cambridge, Mass.: Harvard University Press, 1971). See also idem, *Political Liberalism* (New York: Columbia University Press, 1993).

41. Thomas Nagel, *Equality and Partiality* (New York: Oxford University Press, 1991), pp. 142–144.

42. T. M. Scanlon, "Contractualism and Utilitarianism," in Amartya Sen and Bernard Williams, eds., *Utilitarianism and Beyond* (Cambridge: Cambridge University Press, 1982), p. 110. See also T. M. Scanlon, "Rights, Goals, and Fairness," in Jeremy Waldron, ed., *Theories of Rights* (Oxford: Oxford University Press, 1984), pp. 137–152.

43. Of course, if nonhuman kinds have no rights, they need not be parties to the contract. But they (or their surrogates) cannot be excluded from the negotiation on the ground that they have no rights and then be denied any rights because they did not participate. The question whether nonhuman kinds have rights typically is not part of the discussion at all.

44. Thomson, *The Realm of Rights*, p. 373.

45. Ibid., p. 77.

46. Compare Jeremy Waldron's observation that "moral facts" as something that motivates to action are "something queer," which look as though "the metaphysical account of them has been cobbled together in an *ad hoc* way." Jeremy Waldron, "The Irrelevance of Moral Objectivity," in Robert P. George, ed., *Natural Law Theory* (Oxford: Clarendon Press, 1992), pp. 168–169.

TWO. HUMAN RESPONSIBILITY

1. A closely similar question is, however, raised in Greek tragedy, for example by the problem of Oedipus' and Creon's acceptance of personal responsibility for the tragic outcomes in *Oedipus the King* and *Antigone*.

2. When we think about slavery, we commonly think about legal rights; the argument that persons are *naturally* slaves has rarely been made, Aristotle being the notable, problematic instance. For a more recent example, an antebellum argument defending the practice of slavery in the United States, see George Fitzhugh, *Cannibals All!* (Cambridge, Mass.: Harvard University Press, 1960), pp. 199–203. The wrongfulness of slavery is that it denies legal rights to beings who we know are responsible and do have rights. For that reason, whatever one's view about animal rights, their denial is not the same kind of wrong as slavery. If we praise the noble slave, it is because the terms of his enslavement do not oblige him to conduct himself nobly but give him the right to do so or not; he is, therefore, responsible for his noble conduct. Were he obliged so to act he would not have the right not to do so or, in any meaningful sense, to do so; and his doing so, without responsibility, would not be a mark of nobility.

3. See Chapter Five.

4. Cf. cases in which the Supreme Court has said that the government may not "put a price" on the exercise of a constitutional right. E.g., United States v. Jackson, 390 U.S. 570 (1968) (capital punishment provision of Federal Kidnaping Act put "impermissible burden" on exercise of right to trial by jury). But compare the attitude toward commission of a so-called civil, i.e., noncriminal, "wrong." Does one who breaches a contract or commits a tort *ipso facto* commit a wrong? Or does one who enters into a contract have a right *either* to carry out his promise *or* not to carry it out and pay damages? Does one have a *right* carelessly or deliberately to damage a neighbor's property provided appropriate compensation is paid? Views differ. The jurisprudential school of law and economics strongly suggests that provided there is a compensatory payment, it is misleading to speak of a "wrong" in either situation. An indication, others think, of what is wrong with law and economics.

5. I am, of course, relying on that knowledge when I give the preceding self-referential description of what responsibility and agency are.

6. Recent studies suggest that some forms of drug addiction are more within the deliberate control of the addict than had been thought. See, e.g., John Kaplan, *The Hardest Drug* (Chicago: University of Chicago Press, 1983), pp. 32–42. One may believe that the tilt of answers to questions of that kind is more political than empirical.

7. The King v. Creighton, 14 Can. Cr. Cas. 349, 350 (Owen Sound Assizes, 1908).

8. See, e.g., Powell v. Texas, 392 U.S. 514 (1968). The broadest ground of excuse is insanity. Even the insanity defense is tied to the defendant's allegedly criminal conduct; it is not inconsistent with his having responsibility in other respects. See generally Lloyd L. Weinreb, "Desert, Punishment, and Criminal Responsibility," *Law and Contemporary Problems* 49 (Summer 1986):61–63.

9. The literature about the problem of free will is vast. Most of the modern "solutions" and a good many of the older ones seem more concerned to find a verbal formula that papers over the gap in our understanding than to eliminate it. The short of the matter, it seems to me, is, as I have observed elsewhere: "Acting freely means that how I act is up to me as an initiating, self-determining agency, no more or less. A complete causal explanation does not leave the matter up to me or anything else. So far as freedom in that sense—which is the only sense for the present purpose—is concerned, it is all up." Lloyd L. Weinreb, *Natural Law and Justice* (Cambridge, Mass.: Harvard University Press, 1987), p. 201n. None of the more restrictive analyses of freedom, such as an absence of "external" constraint, that make it compatible with cause, satisfies the actual experience of agency, when we feel ourselves to be or observe others to be determining the course of events in the full sense.

10. Sophocles tells this part of the history of the house of Laius in the *Antigone*. The events occur after the events in *Oedipus the King*; but the tragedy was written earlier.

11. I have been taken to task for disregarding "the worldview in which original sin *and* moral freedom belong." See James G. Hanink, review of *Natural Law and Justice*, *Ethics* 49 (1989):436. I did not disregard that world view in my earlier work, nor do I disregard it here. Then and now, my point is precisely that the two—although I should not use the term "original sin"—do coexist. But to suggest that, religious faith aside, Christian doctrine worked out the terms of coexistence better than the Greeks did is wishful thinking. How does original sin (with or without reward and punishment after death) cohere better with moral freedom than the surely more straightforward Greek way of putting it?

12. The argument is elaborated in Immanuel Kant, *Groundwork of the Metaphysic of Morals*, trans. H. J. Paton as *The Moral Law*, 3rd ed. (London: Hutchinson's University Library, 1956). See also idem, *Critique of Pure Reason*, trans. Norman Kemp Smith (London: Macmillan, 1958), pp. 467–479.

13. See, e.g., P. F. Strawson, *Skepticism and Naturalism: Some Varieties* (New York: Columbia University Press, 1985), pp. 31–50; Thomas Nagel, *The View from Nowhere* (New York: Oxford University Press, 1986), pp. 110–

137. Strawson develops the argument somewhat differently in P. F. Strawson, "Freedom and Resentment," in idem, *Freedom and Resentment* (London: Methuen, 1974), pp. 1–25.

THREE. INDIVIDUAL RESPONSIBILITY

1. There is not a clear rule about whether to regard as the cause of an event conduct that is sufficient but not necessary to bring it about. Ordinarily, we avoid the question by referring to only one of two or more sufficient causes as the cause and to the others as attendant circumstances. Theoretically, though extremely rarely in practice, the law (which makes it possible procedurally to consider each alleged cause separately from the rest) accepts the possibility of more than one cause. See, e.g., State v. Batiste, 410 So.2d 1055 (La. 1982).

   This book is not about causation. Here and elsewhere, I pass by qualifications and complexities that have filled volumes. I do not think that, for the present purpose, I have oversimplified or evaded complexity relevant to the argument.
2. Cf. United States v. Park, 421 U.S. 658, 673 (1975), stating that criminal liability as a responsible corporate agent "does not require that which is objectively impossible" and permits a defendant to raise the defense that he was powerless to prevent the criminal violation.
3. See, e.g., People v. Chavez, 77 Cal. App.2d 621, 628, 176 P.2d 92, 96 (1947), in which the court sustained a mother's liability for the death of her child during childbirth on the basis of a duty that was "*naturally* required of her" as the child's mother (emphasis added).
4. Whether a person ought to be *held* responsible if he is in fact responsible—or conceivably if he is not—is a different question.
5. See Model Penal Code § 210.3(1)(b) and commentary, 1 *MPC Part II Commentaries* 49–50. For some cases (voluntary manslaughter), see Lloyd L. Weinreb, *Criminal Law*, 5th ed. (Mineola, N.Y.: Foundation Press, 1993), pp. 88–97.
6. *Aristotelian Society Proceedings* 57 n.s. (1956–57):1–30, reprinted in John L. Austin, *Philosophical Papers*, 3rd ed. (Oxford: Oxford University Press, 1979), pp. 175–204.

FOUR. OEDIPUS AT FENWAY PARK

1. John Locke, *Second Treatise of Government*, §4, in idem, *Two Treatises of Government*, ed. Peter Laslett, 2nd ed. (Cambridge: Cambridge University Press, 1967), p. 287.

FIVE. RESPONSIBILITY AND RIGHTS

1. Although the connection is mostly taken for granted when it is asserted with respect to a particular (human) individual, it is highly controversial when applied rigorously in gross, as it were, to *kinds* of beings—animals and others—that are not (regarded as) responsible. See Chapter Six.

2. Both one's capacity and one's interests may be regarded as very extended, in however attenuated a form, in a community having a democratic government. Some claims of individual responsibility and rights under democracy stretch the concepts to their breaking point and, it seems to me, are in truth only metaphoric: for example, that democracy is government by consent.

3. Another guard who also fired but did not hit the person was convicted of attempted manslaughter. Pronouncing the sentences (three and a half years in prison for the first guard and a year's suspended sentence for the second), the judge said, "Not everything that is legal is right," and asserted that although the defendants were "at the end of a long chain of responsibility," they had violated "a basic human right." *New York Times,* Jan. 21, 1992, p. A1.

4. It is a matter of controversy in jurisprudence how the conflict is best expressed. A legal positivist would say that there is a legal duty, which is overridden by the moral obligation (and nonlegal right). The standard natural law position is that in view of the moral obligation (and nonlegal right), there is no legal duty, or no valid legal duty. See the exchange about Nazi laws in H. L. A. Hart, "Positivism and the Separation of Law and Morals," *Harvard Law Review* 71 (1958):593–629; Lon L. Fuller, "Positivism and Fidelity to Law—A Reply to Professor Hart," *Harvard Law Review* 71 (1958):630–672.

5. Compare the arguments of the majority and dissenting justices in Bowers v. Hardwick, 478 U.S. 186 (1986), about whether the case concerned a "right of homosexuals to engage in acts of sodomy" (478 U.S. at 191) or "'the right to be let alone'" (478 U.S. at 199; dissenting opinion). See Chapter Nine.

6. We can also ask whether a person ought not to be more responsible, meaning that he ought to pay more attention to the responsibilities that he has. In very special circumstances, one might ask whether a particular human being or group of human beings ought not to be more or less responsible in the future, in general or in specific circumstances. We have a limited capacity to develop or to impede human responsibility or to eliminate it altogether by physiological and psychological means.

7. See the discussion of legal rights in Chapter One.

8. David Hume, *A Treatise of Human Nature,* ed. L. A. Selby-Bigge (Oxford: Clarendon Press, 1888), bk. 1, pt. 4, §6, pp. 251–263.

9. Max Beerbohm, *Zuleika Dobson* (New York: Boni & Liveright, 1911).

10. A man who signed himself "Toad of the Road" wrote to Ann Landers that he had strong "sexual urges for very young females." He met a divorced woman who had young daughters, to whom he was physically attracted. His relationship with the woman progressed, and she wanted to marry. Against his better judgment, he moved in with the woman and found himself sexually aroused by her daughters. The letter continues: "After several months of walking this sexual tightrope, I realized that a tragedy was on the brink of occurring. I moved out and terminated the relationship. I know that my leaving hurt this lovely woman and her daughters, but they'll never know how lucky they were to be rid of me." *Boston Globe,* June 16, 1993, p. 54.

11. But see Robert Nozick, *Anarchy, State, and Utopia* (New York: Basic Books, 1974), p. 172.

12. See, for example, ibid., pp. 265–268.

13. E.g., California Government Code § 27491.47; Michigan Compiled Laws §333.10202.

14. That is the state of nature as Hobbes conceived it, in which "the life of man, [is] solitary, poor, nasty, brutish, and short." Thomas Hobbes, *Leviathan,* ed. Michael Oakeshott (Oxford: Basil Blackwell, 1957), chap. 13, p. 82. Locke's state of nature is not so bleak, because it is infused with the "Law of Nature," a source of rights. John Locke, *Second Treatise of Government,* §6, in idem, *Two Treatises of Government,* ed. Peter Laslett, 2nd ed. (Cambridge: Cambridge University Press, 1967), p. 289.

15. It is a difficulty of just that kind that makes the tragedy of Oedipus at once so problematic and so powerful. But for our identification with Oedipus and recognition of his suffering and an assumption foreign to the Greeks that cosmic justice, if there is any, must be comprehensible in human terms, we might perceive the tragic ending as a demonstration that right triumphs. For Sophocles, the ending affirmed that there is normative order—not the triumph of right as we think of it, but an affirmation nonetheless. All the same, the Greeks were not without a strong conception of personal responsibility. No less than we do ourselves, they started from the experience of persons and things, which preserves a distinction between moral responsibility and causal determination. When Oedipus learns from the oracle that he is fated to kill his father and commit incest with his mother, he does not wait around for it to happen; he flees from the place where those whom he believes to be his father and mother are.

16. Kant's noumenal moral agent, lacking all phenomenal attributes, is suggestive. From our (admittedly unavailing) vantage, one noumenon must be like every other. How does responsibility attach to anyone? Rawls's notion of an agent operating behind a "veil of ignorance" about his own attributes and

interests is devised to a similar purpose and subject to the same objection. See Chapter Eight.

17. There is preserved, therefore, a formal equality, despite unequal individual endowments for which the persons are not themselves responsible. Each person is permitted to make—limited to making—the most of what he has. We call that "equality of opportunity."

    In practice, we commonly seek to provide a minimum level of well-being for all while preserving for some the much greater well-being that they are able to provide for themselves. There is no practical contradiction between the bare propositions, on one hand, that every person ought to be endowed with some minimum capacity, which the community ought to provide for those whose natural endowment is less, and, on the other, that a person ought to have the benefit of his natural endowment, however large. The provision for those who have less need not be obtained out of the "surplus" provision of those who provide for themselves. Food stamps, for example, are funded by taxes, an undifferentiated source, rather than by a requirement that the wealthy turn over some of their food and eat less. The health of the sickly may be improved without the health of those who are well being put at risk. In extreme circumstances, provision of a minimum may be defended as a human right, because without that much the capacity for self-determination generally is undermined. See Chapter Seven. Retention of an endowment above the minimum has to be defended on a different basis, whether as a civil right, as to which see Chapter Eight, or as a matter of social policy (either of which may be the basis of a legal right).

18. See, e.g., Kelley v. Johnson, 425 U.S. 238 (1976), in which the Supreme Court upheld a police commissioner's regulation prescribing the style and length of policemen's hair, sideburns, and mustache, against the challenge that it violated the policemen's constitutional rights. See also Breese v. Smith, 501 P.2d 159 (Alaska 1972), one of a number of cases challenging a regulation about the length of schoolboys' hair. The regulation, which provided that "hair must not be down over the ears, over the eyes . . . [or] over the collar," was struck down.

    The *Times* (London) reported that the French courts had upheld a dwarf's "right to be thrown against a wall covered in inflatable mattresses," against a municipal order prohibiting the "so-called sport" of dwarf-throwing. Feb. 27, 1992, p. 1.

SIX. WHAT HAS RIGHTS

1. The examples are not so far-fetched. Funds frequently are set aside for maintenance of a natural "wonder" or building, an arboretum or wildflower

preserve, and so forth. See the stories "New York's Historical Trees Honored with New Registry," *New York Times,* Aug. 6, 1990, p. B2; and "A New Theory: A Beach Has a Right to Its Sand." *New York Times,* Nov. 29, 1991, p. D12. See generally Christopher D. Stone, "Should Trees Have Standing?—Toward Legal Rights for Natural Objects," *Southern California Law Review* 45 (1972):450–501, reprinted as *Should Trees Have Standing?* (Los Altos, Calif.: William Kaufmann, 1974).

2. Joel Feinberg, "Is There a Right to Be Born?" in James Rachels, ed., *Understanding Moral Philosophy* (Encino, Calif.: Dickenson Publishing, 1976), p. 347, reprinted in Joel Feinberg, *Rights, Justice, and the Bounds of Liberty* (Princeton: Princeton University Press, 1980), p. 208.

3. Joel Feinberg, "The Rights of Animals and Unborn Generations," in William T. Blackstone, ed., *Philosophy and Environmental Crisis* (Athens: University of Georgia Press, 1974), p. 49, reprinted in Feinberg, *Rights, Justice, and the Bounds of Liberty,* p. 165.

4. Ibid.

5. Albert Schweitzer, *Out of My Life and Thought,* trans. A. B. Lemke, rev. ed. (New York: Henry Holt, 1990), pp. 155–159, 232–238.

6. "To undertake to establish universally valid distinctions of value between different kinds of life will end in judging them by the greater or lesser distance at which they stand from us human beings. Our own judgment is, however, a purely subjective criterion. Who among us knows what significance any other kind of life has in itself, as a part of the universe?" Ibid., p. 235.

7. Writers of fiction have occasionally played with the issue, in a variety of ways. E.g., Vercors [Jean Bruller], *You Shall Know Them,* trans. Rita Barisse (Boston: Little, Brown, 1953) (chimpanzee); Douglas Orgill and John Gribbin, *Brother Esau* (New York: Harper & Row, 1982) (creature having common ancestor with human beings and evolving differently); Pierre Boulle, *Planet of the Apes,* trans. Xan Fielding (New York: Vanguard Press, 1963) (apes); Karel Capek, *R. U. R.,* trans. Paul Selver (New York: Samuel French, 1923) (robot). The most celebrated example is *Frankenstein,* in which the human-like being in question is created in a laboratory. Mary W. Shelley, *Frankenstein,* ed. M. K. Joseph (London: Oxford University Press, 1969).

8. In some philosophic discussions, the concept of personhood is used more restrictively to refer only to beings capable of exercising responsibility. It is evident that I agree with the core of that position. Although it states correctly the essential distinction between persons and things and is sufficient for the principal point being made, it disregards the requirement of responsibility itself (elaborated in Chapter Five) that freedom be exercised within a determinate causal order and the impact of that aspect of responsibility on our use of the concept of a person, elaborated later in this chapter.

9. As in Boulle, *Planet of the Apes*. In both the book and the movie made from it, there is a further turn of the screw. At the end of the book, the human space explorers return to earth many hundreds of years later (the consequence of traveling in space). They discover that the ascendance of the apes on the distant planet is replicated on earth. In the movie, it turns out that what the explorers had thought was a distant planet was in fact the earth far in the future (another of those quirky effects of space travel). Does distance in time have the same effect as distance in space? Are the terrestrial apes of the future persons? Are the human beings who behave like apes on the distant planet not?

10. For an example, see Repouille v. United States, 165 F.2d 152, 152 (2nd Cir. 1947), involving the deliberate killing of a thirteen-year-old who, the court said, "had 'suffered from birth from a brain injury which destined him to be an idiot and a physical monstrosity malformed in all four limbs. The child was blind, mute, and deformed. He had to be fed; the movements of his bladder and bowels were involuntary, and his entire life was spent in a small crib.'"

SEVEN. HUMAN RIGHTS

1. The argument that all human beings ought to be *x* because that is God's will can be rendered as a human right to be *x*, according to the nominalist premise that God's will is determinative of reality and prior and superior to any moral argument. Some arguments about human rights do refer explicitly to divine ordinance. I shall not consider such arguments further, except to note that their closest nontheological analogue seems to be an argument of the kind that I have made here, that rights are a function of responsibility, which is a matter of fact.

2. Once the idea of responsibility has been acquired, it does not depend on the possibility of communication to other similarly responsible beings. See Chapter Eight. All the same, were communication possible but severely restricted, the scope of individual responsibility would almost certainly be greatly diminished. On that basis (aside from any other, utilitarian basis), the special constitutional place of freedom of expression is justified.

3. See, e.g., Jean Piaget, *The Moral Judgment of the Child*, trans. Marjorie Gabain (New York: Free Press, 1965); Carol Gilligan, *In a Different Voice* (Cambridge, Mass.: Harvard University Press, 1982).

4. The difference has been recognized in the criminal law as the defense of diminished capacity or diminished responsibility. See, e.g. People v. Wolff, 61 Cal.2d 795, 394 P.2d 959 (1964). See generally, rejecting the defense, Bethea v. United States, 365 A.2d 64 (D.C. 1976). The defense, in one form

or another, was quite widely accepted in the 1960s and 1970s. Since then it has lost ground, one among many indications of public sentiment that persons who commit harmful acts should be held responsible, without too much concern for whether they are fully responsible as individuals or not.

5. See Jean-Jacques Rousseau, *Considérations sur le Gouvernement de Pologne,* in idem, *Oeuvres Complètes,* 4 vols. to date (Paris: Pléiade, 1959–1969) III (1964), 966, translated in idem, *Political Writings,* trans. and ed. Frederick Watkins (Edinburgh: Nelson, 1953), p. 176; George Orwell, *1984* (London: Secker & Warburg, 1949).

6. That is the right claimed by John (the Savage) in Aldous Huxley's *Brave New World* (Garden City, N.Y.: Doubleday, Doran, 1932).

7. John Locke, *Second Treatise of Government,* chap. 5, in Locke, *Two Treatises of Government,* ed. Peter Laslett, 2nd ed. (Cambridge: Cambridge University Press, 1967), pp. 303–320; quotation, p. 306.

8. See Robert Nozick, *Anarchy, State, and Utopia* (New York: Basic Books, 1974), p. 169. Nozick observes that "taxation of earnings from labor is on a par with forced labor." Ibid.

9. John Rawls, *A Theory of Justice* (Cambridge, Mass.: Harvard University Press, 1971), pp. 103–104. See generally Lloyd L. Weinreb, *Natural Law and Justice* (Cambridge, Mass.: Harvard University Press, 1987), p. 237–240.

10. See Judith Jarvis Thomson, *The Realm of Rights* (Cambridge, Mass.: Harvard University Press, 1990), p. 205–226. ". . . people's bodies are their First Property, whereas everything else they own—their houses, typewriters, and shoes—is their Second Property." Ibid., p. 226.

11. It is perhaps more precise to say that all persons have an equal right to *x,* rather than that all persons have a right to equal *x.* The distinction may be insisted on strongly. It depends, however, on an arbitrary specification of what counts as "a" right. An equal right to *x* will or will not be the same as a right to equal *x,* according to how *x* is defined, which is not determined by any independent criteria. The weight that has been attached to the distinction betrays the inaptness of equality as such as a human ideal altogether. See Weinreb, *Natural Law and Justice,* pp. 159–183.

12. Ronald Dworkin, *Taking Rights Seriously* (Cambridge, Mass.: Harvard University Press, 1977), pp. 272–278. See also idem, "Rights as Trumps," in Jeremy Waldron, ed., *Theories of Rights* (Oxford: Oxford University Press, 1984), pp. 153–167.

13. Dworkin, *Taking Rights Seriously,* p. 275.

14. Ibid., pp. 275–276.

15. See Weinreb, *Natural Law and Justice,* pp. 135–141.

16. Lewis Carroll, *Through the Looking Glass,* chap. 4, in *Alice's Adventures in Wonderland* (New York: Heritage Press, 1941) pp. 68–72.

17. Even if it can plausibly be said that at some time in the past such a belief was thought to be well-founded, one may doubt that errors of that kind generally qualify as "honest mistakes." Given the consequences for the disfavored group, "honesty" demanded at least a conscientious effort to test the belief; and, for the most part, there was none. In any case, whatever their basis in the past, such beliefs are not now thought to be soundly based.

18. See the discussion of affirmative action in Chapter Nine.

19. For a strong argument to the contrary, that the deliberate taking of human life is never justified, see John Finnis, *Natural Law and Natural Rights* (Oxford: Clarendon Press, 1980), pp. 86, 118–125. Although Finnis' principle is entirely clear, its basis and its application are less so. He purports not to rely on a theological premise that, according to its content, might provide a basis for the argument; but one may be somewhat doubtful about the disclaimer, in view of his arguments elsewhere. See, e.g., ibid., pp. 378–410. The application of the argument is uncertain because Finnis accepts and relies on the notion of "double effect," which is itself anything but precise. See ibid., pp. 122–124.

20. See Stanley I. Benn, *A Theory of Freedom* (Cambridge: Cambridge University Press, 1988), p. 16.

21. Compare Thomson's discussion of the person "hooked up" to a famous violinist in order to preserve the latter's life. Judith Jarvis Thomson, "A Defense of Abortion," *Philosophy and Public Affairs* 1 (1971):47–66, reprinted in idem, *Rights, Restitution, and Risk* (Cambridge, Mass.: Harvard University Press, 1986), pp. 1–19.

22. 410 U.S. 113 (1973).

23. See, e.g., Robinson v. California, 370 U.S. 660 (1962). A person may not be executed unless he is then responsible. See Ford v. Wainwright, 477 U.S. 399 (1986).

24. Compare Benn's discussion of the psychopath in *A Theory of Freedom*, pp. 101–102.

25. Immanuel Kant, *The Metaphysical Elements of Justice (The Metaphysics of Morals: Part One)*, trans. John Ladd (Indianapolis: Library of Liberal Arts, 1965), pp. 100–101.

26. See, e.g., In re Blodgett, 112 S.Ct. 674 (1992); McCleskey v. Zant, 111 S.Ct. 1454 (1991).

EIGHT. CIVIL RIGHTS

1. John Rawls, *A Theory of Justice* (Cambridge, Mass: Harvard University Press, 1971).

2. See John Rawls, *Political Liberalism* (New York: Columbia University Press, 1993).

3. Robert Nozick, *Anarchy, State, and Utopia* (New York: Basic Books, 1974).

4. The preface of *Anarchy, State, and Utopia* begins: "Individuals have rights, and there are things no person or group may do to them (without violating their rights)." P. ix.

5. See Alasdair MacIntyre, *After Virtue,* 2nd ed. (Notre Dame, Ind.: University of Notre Dame Press, 1984); Michael J. Sandel, *Liberalism and the Limits of Justice* (Cambridge: Cambridge University Press, 1982).

6. Whether she would abstract from concrete situations and could be said to have a conception of causal agency or a general conception of herself and others as agents is problematic. Since she is entirely alone, the puzzling issue of "private language" would extend to all her experience. See generally Ludwig Wittgenstein, *Philosophical Investigations,* trans. G. E. M. Anscombe (Oxford: Basil Blackwell, 1958), §§243 ff. Although my description suggests that she may have such conceptions, I do not intend to take any position on that issue. My point is, rather, that even making the largest concession to that possibility, she would not entertain the idea of an "objective" evaluation, i.e., one tied to no point of view.

7. At this point, both persons have got beyond any restriction to private language, if there is such. Communicating with each other about their common experience, they have a capacity to abstract and conceptualize. Somewhere in the shift from one alone to two (or more) together, the capacity for distinctively human language has arisen. The acquisition of language is critical to the transformation that I envisage; but *how* it is acquired is not. Whatever scenario one adopts, it seems to me that moral awareness depends on the possession of language in the full sense and, therefore, on membership within a human community.

8. In classical Greek thought, the idea of normative *natural* order underlies the conception of justice and dispenses with a distinct conception of rights. See, e.g., Plato, *Laws* 10.903. The connection is evident in Aristotle's writings, in which the normative natural order has become scarcely more than a logical abstraction and is replaced in his account of justice, albeit ambiguously and inexplicitly, by something akin to rights. I am not here defending the kind of "right-based morality" to which Joseph Raz and others have raised substantial objections. See Joseph Raz, "Right-Based Moralities," in R. G. Frey, ed., *Utility and Rights* (Oxford: Basil Blackwell, 1985), pp. 42–60. My point is not that the foundational *content* of morality is composed exclusively of rights but that morality assumes the existence of moral beings—beings who are responsible and, therefore, have rights.

9. Thomas Hobbes, *Leviathan,* ed. Michael Oakeshott (Oxford: Basil Black-well, 1957), chap. 13, p. 83.

10. "But a man may here object, that the condition of subjects is very miserable; as being obnoxious to the lusts, and other irregular passions of him, or them that have so unlimited a power in their hands . . . not considering that the state of man can never be without some incommodity or other; and that the greatest, that in any form of government can possibly happen to the people in general is scarce sensible in respect of the miseries, and horrible calamities, that accompany a civil war, or that dissolute condition of masterless men, without subjection to laws, and a coercive power to tie their hands from rapine and revenge." Ibid., chap. 18, p. 120.

11. Neither of the Greek concepts can be rendered fully in modern terms, which will not contain together both the descriptive and the normative elements. Casting aside the latter, we usually translate *physis* as "nature" (hence the modern "physics," "physical," etc.) and *nomos* as positive "law" or "convention." The term *nomos* especially was full of ambiguity, not unlike our own term "law."

NINE. APPLICATIONS

1. The rights discussed in this chapter are those that I have called simply "nonlegal" rights: rights that a person has as a matter of fact, not dependent on law. Although we commonly talk about such rights without further qualification, in modern rights talk the specific category that comes closest, as elaborated in Chapter Eight, is civil rights. Human rights, which are a special category of nonlegal rights, on one hand, and legal or quasi-legal rights, on the other, are not the subject of this chapter. The former are discussed in Chapter Seven and the latter very briefly in Chapter One. Human rights are universal and do not depend for their validity on the *nomos* of the community. As human rights, however, they are very general, and they acquire specific content as rights in the manner described here. Although every human being has a right to education, for example, the content of the right varies from one community to another. One would normally expect the right to education to be a civil right and to be legally protected; but it might in some respects be a civil right without legal protection or be protected legally beyond its status as a civil right.

2. See generally Lance Liebman, "Too Much Information: Predictions of Employee Disease and the Fringe Benefit System," *University of Chicago Legal Forum* 1988:57–92.

3. The New York Court of Appeals held that an employer violated the state's

Human Rights Law, which prohibits employers from refusing to employ persons with a "disability," when it refused to hire a worker because of her "gross obesity," unrelated to any other diagnosed medical condition. State Division of Human Rights v. Xerox Corp., 65 N.Y.2d 213, 480 N.E.2d 695 (1985).

4. An official in the U.S. Department of Education once asserted publicly that physical handicaps due to birth defects and the like are constitutive and reflect a person's inner worth. She was excoriated in the press and finally left her position. See *New York Times,* April 17, 1985, p. B4; April 18, 1985, p. A26; April 19, 1985, p. A19; *Newsweek,* April 29, 1985, p. 33.

5. 478 U.S. 186 (1986).

6. The Court's opinion refers to sodomy, which the statute in question defined to include oral sex. The act for which the defendant was prosecuted was oral sex.

7. In the aftermath of *Hardwick,* some advocates of gay rights have argued that the equal protection right not to be discriminated against because one is homosexual ought to be regarded as primary. This position is plausible as a matter of constitutional law if the discrimination is practiced against persons who are homosexual or have a "homosexual orientation" without proof that they have engaged in the conduct prohibited by the law upheld in *Hardwick.* Some persons, presumably a small group, would be among those subject to discrimination, although they do not engage in the prohibited conduct. See Watkins v. United States Army, 847 F.2d 1329 (9th Cir. 1988), *withdrawn,* 875 F.2d 699 (9th Cir. 1989). See generally Cass R. Sunstein, "Sexual Orientation and the Constitution: A Note on the Relationship between Due Process and Equal Protection," *University of Chicago Law Review* 55 (1988):1161–79.

8. Patrick Devlin, *The Enforcement of Morals* (London: Oxford University Press, 1965), pp. 1–25.

9. See H. L. A. Hart, *Law, Liberty, and Morality* (Stanford: Stanford University Press, 1963), pp. 48–55.

10. Since the Court concluded in *Hardwick* that a fundamental right is not involved, a prohibition justified as a health measure would presumably survive *constitutional* challenge, as a rational legislative response to a perceived social need. But see City of Cleburne, Texas v. Cleburne Living Center, Inc., 473 U.S. 432 (1985), holding that the requirement of a special use permit for operation of a home for the mentally retarded violated the Equal Protection Clause. The AIDS argument would in any case be vulnerable at the legislative level.

11. Bowers v. Hardwick, 478 U.S. 186, 191 (majority), 199 (dissent: the "'right to be let alone'") (1986).

12. John Stuart Mill, *On Liberty,* in *Utilitarianism, Liberty, and Representative Government* (New York: E. P. Dutton, 1951) pp. 95–96.

13. See Powell v. Texas, 392 U.S. 514 (1968) (5–4).

14. 478 U.S. at 198 n.2 (concurring opinion).

15. In one collateral respect, the prohibition of homosexual sexual conduct is not abstract. Such laws provide a ground for laws that discriminate against homosexuals or persons who commit homosexual sexual acts. (But see note 7 above.) If prohibitory laws were simply repealed without having been declared unconstitutional, discriminatory laws would remain valid theoretically; but it would be much more difficult to defend them.

16. The guidelines that were later declared to implement the policy are on their face less reflective of a general pulling back than of a (small) shift of the line defining the conduct that merits discharge. One may hope and, I think, expect that once the matter has receded from public attention, guidelines or no, the actual implementation of the policy will be as I have suggested.

17. Recent legislative and other measures in a few states and local communities that express opposition to homosexuality are not, I think, strong evidence to the contrary. The measures do not prohibit homosexual sexual conduct. For the most part, they attempt to characterize homosexuality as aberrant and wrong. Although the measures understandably offend homosexuals, that and the satisfaction they give to their proponents seem to be their principal purpose and effect.

18. As a matter of constitutional law, were the right to engage in homosexual conduct recognized, the equal protection clause might require equivalent treatment of heterosexual and homosexual persons in such matters. See note 7 above.

19. In this context, discrimination almost always refers to the denial of opportunities rather than to the appropriation of goods belonging to members of the disfavored group. The latter kind of discriminatory action may call for a remedy long afterward even if the beneficiary of the appropriation cannot be identified, on the basis of a (not incontestable) assumption that the goods or their equivalent value would not have been lost or voluntarily alienated.

20. Ronald Dworkin, *A Matter of Principle* (Cambridge, Mass.: Harvard University Press, 1985), p. 297.

21. Dworkin leaves no doubt that that is his position. He says that although Allan Bakke, the rejected white applicant to medical school who attacked an affirmative action program in Regents of the University of California v. Bakke, 438 U.S. 265 (1978), was understandably disappointed, no right of his was involved. Dworkin considers and rejects the principles that he thinks might be supposed to support an applicant's right to be admitted, including "a right

to be judged on his merit." Dworkin's conclusion is: "In spite of popular opinion, the idea that the *Bakke* case presents a conflict between a desirable social goal and important individual rights is a piece of intellectual confusion." Ibid., p. 298.

22. One might conclude that the two practices merge, since in both cases an applicant's career plans would be taken into account. It might be the case, however, that group-based admissions were as likely or even more likely to yield the best "mix," with less expenditure of resources to determine who was admitted.

23. The use of a lottery to select those who are drafted into the army is a dubious policy for those reasons, although as actually carried out before the draft was ended in 1973 it was idiosyncratic as social policy and, at that, riddled with exceptions (themselves not notably just). Even so, there is evidence that the "just world phenomenon"—belief that random events somehow reflect individual desert—was at work. See Melvin J. Lerner and Dale T. Miller, "'Just World Research' and the Attribution Process: Looking Back and Ahead," *Psychological Bulletin* 85 (1978):1030–51. More recently, the use of a lottery to select those illegal aliens who are given permanent resident status raises the same questions.

24. William James, *The Varieties of Religious Experience* (Cambridge, Mass.: Harvard University Press, 1985), p. 400.

Index